Aeschylus

Twayne's World Authors Series

Ruth Scodel, Editor of Greek Literature

Harvard University

TWAS 675

A Paestan red-figure bell-krater by Python (British Museum, 1917, 12–10.1) illustrating Orestes at Delphi flanked by Athena and Apollo, but threatened by the Furies from above the tripod and beside Apollo. Photograph courtesy of the Trustees of the British Museum.

Aeschylus

By Lois Spatz

University of Missouri–Kansas City

Twayne Publishers • *Boston*

Aeschylus

Lois Spatz

Book Production by John Amburg

Book Design by Barbara Anderson

Printed on permanent/durable acid-free
paper and bound in the United States of
America.

**Library of Congress Cataloging in
Publication Data**
Spatz, Lois.
   Aeschylus.

(Twayne's world authors series;
TWAS 675)
Bibliography: p. 195
Includes index.
1. Aeschylus—Criticism and interpretation.
I. Title. II. Series.
PR3829.S56   1982   882'.01   82-12032
ISBN 0-8057-6522-0

To Jonas
ou gar dokein aristos all' einai thelei

Contents

About the Author

Dr. Lois Settler Spatz was graduated from Goucher College in 1960 as a Phi Beta Kappa with Honors in Classics. She received the Ph.D. in Classics from Indiana University in 1968. After teaching at Brooklyn College and Park College, she is now an Associate Professor of English at the University of Missouri–Kansas City, where she specializes in courses in drama, mythology, and ancient literature in translation. She has reviewed several books on these subjects for *American Classical Review* and *Classical Journal*, as well as publishing "Metrical Motifs in Aristophanes' *Clouds.*" *Quaderni Urbinati* 13 (1972):62–82. Dr. Spatz has also written *Aristophanes* for the Twayne World Authors Series.

Preface

New readers of Aeschylus frequently respond ambivalently to his plays. They appreciate the excitement of the dramatic situation and the beauty of the lyrics. Yet they are disturbed by the difficulty of the poet's imagistic language and the strangeness of the myths on which he based his plots. In order to make Aeschylus more comprehensible to modern readers, this study has placed his dramas in the context of the general development of Greek tragedy and against the background of the political and social life of Athens in the first half of the fifth century B.C.

The introductory chapter explains the connection between Greek tragedy and the public life of the polis (city-state). Aeschylus's plays were produced by the citizens of Athens as a means of worshiping their nature god Dionysus in the decades after they had defeated the Persian Empire and were building their city into the cultural and political center of the Mediterranean world. Within the context of the religious festival, Aeschylus used the myths of an earlier age and the familiar lyric forms of public ceremony to dramatize the problems, fears, and aspirations of his own generation.

Aeschylus's plays, however, must not be read as historical documents or period pieces. The tragic dilemmas encountered by his characters reflect the situation of the ancient Athenians in their greatest moment of glory. But because the Athenians were innovative and yet fearful of change, proud of their achievements yet reverent and self-critical, the tragedies of their spokesman, Aeschylus, communicate across the centuries to modern men who must confront similar problems as they pass through significant changes. Each play will thus be treated both as a product of its own time, reflecting specific topical concerns, and as a dramatization of ageless and universal themes. Aspects of production and style (e.g., the transformation of myth, diction, the trilogy form, and spectacle), which must have elucidated the poet's ideas and moved his audience, will be considered along with subjects of special interest to twentieth-century readers such as symbolism, imagery, and character motivation. I have also included the interpretations of modern psychoanalytic critics, although the fifth-century Greeks, if they were aware of such implications, probably would have stated their awareness differently. I hope that readers will understand what Aeschylus's tragedies meant to contemporary Athenian spectators and at the same time appreciate the poet's timeless artistry and honest portrayal of the human condition.

I have emphasized the literary and social aspects of Aeschylean drama at the expense of the more technical problems that concern classical scholars. Although textual difficulties abound, I have relied primarily on the 1972 Oxford edition by Denys Page and discuss only those passages where lacunae or variant readings affect my analysis. Questions about the date or authenticity of a play, the interpretations of single plays as parts of lost trilogies, and debatable aspects of Greek religion have been given greater attention to reveal the assumptions on which my interpretations are based. Because the treatment of these significant areas of dispute is necessarily cursory, however, fuller discussions have been relegated to the notes.

A few works have been particularly helpful. In *The Stagecraft of Aeschylus: The Dramatic Uses of Entrances and Exits in Greek Tragedy* (Oxford: Clarendon Press, 1977), Oliver Taplin has analyzed questions related to production and significant problems of text and interpretation, with critical surveys of the bibliography and comparisons to the later dramatists. Any investigation of Aeschylus, or indeed of Greek tragedy in general, must heed this monumental work of scholarship. The translations in the Prentice-Hall Greek Drama Series, all by noted Aeschylean scholars, are especially valuable to those who do not know Greek because they include line-by-line commentaries on the nuances of diction and allusion, as well as excellent introductions.

I would like to thank the typing pool in the Office of the Dean of Arts and Sciences at the University of Missouri–Kansas City. To Dr. Jonas Spatz of the English Department of the University of Missouri–Kansas City I owe a special debt of gratitude for his professional help with style as well as for his affectionate support and encouragement. Finally, I would like to express my appreciation to Professor Ruth Scodel, the editor of this series, for her careful reading and constructive advice.

University of Missouri–Kansas City

Lois Spatz

Chronology

Chapter One
Aeschylus: Citizen and Poet

Life and Times

This monument covers Aeschylus the Athenian, Euphorion's son, who died in the wheatlands of Gela. The sacred grove of Marathon with its glories can speak of his valor in battle. The long-haired Persian remembers and can speak of it too.

So reads the epitaph of Athens's first great tragic poet. This verse was composed by Aeschylus himself, according to Pausanias, the second-century A.D. geographer who wondered why the playwright neglected to mention his tragedies.[1] But it is not surprising that this particular poet who witnessed the birth of the Athenian democracy and then participated in its astounding defeat of the Persian Empire would define himself primarily as an Athenian citizen, a veteran of the battle of Marathon (490 B.C.). From his extant plays, it is clear that Aeschylus saw in these events a moral lesson which affected the choice and interpretation of the myths he dramatized for his fellow citizens. And it is also possible that he viewed his poetry as part of his duty as a citizen. In his comedy *Frogs* (405 B.C.), Aristophanes defined the best dramatist as the one who could make the Athenians better citizens and offer the city the best advice (11. 1009–10). On the eve of the Athenian defeat by Sparta, Aristophanes chose to bring Aeschylus, the symbol of the Marathon generation, back from Hades to save the state again.

Aeschylus did not witness the war with Sparta. He was born almost a century earlier, in 525 B.C., in nearby Eleusis, the center for the worship of Demeter and the Eleusinian Mysteries. The facts about his life are sparse.[2] His father was Euphorion, a member of a noble family. His brother, Cynegirus, died at Marathon and he himself may have fought at Salamis and other battles in the Persian War. He probably began to present tragedies early in the fifth century and won his first victory in the annual dramatic contest conducted by the city of Athens in 484. Five of his seven extant plays can be dated with certainty: *Persians* in 472, *Seven Against Thebes* in 467, and the three plays of the *Oresteia* (*Agamemnon, Libation Bearers,* and *Eumenides*) in 458. *The Suppliants* may have been produced in the 460s, whereas *Prometheus Bound* seems to be one of his latest plays (if it was in fact composed by Aeschylus).[3] We do not know how many plays Aeschylus actually wrote; fragments from over fifty plays survive, and ancient sources list nearly ninety titles. Nor is it clear how many victories he won in the contests; perhaps he received thirteen first prizes during his lifetime, and then fifteen more were awarded to revivals of his plays after his death. There is also some confusion about Aeschylus's membership in the Eleusinian Mysteries. Although Aristophanes' *Frogs* (11. 885–87) suggests the poet was an initiate of the cult, Aristotle implies (*Nichomachean Ethics*, 3.1) that Aeschylus accidentally exposed one of its secrets. And, to defend himself against the charge of revealing the Mysteries, according to Clement of Alexandria (*Stromateis* 2.461), Aeschylus proved he never was an initiate. The poet probably traveled twice to the court of the tyrant Hieron of Syracuse in Sicily. On his first visit, he wrote a play in honor of Hieron's foundation of the new city of Aetna (476) and put on a performance of *Persians* for the ruler. He died at Gela during his second visit in 456. According to the ancient *Life of Aeschylus*, the grieved Athenians voted that anyone who wished to produce one of his plays at festival time should be granted a chorus by the official in charge.

In his lifetime, Aeschylus saw Athens develop from an insignificant polis (city-state) ruled by a tyrant into an energetic democracy which led the fight agains the Persian attempt to dominate Greece.[4] While Aeschylus was still a youth, the tyrant, Hippias, the son of Pisistratus, was driven out (510). Clisthenes, the leader of the reform, organized the citizens into ten new tribes with new officers, in order to unify the population of Attica and to break the power of the nobility. He also expanded the People's Council, which served as a steering committee for the Popular Assembly composed of all citizens (508). A reform instituted after Marathon opened public office to nonaristocratic land-

owners and thus reduced the nobles' control of the Council of the
Areopagus, a body of ex-magistrates which functioned as a supreme
court able to declare the assembly's laws or proceedings unconstitu-
tional. By 462, Ephialtes passed a law which deprived the Areopagus of
all judicial powers except those related to premeditated murder. Thus,
the assembly, with its annually elected council and its own People's
Court, gained complete control of the government. A few years later,
the magistracies themselves, now offices for executing the assembly's
will rather than initiating policy, were opened up to all citizens.
Although hostility between the *demos* (common people) and nobles
smoldered constantly and burst into crisis from time to time under rival
leaders, the new democratic institutions worked in practice. Moreover,
the *demos*, now directly responsible for policy and public affairs, became
an experienced, informed, energetic, and patriotic citizen body.
Herodotus reports on the effect of the political change.

Thus Athens went from strength to strength and proved, if proof were
needed, how noble a thing freedom is . . . ; for while they were oppressed
under a despotic government, they had no better success in war than any of
their neighbors, yet, once the yoke was flung off, they proved the finest
fighters in the world . . . so long as they were held down by authority, they
deliberately shirked their duty . . . ; but when freedom was won, then every
man amongst them longed to distinguish himself.[5]

The heroism of the Athenian response to the Persian invasion proves
his point. When, in 500 B.C., their fellow Greeks in Asia Minor and
the islands revolted against Persian taxes and tyranny, Athens and her
ally Eretria were the only mainland Greeks to help the Ionian rebels.
The revolt was a failure, but the Athenian intervention attracted the
enmity of Persia. Ten years later, the Persians set out to avenge the
interference. When they landed on the plain of Marathon, twenty-six
miles from Athens, the citizen army, led by Miltiades, met and
defeated a greatly superior Persian army. As the Persians retreated
toward Athens, the Athenians suspected that aristocratic traitors were
about to surrender the undefended polis. They marched back in such
haste that they arrived in Athens before the Persian fleet. Seeing them

camped outside the city walls, the Persians turned around and set sail for Asia.

Xerxes, the son of Darius, began a massive invasion of Greece in 483. While most mainland Greeks could not decide whether to fight, Athens, under the brilliant leadership of Themistocles, was already preparing its naval defense. When the brave Spartan troop under Leonidas was defeated by treachery at Thermopylae and the Athenian fleet could not stop the Persian ships at Artemision, the allied navy gathered at the gulf of Salamis to decide whether to make their next stand there or closer to their homes, in the Peloponnese. Themistocles prevented them from dispersing and leaving Attica undefended. Earlier he had evacuated his civilian population to Troezen and Salamis, interpreting the "wooden walls" the Pythia at Delphi had promised would survive the war as the ships of the Athenian navy. Now he manipulated the Persians into fighting the decisive sea battle at Salamis under conditions most advantageous to the Greek fleet. The result was a disaster for the Persian navy. Although the Persian infantry sacked Athens, desecrated its temples, and burned the Acropolis, they could not win the war after the Greek naval victory. With most of their ships destroyed, the Persian fleet withdrew and its army evacuated Athens for the winter. The Persians were able to reoccupy the city in the spring, but an alliance of Athenians and Spartans finally defeated them in a land battle at Plataea in 479. About the same time, an allied navy defeated the remnants of the Persian fleet at Mycale. At home, the Athenians began to rebuild their city. On the seas, the Athenians and Spartans joined with the Greeks of Asia and the islands in an alliance known as the Delian League to push the Persians back from the coast of Asia Minor. But when the allies became dissatisfied with the Spartan commanders, Sparta, with trouble at home, willingly withdrew and left Athens in control. Leadership of the Delian League brought a new set of problems, but the victory over Persia was complete.

The magnitude of the Athenian success was interpreted as a sign of divine intervention in history. Herodotus reports Themistocles' reaction to the Persian withdrawal from Salamis.

Indeed it was not we who performed this exploit; it was God and our divine protectors, who were jealous that one man in his godless pride should be king of Asia and of Europe too—a man who does not know the difference between sacred and profane, who burns and destroys the statues of the gods, and dared to lash the sea with whips and bind it with fetters. (*The Histories.* 8.109, 535)

Aeschylus, an eyewitness to the events, dramatized this moral lesson in his historical tragedy, *Persians*. Godless pride inevitably brings divine jealousy and punishment to men. The cosmic justice illustrated by the divine response reaffirms the moral order and validates the political ideals that support it.

But Aeschylus may have feared that those political ideals were in jeopardy once the immediate danger of foreign intervention disappeared. Success against Persia was followed by intense rivalry for leadership at home (first between Themistocles and Cimon, with the support of Aristides, and then between Cimon and Ephialtes, whose successor was Pericles) and by disturbing changes in relations with Sparta and with the allies in the Delian League. Against this background of the polis in transformation, Aeschylus, in *Persians* and in his tragedies derived from myth, dramatized both the suffering of the past and the hope for honorable compromise that would preserve those Athenian ideals which were the source of their success.

Tragedy as Public Worship

Noted classicists such as Gilbert Murray and Gerald Else have termed Aeschylus the father of tragic drama.[6] His *Persians* is the earliest Greek tragedy that has come down to us. It is a sophisticated play, where choral odes with elaborate meters alternate with episodes of dialogue between actors, which forces participants and spectators to examine the universal principles of morality and cosmic justice. Yet its antecedents are almost entirely unknown apart from the few titles of plays by earlier tragedians and the speculations of much later Greek and Roman writers.[7]

We can discern, however, some important differences between the ancient Greek theater and our own. First of all, it is clear that the origin and development of Attic tragedy are closely connected to the religious and political life of the people. According to the Parium Marble (almost the only universally accepted piece of evidence), Pisistratus, the tyrant of Athens, in honor of the god Dionysus, established in 534 B.C. the Great or City Dionysia, an elaborate state festival culminating in several days of performances of tragedy. Throughout the classical age, plays were produced in places sacred to the gods on specific days set aside for worship. In the festivals at Athens, the citizens paid for, participated in, watched en masse, and then judged the performances and the performers. Thus, unlike our modern theater, Greek drama was religious rather than secular, a community product rather than an esoteric art form, and a state-supported rather than a commercial enterprise.

It is difficult to explain exactly why and how Dionysus, the god of wine and agriculture, became the patron deity of drama.[8] Only one extant tragedy, Euripides' *Bacchae*, actually dramatizes a myth about him. His worship was tied to that of the grain goddess Demeter and the cycles of nature, to winter and summer, to planting, which the ancients viewed as the death of the seeds buried in the earth, and harvesting the crop, which they considered the rebirth of the seeds as vegetation. Typical Dionysiac myths show the god, who is himself killed and reborn in two versions, arriving at a new place, meeting resistance, and then finally overcoming the opposition (e.g., *Bacchae*). Behind these tales, some scholars suppose a ritual reenactment or cultic narrative of the forces of life struggling against and ultimately defeating the forces of death. Although the playwrights introduce so many innovations in the myths that tragedies cannot be considered rituals or reenactments, the typical tragic conflict which leads to a hero's struggle and defeat may have antecedents in the winter/resistance phase in the Dionysiac legend. Interestingly enough, after 486, comedy, which completes the cosmic cycle by celebrating the life force through the success of its lusty heroes, was added to the day's presentation of tragedies.

The seeds of the subject matter may be in the myths about Dionysus, but the devices and effects of drama probably go back to the way he was originally worshiped. Dionysus's cult was escstatic; participants used loud music, dancing, and, of course, wine, to liberate themselves from their individual identities. By putting on costumes, skins, and masks, they could transform themselves into the animals or heroes associated with Dionysus.[9] Thus they were able to commune with and even take on the powers of the deity. The later dramatic festival supervised by the state, complete with sacrifices, processions, mummery, and drinking, channeled the religious drives toward ecstasy and communion into an orderly and socially cohesive form. The climax of the festival in the performances would offer the citizen an opportunity for a shared release from his limited private self. Actors, chorus, and audience together became participants in a dramatization of an event in sacred time which connected them to each other as well as to the ambiguous potency of divine and eternal nature.

The Great Dionysia was held at the end of March.[10] As a preliminary to the celebration, Dionysus's statue was escorted by a torchlight procession from outside the city to his theater. Just before the official opening, the poets appeared with their actors to announce the subjects of the plays to be performed (*proagon*). The festival proper began with another procession, known as the *pompē*, which culminated in sacrifices in the god's sacred precinct. On the following days, the contests were held. The exact schedule is uncertain. At the time of *Persians*, three days were devoted to tragedy with each poet being assigned one separate day to present three tragedies and a satyr play. (The group was called a tetralogy.) A single comedy probably concluded the day's dramas. Each morning at daybreak the ceremonies began; after the theater was purified by a sacrifice and libations were poured, the herald announced the titles of the day's plays. At the end of the series of performances, judges voted on the order of merit and the victorious poet was awarded a crown of ivy in the theater. Official records of competitors and victors were inscribed in stone. Private individuals, proud of their participation, set up monuments to commemorate their contributions.

The entire community was responsible for the success of the Great Dionysia. The magistrate known as the *archon epynomous* had charge of the procession and the contests. He selected the poets for the competition and appointed the *choregus* or sponsor who would pay for the costuming and training of the chorus for one tetralogy. (The richest citizens were required to underwrite the performances in turn as a kind of income tax.) The choregus had to pick his chorus and its trainer from among the citizens. In addition he may have played some role in the choice of plays and selection of the judges. To the poet, and later the archon, belonged the responsibility for the selection, payment, and training of the actors (who were all male and professionals). The state developed procedures to ensure that the performances were evaluated fairly. The citizens who were selected as judges, by lot according to tribe from an approved list, had to swear they would give an impartial verdict. At the end of the Great Dionysia, the assembly scrutinized the conduct of both the officials and private citizens during the festival. The examination of public records, prosecution for misconduct (such as assault while intoxicated or seat-stealing), and the granting of public honor for extraordinary efforts assured the propriety of the celebration.

The dramatization of myth, which Pisistratus made the keystone of the festival, probably arose from the combination of two earlier and familiar modes of public communication: choral song and individual recitation. By the end of the sixth century B.C., group singing and dancing had developed from impromptu expressions of emotion into an elaborate genre which combined poetic or imagistic diction and structure, complex lyric meters, stylized dance steps, and accompaniment by a flutist.[11] Such choral odes would be performed at public occasions like funerals, anniversaries of the deaths of heroes, and religious festivals. Tragic poets themselves incorporated these familiar forms into the lyrics of their dramas.[12] The entrance song of the chorus in *Bacchae* imitates the cult song of a Dionysiac procession, whereas Aeschylus ends *Persians* and *Seven Against Thebes* with dirges similar to his audience's own funeral laments.

The actors' sections are different from the choral odes. The lines are spoken, or sometimes declaimed or chanted, in stichic verses imitative of the rhythm, diction, and logic of conversation or debate. Moreover, whereas the chorus narrates, witnesses, or reacts to important events, the actors perform as if they were the very characters involved in the crisis. This aspect of the drama has been traced to two main sources.[13] Traveling bards (rhapsodes) who recited Homer changed their voices and expressions to match each character in the conversations and arguments of epic. Lyric poets too performed their compositions as people describing personal experience rather than narrating events. Early in the sixth century B.C., Solon, the lawgiver of Athens, had already used the verse forms which later appeared in the episodes of tragedy to defend his ideas to the public in his own person.

Other Greek city-states had the same kinds of public processions, emotional forms of worship and lament, and rhapsodes and poets. Yet only in Athens were these diverse elements combined to produce tragedy. Although it must have already had some artistic merit and popularity to attract Pisistratus's patronage, the first tragedy is attributed to Thespis in the Sixty-first Olympiad (536–533 B.C.), which corresponds to the date for the establishment of the Great Dionysia. Who Thespis was, and whether or why he created the form must always remain unknown. Scholars have speculated, however, that Pisistratus's motives for encouraging its development were political. At a time when the tyrant needed support to remain in power, he built up civic pride and patriotism by instituting great city festivals. He chose Dionysus as the patron of one because this agricultural deity was popular with the small landholders. He selected the new form tragedy because it had no association with the older aristocratic public celebrations. But whatever his reasons, the Athenian population responded with enthusiasm and support. New plays continued to be written by respected citizens of the polis, and contests for actors as well as poets were instituted. Gerald Else explains the effect of tragedy on the Athenian audience:

The *Iliad* with its dual vision of heroism and the tragic limits of heroism is the root of all tragedy. . . . But it took Thespis' act of genius to bring the Homeric vision into focus for a new age. The *Iliad* deals only with heroes; the common man is present only as a backdrop, stage setting, or else as the audience sitting and listening to a far off tale of long ago. Tragedy for the first time brought the far away directly into the present and the great man into direct contact with the little man. It did these two things through the twin devices of the "actor" and the chorus. Through the actor, who was the hero, standing before him, and the chorus, which was "like himself," the ordinary Athenian was enabled to feel, to sympathize with the hero in a new way. Here all Athenians, noble and common alike, could meet on a common ground, in a common surge of emotional identification with the heroic spirit. All of this was done through forms—iambic verse, *rhesis* (speech), hymn, *threnos* (lament)—a living part of Athenian experience, and therefore sure of their emotional effect. Tragedy represented, in effect, the beginning of a new spiritual unification of Attica.[14]

Form and Performance

The theater of Dionysus in which Aeschylus's plays were performed differs considerably from our standard theater building, housing a raised stage with a proscenium arch, curtains, and artificial lighting.[15]

The Athenian audience sat outside on benches set in semicircular rows on the southeast slope of the Acropolis. They looked down on the playing area at the foot of the hill, a huge round dancing floor fifteen feet in diameter called the orchestra (from the Greek verb *orchēomai* meaning "I dance"). Ramps on either side, known as *eisodoi* or *parodoi* ("entrances") provided passageways for most of the entrances and exits required by the performers. At the time of the *Oresteia*, if not before, a stage building (*skēnē*) sat on the far side of the orchestra opposite the spectators. Its inside was used by the actors as a changing room. Its facade fronting the audience contained at least one door and provided a scenic background such as the entrance to a temple or palace. The door itself could be used by the actors for entrances and exits into a building, whereas the roof might be employed as an additional playing area. The structure may have stood on some sort of platform of two or three steps which provided a further playing area or stage, slightly raised but easily accessible to the orchestra. Two devices were employed in connection with the *skēnē*. To reveal a tableau of a scene described as having taken place within the building, a shallow platform on wheels, called the *ekkyklema*, could be rolled out of the opening in the facade. Hidden behind the *skēnē*, a huge crane, called the *mēchanē* or *geranos* or *kiadē*, requiring a firm foundation and a system of pulleys, functioned as a device to fly in gods for epiphanies. Although Aristophanes ridicules Euripides' excessive use of these devices, it is not clear whether a playwright as early as Aeschylus would have employed them.

By the time of Aeschylus's *Persians*, the play the audience watched had reached its classic form.[16] Generally, but not always (v. *Persians, Suppliants*) it began with a prologue spoken by one or more actors who set the scene and provided background information. Then the chorus entered the orchestra and sang a lyric known as a parodos, probably from the passageway they came through. From then on choral odes, each called a *stasimon* (because the chorus remained in the orchestra to sing it), alternated with scenes of dialogue called episodes, with the division between the two parts usually marked by the entrance or exit of the actors. Sometimes the chorus and actor sang together in a lyric exchange called a *kommos* or lament. An actor himself might also sing or chant in lyric rhythms (recitative or *parakatalogē*) to express his intensely emotional state. On the other hand, when the chorus leader conversed with an actor within an episode, he would speak the verses the actors used. When the chorus sings lyric to which the actor responds with dialogue verse, the scene is called epirrhematic. The play concluded with an exodus, the ode sung by the chorus as it left the orchestra.

No more than three actors ever converse in the same scene in any Greek tragedy (although there may have been any number of nonspeaking extras). Moreover, tradition records that whereas Thespis invented the first actor, Aeschylus introduced a second, and Sophocles added the third and last. Thus, there must have been a rule or convention which limited the number of actors in each play to three. Perhaps the restriction developed as a means of controlling the expense or insuring that the poets entered the contest with the same limitations. (Probably for similar reasons, the number of chorus members was restricted.) But the fact that only three actors could speak in any one scene did not limit the number of speaking roles in a given play. Each actor could play several parts by changing his mask in the *skēnē* between episodes. The first actor, always the most important and the only one who could win a prize, generally portrayed the character who appeared on the stage in the most episodes. The second actor would play the other interlocutors, changing his identity as often as necessary. When an episode required still another speaker, the third actor would be employed. *Libation Bearers* is the only extant Aeschylean play that contains a three-way scene. In *Agamemnon* and *Prometheus Bound*, however, Aeschylus introduced the third actor to make dramatic use of the silence of an important character who would speak later.[17] But, in general, Aeschylean tragedy consists of scenes of confrontation between two actors or one actor and the chorus.

From the beginning of tragedy, the actors wore masks, perhaps because as sacred objects in earlier forms of worship, they could magically transform the actor into the character.[18] But masks also had a more practical function; their use permitted an actor to play more than one role. Vase paintings and terra-cottas from the fifth century indicate that the mask-makers aimed at naturalism; they attempted to convey general characteristics such as sex, age, status, and even personality type. Thus, they varied the shade of the complexion, or the style and color of the hair, or slightly changed the cast of the eyebrows or mouth, or added a beard or wrinkles rather than actually distorting or exaggerating features. Sometimes additions such as a wreath for a herald, a tiara for royalty, or an exotic headdress for a foreigner further identified the character.

Although the tragic costume became standardized (as a long elaborately patterned tunic with long fitted sleeves) by the end of the fifth century, it is hard to determine exactly what Aeschylus's actors wore.[19] Their garments were probably extensions of ordinary Athenian dress. Whether portraying men or women, all the actors wore the standard Greek undergarment, a tunic called a *chiton*, which could be belted with a girdle, and might be long or short, depending on the age, sex, and status of the character. In addition, one might wear or carry the common outer garment, the *himation*. There is some indication that tragic actors wore colors keyed to their roles; i.e., purple for kings, white for priests, yellow for young girls, or black for mourners, Cassandra, in *Agamemnon*, dresses in the special outer garments of a prophetess, whereas the characters and chorus of *Persians* probably had headdresses and *chitons* as well as tunics with patterns or lengths to indicate their oriental origins. A special boot called a *cothurnus* also was associated with the tragic costume. It had a normal sole and high uppers which were laced tight on males, but left loose on females.

Since actors wore masks which hid their facial expressions, they had to develop their characters by relying on their voices and gestures.[20] The theaters were large and the spectators in the last rows were far from the playing area. Thus, although the acoustics were excellent because the mountain slope itself and later the *skēnē* formed sounding boards, the actor had to learn to throw his voice clearly. He also had to be able to change his voice when he changed his role in the course of a play. Not only did the actor speak in rhythms close to conversation, but he often recited more elaborate verses to the accompaniment of a flute (recitatives) and sometimes even sang in lyric rhythms. Thus, his vocal skills were more like those of an opera singer's, and he was judged in similar terms. Moreover, he had to develop skill in using gestures and rapid movements to compensate both for the absence of facial expression and the distance from his audience. The clarity of his gestures would be particularly important since his adherence to or deviation from his society's fixed procedures for approaching others (i.e., the rituals of supplication, libation, prayer, mourning) would convey to the audience the gravity of the situation and his own attitude to the established rules of behavior.[21] Indeed, some scholars have suggested that the three-actor limit evolved naturally because it was difficult to find men with so many talents.

In Aeschylus's time, the chorus was as important as the actor and far more difficult to prepare for the production.[22] It was composed of twelve men (fifteen in Sophocles and Euripides) who were chosen from a pool of citizens skilled in singing and dancing. The chorus probably dressed in simple costumes and masks which identified their sex and station. Exactly how they performed is not certain.[23] They were led into the orchestra by a more elaborately dressed flutist who accompanied their songs. Once there, they grouped themselves into a rectangular formation, according to ranks and files. The leader of the chorus, the *coryphaeus*, who spoke for the group would probably be in a prominent position, visible whether addressing his companions or the actors. Although the stanzas of a choral ode are usually divided into two metrically corresponding parts (strophe and antistrophe), there is no evidence to suggest that the chorus divided in half to sing or dance to each other. Aeschylus himself is said to have invented many of the movements and gestures which became standard accompaniments to the odes. These dances probably consisted of a combination of steps and turns with fixed poses or attitudes (*schemata*) that imitated the gestures expressive of common activities or emotions. Dirges must have been accompanied by the beating of breasts and the tearing of hair and cheeks, and perhaps even bending, kneeling, or falling to beat the ground to arouse the dead or depict despair.

We can assume that the producers of Greek tragedy were aiming in part to create an illusion of reality.[24] The audience, used to imagining the picture from the word, would not expect scenic realism as we define it today, but, in fact, most actions described in the text as occurring before the spectators' eyes could be easily performed by the actors. Events which could not be represented believably in the playing area (i.e., murders, storms, battles) usually happened "off-stage" and were described by messengers. Nonetheless, several conditions in the theater required that the audience accept certain conventions about the performance.[25] The plays were acted out in broad daylight in an open area without curtains, a roof, or artificial lighting. The audience had to imagine there was darkness if a performer carried a lantern or announced that it was night. They had to visualize the open space, or altar, or later the facade of the *skēnē* as whatever setting the drama required. In the early plays, the audience's imagination was limited only by the text. They could visualize the open space as any interior room or outdoor scene the characters indicated. Once the *skēnē* was used to represent a building, however, the audience was by definition outside. They had to accept the presentation of intimate conversation as taking place outdoors in public or the representation of the interior scenes in tableau on the platform (*ekkyklema*).

Any theater audience must pretend that the actors are the characters they represent rather than the people they know they are. In the modern theater, whether arena or proscenium, the darkened auditorium separates the spectators, psychologically as well as physically, from the illuminated playing area. No such barrier existed in the Greek theater; the daylight shone on both the orchestra and the benches; the first rows of patrons were on the same level as the chorus, and the spectators, like the performers, were citizens who might be participants in the next dramas of the Great Dionysia. Perhaps the depersonalized masks and costumes, as well as the dancing and music, helped to create the illusion that transported the audience from the busy world of contemporary Athens to the timeless realm of myth. In tragedy, this barrier between the two worlds is never broken by direct communication between the performers and the audience, by topical allusions, or even by references to the "theater" as a metaphor for life.[26] Thus, the audience never participates or is made self-conscious by the performance, as happens frequently in Old Comedy. Rather, the audience at a tragedy loses its own identity in the sustained dramatic illusion and empathizes with the heroes and chorus of a sacred past which it recognizes as its own.

Information about the audience, like everything else, comes from later sources and may not reflect its constitution and character in Aeschylus's lifetime.[27] The stone theater must have accommodated about 15,000 seats with standing room for a few thousand more. In the beginning, the spectators were citizens of Athens who knew one another and shared a common political and public life. Women and boys were probably admitted as well, although they might have been required to sit high up in back, separated from the men. The best seats, those in front, nearest the orchestra, were reserved for important public officials and visiting dignitaries. When Athens, as ruler of the Delian League, became the center of the Greek world, the Great Dionysia was crowded with ambassadors and private citizens from city-states throughout the Mediterranean.

The audience arrived at dawn and sat through three tragedies, a satyr play, and one comedy. This feat demonstrates their stamina at the very least, but does not indicate what the spectators took away from the drama. Anecdotes related by the ancient commentators indicate that audiences were very noisy when they wanted to show their disapproval; they hissed, whistled, or kicked their heels against the backs of their seats. On the other hand, a good actor or a moving plot could draw tears. In addition, we read that the audience reacted to individual lines; for example, they interpreted verses of praise for the character Amphiaraus in *Seven Against Thebes* as a description of Aristides the Just, who was present at the performance (Plutarch, *Life of Aristides*, 3). Aristophanes compliments the Athenians on their ability to recognize allusions and judge the technical elements of tragic poetry in *Frogs*, but we cannot really assess their critical faculties from his broad parodies of tragic style.

The fact that Old Comedy does parody the plays and the playwrights, however, testifies to the enormous interest they generated. Many critics, ancient and modern, have attempted to understand the way the best tragedies affected the audience.[28] While Aristophanes emphasized their social role in making the spectators better citizens, Gorgias, Plato, and Aristotle analyzed their ability to stimulate feelings of horror, pity, indignation, and compassion by dramatizing the suffering of others. Recently Oliver Taplin has stressed the complexity of the emotions aroused: the way the audience both fears and desires the terrible event, the "paradoxical pleasure" of these "doleful feelings."[29] But he points out that the emotional is indivisible from the intellectual effect. The focus on the suffering of strangers creates a distance from the trivia and traumata of private life which enables the audience to view suffering from a different and broader perspective. Moreover:

. . . the events of the tragedy are in an ordered *sequence*, a sequence which
gives shape and comprehensibility to what we feel. And, most important of
all, the affairs of the characters which move us are given in a moral setting
which is argued and explored in the play. They act and suffer within
situations of moral conflict, of social, intellectual, and theological conflict.
The quality of the tragedy depends *both* on its power to arouse our emotions
and on the setting of those emotions in a sequence of moral and intellectual
complications which is set out and examined. . . . Tragedy makes us feel
that we understand life in its tragic aspects. . . , that we can better sympathize with, and cope with suffering, misfortune, and waste.[30]

In the ensuing chapters, we shall examine how Aeschylus created,
through story, poetry, and production, emotional experiences which
his fellow Athenians appreciated as beneficial and which still have the
power to affect us today.

Chapter Two
Persians: Monodrama

Plot Summary

Persians was produced for the Great Dionysia of 472 and was awarded first prize. It was presented as the second play of a tetralogy and seems to have had no relation in plot or theme to the other three plays of the group, *Phineus, Glaucus Potneius*, and the satyr play *Prometheus*.[1] The drama begins with a parodos in which a chorus of Persian elders enter the orchestra, and explain that they were left behind to watch over the empire while Xerxes led his mighty forces against Greece. By now they have become anxious because they have heard no news of the expedition. As they speculate on the outcome, Atossa, the queen mother, enters to express her own anxieties. Her fear for her son and the nation has been intensified by a recurring dream. In the dream, she sees an argument between two sisters, one dressed as a Greek and the other as a Persian. Xerxes, trying to yoke the sisters under the chariot, as if they were horses, is thrown by the Greek one, while Darius, his dead father, stands by, pitying but helpless. To avert the catastrophe portended by the dream, the queen had gone to make offerings to Apollo. At his altar, however, she watched terrified as a hawk tore apart an unresisting eagle, symbolic of the destruction of the empire. The loyal chorus advises her to supplicate the gods and take offerings to the dead, especially Darius, to counteract the omens. Atossa lingers to question the elders about the purpose of the expedition and the nature of the enemy.

As they converse, a Persian courier runs in to announce that most of the expeditionary force has been destroyed. The chorus laments in a series of brief lyrics to which the messenger responds in iambic couplets. At first, the queen is struck speechless with horror, but she recovers and requests a detailed report from the courier. After assuring

her that Xerxes is still alive, he lists the dead, describes the naval defeat
at Salamis, and recounts the army's disastrous flight from Greece.
When the queen goes back to the palace to offer prayers to the gods, the
chorus sings a lyric lament for the dead, bewailing the loss to families
and the state, and contrasting Xerxes' leadership with his father's. The
queen returns to bring gifts to the tomb of Darius. As she pours out
libations, the chorus calls on the spirit of the dead king for help. The
ghost of Darius rises from the tomb, and questions his wife while the
awe-struck chorus stands by. Darius interprets the disaster as a punishment from the gods brought on by Xerxes' arrogant yoking of the
Hellespont in his lust to join Greece to his Asian realm. He praises the
temporate rulers of the past and then predicts further woe because of his
son's desecration of the Greek shrines. After advising the queen and
chorus to comfort the returning king, Darius departs, and the chorus
sings a eulogy to him. Xerxes then enters, humiliated by the disaster he
has brought upon himself and his country. Together the defeated
monarch and the chorus lament and leave the orchestra as if proceeding
to the palace.

History and Poetry

When Aeschylus chose to dramatize the Persian reaction to the
disaster at Salamis, he was following the precedent of Phrynichus's
Phoenician Women (476 B.C.) to which he alludes in his first line. Many
of the spectators must have participated in the battle (480 B.C.) or at
the very least endured the hardships of the Persian invasion which
culminated in the sack of Athens. Therefore, we can assume that
Aeschylus probably recounted the major events of the naval defeat
accurately; most of the details conform to Herodotus's account. For
dramatic purposes, however, he chose to emphasize and even distort
certain aspects of the conflict between Greece and Persia.[2] First, he
makes Salamis the most important battle, the defeat which lost Xerxes
the war and the empire, and slights two major battles which were
equally important. Plataea, where the Spartans led a land victory on the
Boeotian plain, is barely mentioned, whereas Mycale, a naval victory
off Asias Minor, also led by a Spartan, is omitted entirely. Clearly

Aeschylus wanted to emphasize the battle of Salamis because it was Athens's owns victory, initiated by her leaders who were fighting in her waters for her very survival.

Yet, for a different reason, Aeschylus almost completely ignores Marathon, another Athenian victory (over Darius ten years earlier in 490). To heighten the impression of Xerxes' rashness, Aeschylus created a Darius who by contrast was so wise and temperate that he confined his conquests to Asia and the islands. But in fact the father was as rash as the son. Darius also attempted to yoke together two continents, when he bridged the Thracian Bosphorus in order to invade Scythia, and he too attacked the Greek mainland, to punish Athens's and Eretria's interference in the Ionian revolt. The Battle of Marathon was his disaster. Herodotus reports that Darius eagerly planned a new expedition, but that, ironically, it was Xerxes who, when he came to the throne, was at first unwilling to proceed.

Nor was the defeat as disastrous and Xerxes' flight from the battle as humiliating as Aeschylus maintains. He led his troops back to Thessaly, left part in winter quarters there, and marched most of his army to the Hellespont where they rested until they could enter Sardis, far fewer in number, but in great and orderly splendor. In 472, Xerxes was still on the throne and the fear of new Persian aggression still existed. But the depiction of a total disaster must have provided an illuminating moral lesson for the Athenian audience and diminished their anxiety about the possibility of future confrontations.

Furthermore, by presenting the Athenian victory from the Persian perspective, the playwright was able to praise the ideals and accomplishments of his polis without seeming arrogant and self-serving. The Athenians appear more heroic because the description of their courage, cunning, and prudence comes from the defeated enemy. Even while the chorus glorifies Darius by cataloguing his Ionian subjects, Aeschylus is reminding the audience of the immensity of the Greek victory. These very Ionians, who had fought with Xerxes at Salamis, were liberated by the war. In fact, the poet's use of the name "Ionians" to signify the mainland Greeks who defeated Persia (e.g., 11. 178, 950, 1025) connects these two groups of Hellenes who would be allied in the Delian League.[3]

Aeschylus also builds a contrast between Persia and Athens which justifies the Athenian victory. The constant references to the immensity and extravagance of Persia, symbolized by the abundant gold, create a picture of an entire society which possesses more than its allotted portion (*Moira*). Athens, on the other hand, is small, and its prosperity comes not from gold but silver, symbolic of its public spirit instead of wealth. The audience, hearing the reference to its silver mines, would be reminded that they had followed the advice of Themistocles and built a navy with the profits of a new vein instead of voting to enrich themselves.

The Persian obeisance to their royal family (as if they were gods, not men) provides another implicit contrast. Athens has no single individual as powerful and despotic as Xerxes or Darius. The conspicuous absence of Themistocles' name effectively dramatizes that the Athenians share equal responsibility for the destiny of their polis. More important, its citizens are free; the Persian courier tells the queen, "Slaves of no one, they are called, nor in subjection to any man" (1. 342). But the Persians are not only enslaved to their rulers; they are also the enslavers of others. After hearing the report of disaster, the chorus laments the loss of its empire:

> They throughout the Asian land
> No longer Persian laws obey
> No longer lordly tribute yield,
> Exacted by necessity;
> Nor suffer rule as suppliants,
> To earth obeisance never make:
> Lost is the kingly power—
>
> Nay, no longer is the tongue
> Imprisoned kept, but loose are men,
> When loose the yoke of power's bound,
> To bawl their liberty. (11. 584–94)[4]

Some scholars conjecture that Aeschylus chose his subject to do more than remind the Athenians of their accomplishments.[5] In the 470s, Themistocles' popularity was being undermined by his political rivals,

Cimon and Aristides. By 472, he was on the verge of ostracism and exile. It is possible that Aeschylus wanted to remind the Athenians of their debt to Themistocles in order to prevent his condemnation. Although the poet never mentions the Athenian leader by name, he does focus attention on him in various ways, e.g., by exaggerating the importance of Salamis, by mentioning Themistocles' trick that forced the naval battle (11. 355 ff.), and by alluding to his various policies.[6] But the chronology of Themistocles' fall is too uncertain and the tragedy's references too vague to assess what Aeschylus's position really was. Perhaps the play, in glorifying the Hellenic union at Salamis, is much more a condemnation of the present dissension at home and abroad than a plea for one man's reputation.

In any case, Aeschylus was not writing a history or a political treatise. To enable his audience to recognize the eternally true pattern of life implicit in the specific Persian defeat, the poet had to remove his audience from the battlefield. He accomplishes this separation in several ways. By setting his scene in far-off Persia, he takes the drama out of the familiar environment of Athens and adds an aura of exotic remoteness. In addition, he portrays the famous people of history unhistorically, both by giving them unexpected characteristics and by assigning them roles which transform them from unique personalities into general character types. Moreover, through his imitation of epic style and story, he sets up a parallel between the contemporary event and the events of a more heroic past, ennobling the participants and increasing their remoteness in time. The distance created allows the poet to intertwine human action and divine response so that the audience can appreciate the paradigmatic significance of their history.

The scene of the drama, the Persian capital of Susa, is fabulously wealthy and very un-Greek. The long lists of Persian people and places, the many loan words from the Persian language, and the exotic Persian costumes reinforce the remoteness of the action from Athenian life. Even when the Persian courier must describe the sites and details of the battle, he mentions no Athenians by name.

Aeschylus also endows his characters with features that distinguish them from the real people associated with the event. The male rulers do not appear before the spectators as the mighty despots so hated by the

Greeks. Rather, Darius is a godlike ghost who justifies the Athenian victory, and Xerxes stands before his subjects humiliated and powerless. The chorus are not the dread warriors who sacked Athens and desecrated her shrines; they are wise, reverent old men who recognize divine will in their disaster. Aeschylus intensifies this fictionalization of the Persians by portraying them as general types. Atossa's character provides the best example, since she so clearly reacts to events as a Mother or Wife as well as a Queen. Xerxes and Darius also function as Son and Father as much as Bad Ruler and Good. The chorus, too, as the respected advisor, plays the general role of Citizen.

Allusions to epic increase the Persian's remoteness from contemporary history. Through the use of epic diction and style, the clash between Greece and Persia becomes associated with that grand battle of the past, the Trojan War, fought in a greater time when men were more heroic and gods actually intervened directly in human events. Imitating the formulae of the *Iliad*, Aeschylus catalogues the names of the Persian warriors who marched off to battle or died with honor (11. 21–56, 302–28, 958–99), identifying them with the valiant heroes of the past. Moreover, the poet uses the story pattern of the *Odyssey* and the return sagas of the epic cycle (where the hero struggles to reach home while his subjects and family anxiously await his arrival) to introduce a parallel between Xerxes and Odysseus (or the other heroes of return sagas).[7] Xerxes' return, however, is a tragedy because, in contrast to Odysseus, he cannot set his house in order. He is the destroyer, not the savior, and his arrival confirms rather than allays the Persians' worst fears.

As in epic, so in the battle of Salamis, Xerxes' failure is not ascribed only to Athens's bravery and cunning. In the myths of epic, situations contain more meaning because human behavior provokes a divine response which illuminates the eternal principles of cosmic order. In *Persians,* too, the poet makes clear that the gods themselves were punishing Xerxes for his transgression of eternal laws which bind all men, even emperors of mighty Persia. Since the spectators confront the defeated, who indirectly praise them while praying and lamenting in familiar ways, the spectators can extend their sympathy to these fellow human beings in their suffering, while at the same time approving, as the characters themselves do, the divine resolution. But the spectacle could not lead the Athenians to gloat over their victory because the action forces them to recognize that they are not solely responsible for the outcome of the battle. If they identify with the Persians, they may recognize their own propensity for moral error. Darius proclaims that his nation's fall must serve as a warning against the ambitions of all future nations. Thus, when the temporal event is revealed to have a cosmic significance, the spectators themselves become aware of their participation in the universal moral order.

The awareness of the gods' intervention develops at the same time as the characters' sense of dread increases. The chorus mentions as early as line 93, in a passage about the invincibility of the expedition, that the divine spirit *Atē* (Ruin) often leads men into traps; although they refer here to the Greeks, the lines also ironically allude to the Persian debacle. The courier suggests that some god (*daimon*, 1. 345) defeated the army, and later cut off their escape on the frozen river (11. 495–502, where forms of *theos* appear three times). The strongest evidence of divine concern comes from the gods themselves, however. Atossa's dream and then the destruction of the eagle, the royal bird, at the altar of Apollo are accepted as direct messages from the other world. The Darius who rises from the dead is more than the former king. He confirms his authority with the gods of the dead before he proclaims both Xerxes' responsibility and the gods' partnership in the disaster (11. 742—50, 819–26).

The relation between the temporal and the cosmic is intensified by the way in which the present action, Xerxes' return, is set into a time frame which shifts from immediate past, to more distant past, to present, and even to the future.[8] This is accomplished through such devices as the chorus's memory of the troops' departure, the messenger's report, Darius's survey of the Persian past, and his prediction of the defeat at Plataea. Although there is unity of time in the simple plot of the return, that present moment is connected to all other significant moments in a way that reveals a pattern of relations between the human and the divine. Darius, who summarizes Persian history, also offers a general statement of the unchanging universal:

> Insolence [*hubris*], once blossoming, bears
> Its fruit, a tossled field of doom [atē], from which
> A weeping harvest's reaped, all tears.
> Behold the punishment of these! remember

Greece and Athens! lest you disdain
Your present fortune, and lust after more,
Squandering great prosperity,
Zeus is the chastener of overboastful
Minds, a grievous corrector. Therefore advise
Him [Xerxes], admonished by reason, to be wise,
And cease his overboastful temper from
Sinning against the gods. (11. 821–32; Benardete, trans.)

Live Performance

The play was much more than its plot, however. Aeschylus directed a
performance for an audience who could see and hear the chorus and
characters move in and out and around the orchestra. But we do not
have any stage directions, notes about the dance and musical accompaniment, or even an undisputed reconstruction of the playing area (see
Chapter 1). What we do possess is the text itself, with its lyric rhythms
related to other genres or public ceremonies, and its characters' own
references to their actions, costumes, and companions. From the clues
in the texts, we shall focus on certain features of the total production
which seem to affect the audience's reaction and underline the poet's
themes.

For a modern audience, used to awarding prizes for scene design and
costuming, "spectacle" is the most easily comprehensible element in
the production of tragedy. Although there could be no elaborate set in
the Theater of Dionysus where the chorus had to have room to dance,
Aeschylus was known in antiquity as the most spectacular of tragedians
for his use of visual effects.[9] In *Persians*, three devices reinforce the
impact of the action. The most obvious is the raising of the ghost of
Darius, which is all the more shocking because it is unexpected. We are
awaiting Xerxes, not his father. Although the dead king has been
mentioned earlier in different contexts, we only expect the queen to
make offerings and the chorus to pray for blessings from him. Instead,
she advises the chorus to conjure the dead king, whereupon they sing a
lyric in rhythms and formulae that the Greek audience would recognize
as an invocation of a divinity (*hymnos kletikos*).[10] The preliminaries and

actual arrival confirm Darius's claims that he is a god and thus add
authority to his predictions and moral pronouncements. It is not
exactly clear how the ghost's appearance was staged. The text suggests a
vertical movement; he comes up and goes down. Perhaps some tempor-
ary structure at the edge of the orchestra over an underground passage
or the mound (*pagos*) that was later leveled represented the tomb, and
the actor playing Darius came up from behind it. Or he may have
simply walked in through the passageway.[11]

Darius's appearance brings up a second feature of the spectacle—the
costuming. The dead king appears in all his royal finery, wearing
saffron slippers and an elaborate feathered tiara. (ll. 659–62). It is
assumed by critics, ancient and modern, that the Persian characters
wore Persian garments, that is, unusual headdresses, long-sleeved
ornamented robes, and patterned trousers.[12] Since these would have
seemed very exotic and lavish to the audience, they would increase the
ambience of excess which the words of the text ascribe to Persia. But if
the poet emphasizes their wealth and self-confidence through the
costumes, he turns this device to unusual use. For, when Xerxes returns
in defeat, his finery is probably ragged and tattered. Aeschylus calls
attention to the king's rags in his mother's dream, the messenger's
account of his rending his clothes in response to the battle, Darius's
advice to reclothe him, and Atossa's desire to obtain a fresh garment
suitable to his position. When Xerxes finally appears, the difference
between his rags and his father's royal splendor heightens the contrast
between the old man's stability and success and the youth's folly which
led to disaster. As the chorus escorts Xerxes to the palace, he instructs
them to rend their garments. This gesture, which accompanies their
final dirge, symbolizes the rending of the Persian empire and the
destruction of its good fortune.

Aeschylus was also famous in antiquity for his elaborate entry
scenes.[13] In *Persians,* he uses the audience's expectations about oriental
pomp to underscore the Persians' increasing degradation. As the
characters' hopes fall, the ceremonial splendour of the royal entrances
decreases. The queen's first and second entrances must have been
radically different from each other, for, in lines 607–8, when she
returns from the palace, she mentions that she has come this time

without her former luxury and her chariots. Thus, she probably made
her first entry in a grand procession, in a chariot, accompanied by
servants, and dressed in her official robes. But after the courier has
announced the disaster, she comes without the external symbols of
power and prosperity. Taplin suggests that she may even be wearing the
black robes of mourning.[14] The contrast underlines her change in
fortune while at the same time adds to her dignity since she so nobly
accepts the blow.

Scholars do not agree about the precise manner of Xerxes' entrance,
but it is clear that he comes before the spectators without the authority
and dignity of his mother and father.[15] His arrival, far from trium-
phant, presents an implicit contrast with the way he set out on the
expedition. In the parodos, the chorus proudly describes the departure
of the armament and its leader, emphasizing its size and splendor by
recurring references to numbers and gold and by actually naming the
many subordinates from many lands who led their own troops in
Xerxes' train. Although we cannot see that "gold-laden" army (*poly-
chrusos*, gold-laden, appears in lines 9, 45, and 53), that "solid column
of war" (l. 19), we are impressed by the chorus's picture of its epic
might and magnificence. But the return of the troop is very different.
The text suggests that Xerxes' robes are tattered and that he is alone (l.
1036: "I am stripped of my escort."). The whole lament emphasizes the
heroes who have been lost in battle. To the chorus's recurrent question,
Xerxes must respond with the confirmation of another death. The
chorus ends the long catalogue of fallen warriors with a simple phrase:
"Little left from so many" (l. 1003). In fact Xerxes' present escort
effectively represents his change in fortune. Instead of a huge troop of
young men, the wealth and flower of all Asia, he is now guided home to
a funeral by a small chorus of men too old to fight.

Although we have little information to help us imagine the lyric and
dance, we can point out a few aspects of this part of the production,
from the text and our knowledge of other lyrics. The drama begins and
ends with the chorus. There is no prologue spoken by an actor or actors
to set the scene and situation, as in most other extant Greek tragedies.
Instead, the play opens with the parodos in which the Persian elders

come through the passageway (also called parodos) chanting in anapests, as if marching toward a public building (1. 141).[16] The poet's use of the chorus to introduce this play emphasizes the communal import of the plot. This will be no family tragedy from which the state suffers incidently; rather the fortune of all Persia is at issue, and the chorus represents all Persians, absent and at home.

The variety of rhythms used and the context in which they appear help to underline the change in Persian fortune.[17] The stately anapestic rhythms which open the play suggest public processionals and add dignity and authority to the old men and to the queen whom they greet reverently. This formal rhythm, which the chorus leader uses twice to address the queen, also stresses the distance between ruler and subject in the monarchy. (The same rhythm is used for a song to Zeus in lines 532–47.) The queen and Darius sometimes respond in trochaic tetrameter, a verse form used for formal dialogue. When the disaster is announced, the queen reveals by her silence her horror as well as her dignity.

But the chorus's opening song also contains ionic rhythms, suggestive of the more ecstatic religions of the East. And it is these rhythms that are picked up as the emotional tensions build and the Persians themselves begin to lose the dignity associated with their secure power and prosperity. The ode which follows the courier's bad news contains a greater variety of lyric rhythms punctuated by cries of pains—ee!, ōa!, pheu!. The next ode, the invocation of Darius, separated only by the queen's short speech and their shorter response, builds to a frenzy by means of repeated cries and even repeated words in rhythms associated with the most intense emotion (choriambics and dochmiacs as well as ionics). The chorus's movements probably expressed their frenzy as well; they may have beat the tomb or ground to arouse the dead king. Awestruck by his epiphany and certain of his divinity, they express their fear in ionics instead of the anapests they used for the queen. The predominance of the lyrics over the episodes in this middle section emphasizes their pain and dread. But their next ode, after Darius departs, provides an effective contrast with the preceding and following songs. Their praise of Darius's great deeds and temperate rule is

composed of dactyls, a stately epic rhythm that places Darius firmly in
an honorable past and thus increases our sense of the difference between
then and now, between father and son.

Xerxes' pathetic appearance is matched by his verse. Unlike the other
characters, he has no speech capable of expressing his suffering. He can
only groan and lament in the lyric rhythms of the chorus. Together they
sing their lamentations in the dirge form familiar to the spectators. The
last two hundred lines are in effect a funeral procession in which the
chorus and Xerxes, representative of all Persia, ruler and ruled, beat
their breasts, pull their hair, and rend their robes, having lost
everything—subjects, property, loved ones, even their own
composure.

Diction and Imagery

Aeschylus selects words and images which increase tension and
enhance his themes.[18] In *Persians*, for example, his uncommon diction
combines with the costumes and rhythms to convey the majesty and
remoteness of his characters. His Greek vocabulary includes unusual
words such as heavy, sonorous compounds, neologisms, and rare expressions, and he even borrows words directly from the Persian language. He uses actual Persian names and introduces the royal person-
ages by their formal Persian titles. Aeschylus also borrows epic words
and formulae, such as catalogues and ornamental epithets to suggest
the heroism of the characters and the mythic nature of the action. But
his double-edged use of words conveys disapproval of oriental des-
potism and foreshadows disaster. While the chorus pronounces its
litany of royal Persian titles, it kneels before the queen in a humble
adoration that the Greeks would have rejected (11. 155–7). In addition,
Aeschylus puns on the similarity between the name "Persia" and the
Greek word for "destroy" (*persai*, 1. 178). And the epithets which added
majesty decrease and disappear once the defeat has been reported.[19]

Similarly, Aeschylus's imagery traces the action and illuminates the
themes implicit in the play.[20] *Persians* develops several related image
patterns simultaneously to underline the reversal in fortune and to
suggest the arrogance and excess which brought about the disaster. The
proud descriptions of the Persian expedition—the "gold-laden" arma-

ment, the mass of marching soldiers, the sport of hunting or fishing, the strength of the sea, and the bridge or yoke joining Asia to Greece—change their meanings once the defeat is reported. Aeschylus also inserts funeral images into the parodos and then increases their frequency until the pattern culminates (in the exodus) in the literal singing of the dirge, which symbolizes the death of Persian prosperity.

The expedition sets out as a glorious troop of orderly men. But the early frequency of the word "gold" (and related words such as "delicate" or "luxurious") forces us to recognize Persian prosperity as prideful extravagance. The contrast between the golden armament and the "black-robed heart" develops into a general contrast between radiance and gloom, or dawn and night, as the imagined mourning becomes a reality.

The description in the parodos also creates a vivid image of the infantry as a close-packed troop of men marching in step.[21] The picture of their heavy feet beating the land is fraught with danger, however, for the queen foresees that "great wealth, raising a cloud of dust, will overturn prosperity with its foot" (1. 163). The messenger's account of the retreat describes a literal fall; instead of a body of strong men on foot, the infantry is now made up of stragglers falling over one another (1. 506). The change in posture symbolizes the decline in power as well as order. In the end, Xerxes has lost the strength of his limbs (1. 913) and Asia has been brought to her knees (1. 930).

Images of hunting and fishing also underline the theme of the fall from fortune. The chorus refers to the net of ruin (1. 95) that will engulf the Greeks.[22] The queen confirms the assurance that the Greeks are the unfortunate prey when she asks why her son desired to "hunt down" Athens (1. 233). But the hunters are the ones who are trapped; the courier describes them as "tunnies or a catch of fish in the sea" (1. 424). The change in the image underlines the reversal and reinforces our sense of the inevitability of divine Ruin (Atē, who spreads her net).

The sea itself, the site of the Persian disaster at Salamis, provides one of the primary images of arrogance and reversal.[23] In the parodos, the armament is depicted as a flood of men, an irresistible wave of the sea (11. 89–90), but the sea can change, as Aeschylus implies in a neologism that describes how the wind turns the sea gray (1. 110). And after the messenger has given a factual account of the naval defeat, the

queen describes the news as a "sea of evils" that overwhelms the Persians
(1. 433), and Darius calls it a "fountain of disasters" (1. 743). Ghastly
images of the dead bobbing in the water, dashing against the shore, or
nibbled at by the fish portray the sea as the instrument of the disaster.
As Darius makes clear, the Hellespont is sacred, the Bosphorus the holy
stream, and Poseidon a god not to be overpowered (11. 745, 746, 750).
Moreover the courier and men believe that the gods directly intervened
in the retreat, raising up untimely winter and freezing the flow of the
holy Strymon (11. 495-96). Again the image reinforces a judgment;
despite its strength and self-confidence, the Persian expedition was not
equal to the divine sea.

The yoke and bridge, the most important complex of images,
embrace all these other pictures.[24] To get to Greece, Xerxes had to
bridge the Hellespont, the body of water which separates it from Asia.
His bridge connecting the two continents is described as a yoke by the
chorus (11. 65–72, 126–32) and by his mother (11. 722, 736). But the
yoke, like the net, conveys the idea of capture and enslavement because
of its use in keeping animals in their traces. In fact, the word first
appears in line 50, where Xerxes' troops hasten to cast "the yoke of
slavery around Hellas." In similar words, Xerxes is described as having
cast his yoke around the neck of the sea (1. 72). Thus the political and
metaphysical ambitions are related; Darius judges this bridge the
height of his son's folly:

> . . . , by youthful pride; who hoped
> To check the sacred waters of the Hellespont
> By chains, just as if it were a slave. He smoothed
> His way, yoking Neptune's flowing Bosphorus
> With hammered shackles. Mortal though he was,
> By folly thought to conquer all the gods
> And Neptune . . . (11. 746–50; Benardete, trans.)

The image is directly connected to the action. In the queen's dream,
Xerxes' failure to enslave Greece is foreshadowed by the Greek sister's
refusal to submit to the yoke. Significantly, he is thrown down by her
violent resistance. Like the others, the yoke image in the end redounds
on the Persians. The young widow is left alone in her marriage yoke

(11. 139, 542), the Persian yoke of strength over Asia will be loosened (1. 594), and the bridge that yoked two into one (1. 131) becomes Xerxes' escape route after his ignominious defeat (1. 736). This pattern, developed in relation to the others in the play, aptly illustrates Earp's assessment that "Aeschylus does his serious thinking in images. He creates pictures to convey difficult ideas vividly and boldly."[25] The intertwining of the pictures and their relation to the concrete details of the plot express the complex relationship among the ideas, desires, and events.

Moreover, the blending of actual dirges with ubiquitous images of lamentation engulfs the entire action of *Persians* in an atmosphere of mourning which foreshadows the sense of total destruction at the end.[26] In the first line of the play, the chorus refers to the absent warriors with an ambiguous word which also means "dead and gone." Then they interrupt their description of the golden armament to express their anxiety in the vivid imagery of the dirge. They see their minds as "black-robed" and "rent" and anticipate the cries of the Cissian women's antiphonal wails (11. 115–25). Words referring to the sounds and gestures of wailing punctuate the dialogue as the courier, the chorus, the queen, and Darius discuss the defeat at Salamis and the disastrous flight. Xerxes, watching at Salamis, "shrieked" (1. 465), "tore his robes and screamed out a shrill cry" (1. 468). In response to the report, the chorus first imagines the Persian women's almost soundless sobbing as they tear their veils, and then cries out their own very real lament. When they join their dirge to Xerxes', the antiphonal wailing, long anticipated by words and images, builds to a crescendo which dramatizes their ineluctable grief.

Persian Tragedy and Universal Condition

Xerxes is the first hero in Greek tragedy. His fall from high fortune to low illustrates that universal rhythm in human life that Aristotle later defined as an essential element in the genre. Aeschylus is more interested in the pattern than the man. He emphasizes the fact that Xerxes is the ruler of a mighty nation at the height of its prosperity and strength. Its lust for even more wealth and power has attracted the envy and anger of the gods. In the words of the queen and Darius, both majestic representatives of Persia's more prudent past, the nation had achieved a glorious and god-granted prosperity (*olbos*) which Xerxes in his pride (*hubris*) and lust after wealth (*ploutos*) destroyed, for he became infatuated (*atē*) and tried to accomplish more than any human should (the yoking of Greece to his rule of Asia and the yoking of the sea). As a consequence, he brought divine Ruin (Atē) upon himself and his nation, and all the characters condemn his rashness (*thrasos*).

The extent of Xerxes' fall from fortune is dramatized by the contrast between the ruler described as the leader of the expedition and the ruler we see before us at the end. He is first introduced to us by the chorus with his impressive formal titles: Lord Xerxes, King, Son of Darius (1. 5), as a "furious lord of populous Asia" (1. 74), a "godlike man" (1. 80), an "Ares who conquers with the bow" (1. 85). We are prepared gradually for the change in his situation by the courier's report, and by the reactions of his parents, who, because of their dreams, portents, and prophecies, seem to have a closer relationship to the gods than the "godlike man" of the parodos. But the actual appearance of Xerxes, stripped of everything, ragged, weak-kneed, and wailing, must shock us. We fully understand the extent of his fall and the limitations of his humanity.

We cannot place all the blame on Xerxes, however. As ruler he embodies all Persia's pride in its power and prosperity. And so the chorus which boasts of the expedition, glories in Darius's conquests, and laments the loss of the empire must share the responsibility for the defeat. The chorus represents the condition of the Persian people, themselves enslaved but identifying with their ruler's lust for power over other nations. Too late they (and the queen) recognize the divine response and become appropriately humble.

But Aeschylus makes it possible to pity the defeated enemy for several reasons. In the first place, despite certain implicit political and moral judgments, the Persians are presented as sensitive, noble men of heroic proportions. They deserve our sympathy from the beginning and gain more respect when they acquiesce in the justice of their punishment. Although they are trapped by their own failures, we recognize with horror that the gods have also stalked them, leading them toward the ruin which is the natural consequence of their own folly. Although no one doubts Xerxes' responsibility, all the characters see a god's hand in every stage of the unexpected defeat and disastrous withdrawal. Darius summarizes the moral of the divine/human relationship: "Whenever someone presses on, the gods join with him" (1. 742).

If the reversal of Persian fortune demonstrates the weakness of the mighty when they oppose divine will, the Athenians cannot rest secure in the assumption that their own actions are independent of this universal pattern of reward and punishment. In fact, Darius warns that the pattern is eternal, that the particular defeat at Plataea will be but one more example of a universal moral order. He exhorts future generations to learn from the event that they must curb their own propensity to "think more than mortal thoughts" (1. 819). Athens had just begun to reap the benefits of the Persian disaster and was building its own store of prosperity, as leader of the Delian League. Therefore, Darius's words to his former subjects apply directly to the spectators.

The empathy between the Athenian audience and the Persian characters goes beyond the moral lesson, however. The ordinary citizen might not recognize his own greed and ambition in the actions of the mighty ruler, but the chorus provides the bridge through which he participates in the suffering. Although the Persian elders are loyal and can offer good advice, they are not as close to the gods as the rulers and are more apprehensive of the future. Their lyrical songs of pain imitate the audience's own modes of grieving, and they pray as the Athenians pray. The chorus conveys what the ordinary citizen suffers when the nation marches off to war: the anxiety of parents for their sons, and the grief of brides who must mourn lost mates.

But even the mighty rulers reenact a personal tragedy that lies beneath the political and moral one. The royal family itself exemplifies the family per se and the three characters exhibit concerns and conflicts inherent in relationships among father, son, and mother/wife.[27] The care of the parents for each other and their child is immediately obvious. Both seem to fear for the continuation of the dynasty as well. The prudence of the older generation is dramatized in the royal couple's dignified appearance and acceptance of their suffering. In addition, Darius's careful language, so full of aphorisms and self-confident judgments, confirms his superiority. Darius twice ascribes Xerxes' rashness to his youth and inexperience (11. 741, 782). In comparison to the mature adults around him, Xerxes, the tearful son, can only seem puerile.

But the queen offers a further explanation for Xerxes' rash act: he was taunted by his associates for being a lesser man than his father. Xerxes' invasion of Greece in response to this reproach suggests his desire to outdo his father, or, in the Freudian terms of modern psychoanalytic critics, his oedipal rivalry with him.[28] To them, the queen, who reveals this information, seems herself to have an ambivalent attitude toward her son, alternately praising his ambitious quest for manhood and blaming his inadequacy or mothering him with clean clothes and comfort. The overt meaning of her dream is very clear; Xerxes will fail to conquer Greece. There are sexual overtones, however, in his attempt to yoke the two women/horses.[29] The mother splits herself into two sisters who quarrel because she desires her son and represses that desire by rebuking and censuring him. The political application suggests the mother's additional conflict between ambition for and jealousy of her son's possible success.[30] The son, in turn, wants to yoke (or marry) his father's woman (or land), in other words, to replace his father as a ruler and lover. When the Xerxes of the dream is thrown to the ground, the sight of Darius looking on causes him to rend his garments, presumably in humiliation. Darius, in dream and episode, is so strong and wise that Xerxes appears to be no serious threat. However far one wants to take the psychoanalytic interpretation, the universal tension of the parent/child relationship is part of the drama, and Xerxes, the son who fails to define himself within it, suffers his own private tragedy.

Thus, the spectators at *Persians* could watch the performance and feel pity and fear for the characters as their apprehensions become a reality, and at the same time see a relation between the suffering of the mighty and their own needs and ambitions. If what they view is painful in itself, what they gain is, in Aristotle's words, the "pleasure peculiar to tragedy."[31] Their guilty fear that too much of a good thing is dangerous, their omnipresent awareness of the likelihood of failure, and their subconscious strivings for independence are all validated by the dramatization of this particular story. When the universal pattern of reward and punishment is once again confirmed, the individual also achieves insight into the human condition. To Aeschylus, this insight is grounds for optimism, for it confirms the existence of a providential moral order. The punishment of the Persians is harsh but just, wisdom has come from their suffering, and, with god's help, a more prudent Hellas has emerged victorious.

Chapter Three

Seven Against Thebes: Resolution

Play and Trilogy

Seven Against Thebes, which won first prize in 467 B.C., was produced as the third play in a trilogy about the curse on the House of Laius. The lost *Laius* and *Oedipus* preceded the extant play, and the lost satyr play *The Sphinx* completed the tetralogy. *Seven Against Thebes* may not have been its original title. In the play, the city under siege is called Cadmeia and its citizens Cadmeians. And the seven invaders are not the central characters. Aristophanes, however, referred to the tragedy as "Seven Against Thebes" in 405 B.C. (*Frogs*, 1. 1021), so it must have been known by this name as well, and its original title was lost.[1]

The Theban saga was a popular one; it was the subject of a lost epic, the *Thebais*, two lyrics by Stesichorus, and three extant tragedies by Sophocles (*Oedipus the King*, *Oedipus at Colonus*, and *Antigone*), as well as Euripides' *Phoenician Women* and *Suppliant Women*. Its use by other poets, however, does not help us to understand the content and emphasis of the first two plays in this trilogy. Other extant plays by Aeschylus which are parts of trilogies indicate that the poet was free to invent or change details so that he could shape a familiar myth to his own themes and purposes. Thus, the safest guide we have for determining what events were brought to conclusion by *Seven Against Thebes* is the play itself (in addition to the few extant lines from *Laius* and *Oedipus*).

It is necessary to summarize the high points of the myth, however, in order to understand the impact and imagery of the extant play.[2] The ubiquitous association of Thebes with Cadmus, its founder, alludes to the unusual circumstances of the city's origin. Cadmus, a Tyrian prince, was instructed by Apollo to follow a cow and found a city in Boeotia on the very spot where it came to rest. As he was about to sacrifice the cow to Athena, a serpent who was guarding a spring sacred to Ares attacked and killed most of his men. After Cadmus struck back and killed the snake, Athena advised him to sow the serpent's teeth in the ground. From the soil sprang armed men who began to fight each other. The five who survived when Ares stopped the battle were called Spartoi or Sown Men, and their descendants became the nobles of Thebes. After Cadmus had appeased Ares for the death of his serpent son, he married the god's daughter Harmonia and ruled his new city. Implicit in this story are the ideas that the earth is literally the mother of the Cadmeians, who are thus her crop or fruit, and that the citizens themselves, literal descendants of Ares, are the survivors of an initial fratricide.

Several generations intervened between Cadmus and his descendant, King Laius, the subject of the first play in the trilogy. All we can tell from the *Seven Against Thebes* is that Apollo three times warned Laius to die childless in order to save the city. No reason is given for Apollo's words to Laius, but it has been suggested that Laius was cursed with childlessness because, while a guest, he raped Chrysippus, the son of his host, Pelops. Laius, in a frenzy, ignored Apollo's words and sired Oedipus, but then exposed his son at birth. The Sphinx, called a "reproach to the city" (1. 539), probably was sent by the gods to punish Laius's crime. Perhaps the city was implicated for not punishing Laius itself. In any case, in the first generation, the fate of the city and the fate of Laius's line were intertwined.[3] We cannot know, however, what aspects of the story Aeschylus focused on or how he dramatized the action.

Ironically, it was Oedipus, Laius's own son, who survived to murder him unknowingly and then save the city from the Sphinx. As a reward for its rescue, Thebes made him king and gave him the widowed queen, his own mother, as a bride with whom he unwittingly produced an incestuous progeny. The chorus of *Seven Against Thebes* reveals that Oedipus, at the peak of his prosperity and popularity, discovered his crime and blinded himself with the "hand that slew his father." He then cursed his sons for not providing him with "honorable maintenance" and predicted that "with an arbiter of iron in hand they would someday divide his possessions" (11. 777-90). Part of the second play must have concerned Oedipus's recognition and self-punishment. But we do not know how the playwright treated the paternal curse, which is so important to the third play.[4] It must have been stated as a riddle suggesting a quarrel over the inheritance. Its full meaning, that his sons will literally divide each other's bodies with spears and thus possess their graves as equal shares of the land, becomes clear only in the exodus of the *Seven Against Thebes*. The reason for the curse presents a further problem.[5] The phrase translated as "honorable maintenance" (1. 785) is corrupt. It could refer to the sons' improper respect, misuse of the family property, or acquiescence to the expulsion of their blind father from Thebes. Or it could mean that Oedipus, horrified at his crime, blinded himself and cursed his unnatural offspring. Whatever the reason, the enigmatic curse must have been an important element of the second play. The audience witnessing *Seven Against Thebes* would have been fully aware of Oedipus's words, if not their final significance.

We cannot be sure how Eteocles and Polynices responded to the curse or who was to blame for their quarrel. In one version of the myth, the brothers were twins who agreed to share the rule of Thebes by alternating the kingship annually. When Eteocles refused to abdicate, Polynices attacked the city. It is also possible that Aeschylus chose elements from another version. In a fragment from Stesichorus a woman advises the brothers to avoid their father's curse by dividing the family property so that one would leave the city, taking the most valuable of the family's movable possessions (the necklace and robe of Harmonia, gifts of the gods at her wedding), whereas the other would retain the land and kingship. The standard Athenian procedure for such a division of property would be that of allotment. The parties would agree upon an equal division and then the shares would be assigned by lot. An objective arbitrator would supervise the procedure and mediate any disputes that arose. If the sons of Oedipus followed this procedure (which may be alluded to in lines 727-29), the "allotment by iron" becomes a peaceful settlement with a foreigner from Scythia (famous for iron) as arbitrator.[6] But, according to Aeschylus, Eteocles must have feared more dire possibilities, for he alludes to nightmares at the time of the division (11. 710-11). In the play as in the saga, Polynices, encouraged by Adrastus, his Argive father-in-law, and Tydeus, a fellow exile and brother-in-law, launched an attack against Thebes. Although Polynices claims he was unjustly banished (11. 637 ff.), he is treated as a villain for invading his motherland throughout most of the play.

Seven Against Thebes contains little information about past events in the House of Laius. Instead the first two-thirds of the play concentrates exclusively on Eteocles' defense of his city. The tragedy opens as the Argive expedition, which has been long besieging Thebes, prepares to assault its seven gates. The scene is the acropolis of Thebes, site of the shrine of the gods (whose altars may have ringed the edge of the orchestra) and a high place from which the battle could be seen and described. In the prologue, Eteocles informs a gathering of citizens about the new situation and orders them to their respective defensive positions. Next a scout enters to report on the movements of the enemy; seven heroes, having sworn and prayed for victory, are now casting lots to determine which man shall attack which gate of Thebes. After advising Eteocles to choose the best men to meet these invaders, the scout leaves to keep further watch on events, and the king prays to Zeus, Earth, and the city's gods, as well as to his father's curse, to protect Thebes.

Once the king has exited, a chorus of shrieking women enters the orchestra in a panic; in agitated rhythms (dochmiacs and lyric iambs) they sing about the terrifying sights and sounds of the enemy advance. Several editors have suggested that they actually come running in separately, singing individual verses from lines 7 to 108, until the chorus leader calms them so that they can sing their prayers together.[7] As they pray for their lives, Eteocles returns in haste, furious at their frightened and ill-omened words, which he fears will discourage the soldiers and anger their divine protectors. In an "epirrhematic" scene in which the chorus sings lyrics and Eteocles responds in iambic trimeters, the king gradually succeeds in quieting the women and convincing them to pray instead for victory. After a series of one-line exchanges, he announces that he himself will fight as one of the seven defenders at the gates of Thebes. He then goes off to place his warriors (1. 284).

After the chorus sings a stasimon in which they describe the attack and envision their future suffering, Eteocles and the scout enter from opposite sides, hastening toward each other in their zeal to respond quickly to the enemy's assault. This episode is the center piece of the play. In seven long, paired speeches, each pair interrupted by a brief strophe from the chorus, the scout reports the names and characters of the Argive attackers, describing each primarily by his shield and motto, and the king announces an appropriate Theban opponent. The device of the paired speeches with hero opposed to hero, shield to shield, verbally represents the thrust and parry of the hand-to-hand combat that will take place off-stage.[8] Not until the seventh speech does Eteocles hear that Polynices is at the seventh gate, calling for combat with him. He recognizes his father's curse at work and prepares to enter the battle against his brother. In a second epirrhematic scene, the chorus tries to dissuade him, but, having called for his arms, he answers their protests, probably while dressing for battle, and departs for the seventh gate.[9] The chorus reviews the past history of the House of Laius, and fearfully speculates on the destiny of their cursed king. Then a messenger comes to report the two-fold results: the city has been saved by Theban victories at the first six gates, but the royal brothers have killed each other at the seventh. The chorus is elated by the salvation of Thebes, yet laments the mutual fratricide. As the bodies of the dead sons of Oedipus are carried into the orchestra, the chorus divides in half to sing an antiphonal dirge and to exit in a funeral procession, toward the place of burial.

So it seems that the play should end, with the city saved and the curse which destroys the offspring of Laius fulfilled. But the text of the play adds a new element. At line 861, in the middle of its dirge, the chorus calls attention to Antigone and Ismene, the sisters of Oedipus's dead sons. Then, at line 1005, a herald enters to announce that the council of the Cadmeians has decreed that Eteocles should be buried with honor, but that Polynices, the invader, must be cast out unburied to be left to the dogs. At lines 1026 ff., Antigone argues with the herald and insists that she will bury Polynices despite the decree. Because there are no earlier allusions in the play to Oedipus's other children or to the continuation of the Theban saga, it has been conjectured that these sections are an interpolation added by later actors for audiences familiar with Sophocles' *Antigone* or Euripides' *Phoenician Women*. Aeschylus, of course, knew the end of the saga; he even wrote a tragedy entitled *Epigonoi* (as yet undated) about the sons of the original invaders who returned in the next generation and finally did destroy Thebes. But most of our play emphasizes the safety of Thebes and the destruction of the House of Oedipus. Therefore, it seems best to discuss the *Seven Against Thebes* as if Aeschylus concluded it with the lament for the dead brothers and without reference to Antigone or her illegal burial of Polynices.[10]

The Transition from War to Curse

Aeschylus argues in Aristophanes' *Frogs* (11. 1021–22) that he has made the Athenians better citizens by composing a drama "full of Ares." He insists that anyone who has seen *Seven Against Thebes* would be eager to become a brave warrior. Indeed, the play is "full of Ares"; actors and chorus describe the horrifying sights, the unbearable noise, and the painful consequences of the siege. The fury of the attackers, clear from their violent motion and their blasphemous overconfidence, is set in opposition to the calm valor and prudent self-assurance of the defenders of the motherland. So vivid is the picture of the city protecting itself that critics believe that Aeschylus is drawing on his memory of the Persian destruction of Athens thirteen years earlier.[11] In addition to describing the terror realistically, he has added details of language and battle custom which make the Argives seem more foreign or barbarian than Greek. In contrast, the "Greekness" of Thebes is emphasized when Eteocles describes it as a "free city" (11. 74–75). His metaphorical identification of the city with a ship, and its battlements with plankings (11. 32–33) may even recall the "wooden walls" Athens relied on in the naval victory at Salamis. Aeschylus's audience, fellow citizen-soldiers and victims of invasion, would surely project their memory of the Persians' hubris, the Athenians' patriotism, and the horror of the attack onto his tragic characters and mythic situation. Thus the poet, in retelling the myth, connects the Athenian present to the timeless heroic world.

Aeschylus's emphasis on the war, however, has provoked serious criticism of the play.[12] Some scholars have charged that Aeschylus has used two separate stories, the defense of Thebes and the curse on the House of Laius, without properly blending them. They argue that the first part of the play depicts a city under siege with Eteocles as a firm and rational leader, but that once he learns that Polynices is at the seventh gate, he changes (at line 653) into an insane victim of the curse. Thus the fate of the cursed family, the themes of the first two plays,

displaces the fate of the besieged city, so important to most of the third
play, and the trilogy ends without connecting the two themes.

But an audience who had watched *Laius* and *Oedipus* would surely
consider Eteocles a member of a doomed family as well as the leader of
Thebes and would relate the war to his father's curse. In fact, the
importance of Eteocles is one of the major unifying devices in the third
play, since, as king and son of Oedipus, he represents both the city and
the family. He is the vehicle through which the curse is fulfilled and the
city rescued. The plot is Eteocles' plot, a combination of two story
patterns embodying both his recognition and his self-sacrifice.[13] Eteocles begins by behaving as if the battle is a threat only to the polis. In
fact, as we shall see, he is strangely silent about his family, while the
audience, familiar with the outcome, detects the irony in his situation
with increasing dread. Eteocles perceives gradually, through the shield
scene, that the war is also a private one, which he must fight as a son of
Oedipus. When he is thrown headlong into combat with his brother,
he submits with full will and knowledge to his self-destruction. By his
defense and death, he has saved the city. The two themes are never
separated in fact, although the hero must make the connection.

But none of this is apparent when the play begins. There are only a
few patent references to the family history of Eteocles before the sixth
pair of speeches. Early in the play (1. 70), the leader himself prays for
victory to his father's curse. Twice the chorus addresses him as the son of
Oedipus (11. 203, 372). Even though the shield of the Argive Parthenopaeus depicts the Sphinx devouring a Theban outside the city's walls,
there is no mention of either Laius's or Oedipus's relation to the
monster. The poet does not emphasize the personal and internal dimensions of the crisis, perhaps to make Eteocles' recognition all the more
dramatic and increase the audience's anxiety during the first two-thirds
of the play. Knowing the fratricide was inevitable, they must have
watched with pity and fear as Eteocles unwittingly moved toward it.

Because the Thebans must respond to the immediate threat of the
Argive invasion, Aeschylus only gradually narrows his focus to the
combat between the cursed brothers. The three-part structure of the
play underlines the transition: from mass reaction to individual combat
to the fatal match.[14] In the opening scenes, Aeschylus introduces the

major groups involved in the crisis: the Theban defenders, the terrified women of the city, and the Argive attackers. The shield scene transforms the play from a general description of war to a dramatization of personal combat between individual heroes for possession of the particular city of Thebes. By the sixth set of speeches, the private dimensions of the invasion are patent. In the seventh, the poet finally fixes on the combat between the cursed sons of Oedipus for possession of the motherland. The closing scenes parallel the beginning in structure (an epirrhematic scene between Eteocles and the chorus, another stasimon, a brief episode and then an exodus which balances the chorus's parodos), but the characters and subject have changed. In the opening epirrhemes, the chorus was advised by a pragmatic Eteocles; now in the second exchange the chorus attempts to offer advice of its own to the crazed son of Oedipus. The women's opening odes all described the terror of the war, but their last songs relate the perverse history of the royal house. In the exodus, their lament for the dead brothers signifies the destruction of the family that endangered the city.

The opening scenes introduce the invasion as a common action from the perspective of the besieged, but this presentation is double-edged. On the one hand, the Thebans are clearly distinguished as innocent victims or valiant warriors defending against villainous attackers. But, because all the groups respond en masse, war itself is dramatized as a dehumanizing activity which erases differences between individuals. The first group, the male defenders, represented by Eteocles and the scout, appear efficient, courageous, and modest. In the prologue, Eteocles addresses the citizens like a rational leader in full control of the situation. In quick succession, as if by response to a signal, all move forward to their respective duties. The six heroes Eteocles selects are self-effacing members of a group of patriots stepping out of rank to fight in turn. They display only the characteristics appropriate to brave warriors; they are rational, dispassionate, and devoted to their cause, keeping their fears and individual quirks under firm control in order better to serve the motherland.

The female chorus introduces another side of the Theban response. As passive victims, they convey the terror of the civilian experience. Presumably they are reacting to what they can really see or hear from the acropolis—the deafening noises of the enemy's approach, the snort of horses, the clash of shields, the thud of stones hitting the battlements, the screech and din of the chariots. Through female imaginations, we foresee the possible catastrophe: the victors flooding the streets, raping, plundering, and murdering. These women refer to themselves as young girls, speak in the first person, and even ask, "What will become of me?" (1. 297). Thus they present the selfish and irrational elements the Theban warriors never display. Eteocles calls them an enemy within (1. 196) because their panic threatens to destroy order and alienate the gods.

The enemy outside stands in stark contrast to the Theban defenders. Bloodthirsty and lusting for battle, they are nearly always associated with the fury of the elements and the ferocity of beasts. They are the storm that threatens to capsize the ship of state (1. 64), raging torrents (11. 86, 63), floods of men (1. 80) gone berserk in their zeal to destroy Thebes. The scout compares them to lions (11. 52–53); later on Tydeus and Hippomedon are described as snakes (11. 381, 503, respectively). In the shield scene, the snorting of the enemy's horses and the monsters depicted on their shields emphasize the warriors' bestiality. If the attackers seem human at all, they are barbarians speaking an alien tongue (1. 170).

On one level, the shield scene, the second phase of the play, continues the depiction of war as a mass activity that dehumanizes and destroys men.[15] In several of the speeches, the heroes are described mainly in terms of their weapons, a device which transforms them from flesh and blood into machines of death. Moreover, each group of warriors exhibits common characteristics. The enemy are all bloodthirsty braggarts, so confident that they blaspheme the gods by their words and by the mottoes and symbols on their shields. The Thebans oppose the enemy with strength of character, duty to the motherland, and the help of the gods.

But on another level, the warriors of the shield scene are different from the faceless flood of the opening scenes. For these warriors do have names as well as shields. As Eteocles and the scout discuss the pairings, the warriors emerge as individual personalities with unique histories, quarrels, and destinies. This shift from group to single combat narrows the focus and introduces actions and attitudes that foreshadow the fatal battle between the brothers.[16] The scout's first speech, for example, introduces the play's first personality, the Argive warrior Tydeus. Tydeus is so "enraged and thirsty for battle" (1. 380) that the seer Amphiaraus cannot hold him back. His anger at the seer exposes the dissention behind the facade of unified action. Moreover, in his madness for war, he rushes forward to his death, although forewarned by evil omens. Such behavior presages the enmity between the brothers, their fury for combat, and their own ill-omened destinies.

Other details narrow the description of the battle from a siege which could happen anywhere to a war in a specific place with a particular history. Eteocles frequently refers to his heroes as Sown Men ("whom Ares spared" [1. 412]). These allusions underline the Cadmeians' two-fold heritage as children of the earth and survivors of fratricide. Because the Thebans were literally generated from the soil, Eteocles stresses their debt to Cadmeia as parent. Duty calls Melanippus "to shield his motherland from enemy spears" (1. 416), and "Megareus, Creon's son, from the Sown Men's breed" must be willing to die "to repay his land for nurture" (11. 474–77). By these references, the poet presents the normal relations between citizen and country in terms that indict the House of Laius. These sons of the soil have endangered the city with the Sphinx, the plague, and the failure to provide "honorable maintenance" for a parent. Now Polynices has attacked his motherland with a spear, like an enemy.

Complementing Eteocles' references to the Cadmeian heritage, there is a progressive development in the enemy shield emblems from the war between the elements (Tydeus's moon outshining the starry sky), to a siege of any city (Capaneus's fire and Eteoclus's ladder) to the attack on Thebes itself, whose peculiar past is represented by Parthenopaeus's emblem of the Sphinx devouring a Theban while the besieged citizens pelt the monster from the walls.[17] Parthenopaeus, the fifth Argive warrior, is important because he both bears the sphinx emblem and embodies the principle of debt to the motherland. An Arcadian by birth, he is participating in the invasion to repay his foster-mother, Argos, for his nurture. This enemy's loyalty to his foster-parent brings into bold relief Oedipus's sons' failure to respect their true parent.

Parthenopaeus's emblem draws attention to Thebes (and Oedipus, by association). Its depiction of Thebans pelting a fellow Theban to destroy the Sphinx implies that foreign invasion will soon become civil strife.

The sixth Argive, Amphiaraus, begins the transition to the curse by mentioning Polynices for the first time. Because Amphiaraus is different from the earlier enemy warriors, his situation draws attention to the destiny of individuals and foreshadows Eteocles' fate. Amphiaraus is no braggart; he does not have a motto or emblem. The scout says, "He prefers not to seem but to be the best" (ll. 591–92). Nor is he associated with the ferocity and injustice of the Argives. He considers Polynices' invasion a crime. In the saga, his wife, Eriphyle, bribed by Polynices' promise of Harmonia's necklace, persuaded him to join the expedition against his better judgment. Now he is no coward. He goes to the sixth gate, foreseeing his death that will bring him honor. For the first time, the enemy's defeat does not correspond to his merit. For the first time, Eteocles responds to the scout's report by expressing his personal feelings, sympathizing with the good man trapped by evil associates. Perhaps he suspects a parallel between Amphiaraus's position and his own.

The seventh report, on Polynices, narrows the focus to the family and the curse. Yet, because the enemy has an opportunity to state his case, the concentration on the private dimensions widens the moral and metaphysical complications of the siege. Polynices, like Amphiaraus, is an individual who differs from his colleagues. Although he has been condemned by their villainy and Amphiaraus's accusations, he insists on the righteousness of his cause. He prays to the same gods of family and fatherland as Eteocles, and his shield depicts the goddess Justice leading his invasion. His curse and fury for blood express not blasphemy, but deep feelings of hatred and a desire to avenge his brother's unjust banishment of him. Thus the presentation of the other side expands the war into a clash between principles of justice (although only the gods' justice will be vindicated by the resolution). Because, like Amphiaraus, the two sons of Oedipus appear trapped by their family's past errors, the siege has also become a battle of individuals against their destinies.

As soon as Eteocles recognizes the curse at work, he becomes the son of Oedipus as well as the leader of Thebes. His emotion breaks out in three successive exclamations in which he proclaims his kinship with his hated race and displays the passion associated with his family. But he does not abandon his duty and character as a public figure. Instead, he consciously controls his passion, and, in a speech parallel to the first six, selects himself as the most suitable warrior for the seventh gate. For the rest of the play, he responds like the divided soul he is. Several of his iambic trimeters in the epirrheme with the chorus retain the terse epigrammatic quality characteristic of the dispassionate leader who earlier quieted the women. Yet he also displays violent feelings of hatred (11. 691, 695), and dread (11. 690, 702, 709–11). He recognizes all the levels of his involvement when he announces that he will stand against Polynices as leader against leader, brother against brother, enemy against enemy (11. 674–75).

The emphasis on the curse also adds a cosmic dimension to the battle for Cadmeia.[18] Of course, the gods have been prayed to and mentioned before (primarily by the chorus), but Eteocles has behaved as if he were their equal partner in the defense of Thebes. He first admits their superior power when he learns that Amphiaraus will die despite his merit: "Success for mortals is a gift of the gods" (1. 625). After the scout's seventh speech, Eteocles connects Oedipus's curse with Apollo's hatred for his race (11. 653–55) and, like Amphiaraus, accepts the destiny he assumes the gods demand, insisting to the horrified chorus, "When the gods give evil, no man can escape" (1. 719).

The relation between the fratricide and Apollo's prophecy that Laius must die childless brings the two themes of city and family together. First the chorus fears that the city will be destroyed by the brothers' combat (11. 764–65), but after reporting that the city has been saved by victory at the first six gates, the messenger announces the destruction of the House of Laius, which vindicates the god's warning: "Lord Apollo, Captain of Sevens, took the seventh gate, fulfilling the ancient errors of Laius" (11. 779–81). Despite its grief for the sons of Oedipus, the chorus accepts this resolution as just. The unexpected working out of the curse through the Argive siege has proved the truth of Apollo's words and confirmed the moral order established by the gods.

Imagery

Aeschylus develops several image patterns that underline this transition from war to curse. [19] Although the poet seems to limit his focus by shifting from the group to the family, his use of these images expands the significance of the siege from the merely political or martial to the universal and the cosmic. The three patterns discussed here all arise directly from the action. The first, the association between motherland and mother earth through the imagery of fertility and generation, is related to the founding of Cadmeia. The poet's application of the image of the patriot's love of his country to the sexual sins of the House of Oedipus amplifies the psychological implications of the curse.

Two other patterns underscore the developing awareness of the divine role in human life. The image of allotment, connected to Oedipus's riddle, changes in the course of the play from the literal lot by which the seven Argives are assigned their gates to the shares Oedipus bequeathed his sons and finally to the destiny assigned the brothers by the gods. The crisis is best summarized in the "ship of state" metaphor which first portrays Eteocles at the helm of the city beset by the storm of invasion and finally describes the ship, hastened by the gods, that carries the brothers to Hades.

In the course of the play, Aeschylus extends the Cadmeian kinship between citizen and soil into a general image of fertility and growth. Eteocles prays early that the Gods not "root out" his city (1. 72), the chorus imagines its destruction as a wasting of all the earth's produce, and children are, of course, referred to as the "shoots" or "seed" of their parents. The scout and Eteocles expand the birth metaphor: good counsel is the fruit of Amphiaraus's fertile mind (11. 593–94), "evil fruits not to be reaped" come from evil associations, for "the field of Atē brings forth death" (11. 599–602), and the words of Loxias (Apollo) "bear fruit" (1. 618).

This growth image also emphasizes the perversions of the House of Laius. Amphiaraus, who in death will enrich the soil of Thebes, accuses Polynices of "drying up the mother-source" and "attacking the fatherland with his spear" (11. 584–86). Eteocles' word for this injury, *kakouchia* (1. 668), implies mistreatment of a wife. The choral passage (11. 752–55) connects the motherland to the sexual sin of Oedipus:

> Oedipus who killed his father
> And seeded his mother's
> sacred soil, where he himself was reared,
> accepting the bloody stock
> that grew.   (Dawson, trans.)

Polynices has metaphorically repeated the crime of Oedipus by violating the land of his father, his mother-source, with his spear. The transfer of interest from the shield to the spear reinforces the sexual basis of the family's sins against each other. The fratricide, a "mankilling of bitter fruit" (l. 693), is on one level a rivalry between siblings for the beloved mother.

While Aeschylus dramatizes the human activities associated with the siege, he uses the image of allotment to emphasize the divine involvement in the family curse.[20] The audience has just heard Oedipus's riddle concerning the division of the inheritance. They would also be familiar with use of allotment for assigning property or duty impartially. Unlike a modern audience, however, they would have considered such a procedure as a placing of judgment in the gods' hands rather than a mechanical process representing mere chance. Allotment itself implies an element of divine will. By extension, the Greeks deified luck as the goddess Tychē and connected the idea of the lot with an individual's portion or destiny (*moira*) necessitated by a higher order.[21]

In *Seven Against Thebes* Aeschylus moves from the Argive warriors literally casting lots for positions at the seven gates to the figurative meanings associated with the curse and the brothers' portions. In the early sections of the play, the poet makes clear that the Argive lot to which he frequently refers (ll. 39–68, 125–27, 376, 423, 459) has restricted the Thebans' choices. Thus the actual casting of lots in part determines the match of the warriors. But the poet does not tell us exactly how Eteocles responded to the Argive lot; although the leader exits at line 286 after proclaiming that he will station six champions at the gates with himself as seventh, he returns at line 369 without revealing whether he has actually done this. It is possible that he has assigned all his seven beforehand, perhaps by lot like the Argives, or has chosen only some in the interval and will choose the rest now, or is skillfully positioning each of the seven in response to the scout's report.[22] This vagueness about his procedure suggests a two-fold determination of the action. The scout behaves as if Eteocles is making his choices on the spot, and Eteocles seems confident that he is selecting the most appropriate opponent for each Argive. Yet Eteocles refers to *tychē* (e.g., 11. 505–6, 520), Ares' dice (l. 414), and Hermes, god of luck (1. 508), suggesting that he believes he has enlisted divine chance as his ally.

But Eteocles' confidence that his actions have been blessed by good luck disappears when he learns that the first six pairings have brought him and his brother together at the seventh gate. Now the imagery of the lot refers to the hostile "division of property by iron" implicit in Oedipus's curse (e.g., 11. 711, 715, 729, 735). Both the chorus (11. 727–34) and the messenger (11. 815–20) describe the fratricide figuratively as an equal division of the brothers' bodies by the spear so that each now possesses his grave as an equal share of the land. In the dirge, the chorus expands this allotment image to include *moira*, sent by the gods.

> Full chorus:
>   Now they truly share their blood.
>   Bitter the arbiter of strife, a stranger
>   fire forged, sped from overseas,
>   whetted steel! Bitter, though fair, the divider
>   of their goods, Ares, by whom the father's curse
>   was brought to fulfillment,
> Second semichorus:
>   They hold the lot which they won, unhappy men,
>   of apportionments sent by god,
>   and beneath their bodies earth's
>   wealth will stretch unlimited.
>   (11. 940–50; Dawson, trans.)

The ship of state image encompasses the political, psychological, and cosmic dimensions of the drama. In the prologue, Aeschylus introduces the traditional political metaphor: the city is a ship endangered by a sea of troubles. Eteocles defines himself as the helmsman who must guide his ship of state through the storm of invasion. He and the Thebans are calm, orderly rowers or sailors, whereas the bloodthirsty Argives are identified with the storm, the raging flood, the waves that buffet the ship. As the action develops, however, Aeschylus uses the analogy to indicate that the irrational forces represented by the Argive flood are also present within the city's walls.[23] Eteocles calls the panicky women the enemy within and accuses them of "flooding the city with cowardice", like the raging waters of the Argives (1. 192). The emotionalism of the Argives and the chorus is later associated with the family of Oedipus through variations of the same metaphor. In the second epirrhematic scene, Eteocles and the chorus describe the curse as a sea stirred by the wind and about to seethe and boil over in storm (11. 705–9).

The further development of this image also implies that the Thebans and Argives are on the same ship and that the gods are the real helmsmen. Just before Eteocles recognizes the curse at work, he imagines Amphiaraus, not as one of the Argive flood, but as a seaman like himself. And the Argive invaders have now become a "god-detested breed" of "hot-headed sailors" (11. 602–4), a description which links them with the Thebans and the "god-abhorred" family of Oedipus. Once Eteocles comprehends his situation, he uses the ship metaphor again, but this time the ship is led by god, not himself, and the sea is the wave of Cocytus, the river of death (11. 689–90).

After Eteocles exits to meet Polynices, the political, psychological, and cosmic implications of this image are combined. The chorus connects the family sin with the danger to Thebes, singing that it has brought "waves of evil" which "surge around the ship of state" (11. 758–60). The messenger's announcement of victory recalls Eteocles' opening image.

> The state now has fair weather, and for all
> the waves' buffeting, it has shipped no sea;
> the walls hold tight, the gates had as bulwarks
> champions whom we could trust in single fight.
>   (11. 795–99; Dawson, trans.)

But Eteocles himself is dead. The chorus compares its motions and sounds of mourning to those of the sacred vessel of Apollo which is sailing not to Delos, the island of the god, but to Acheron, the land of the dead (11. 854–60). Its final words (which may not be genuine) mourn Eteocles as the one who

> next to the Blessed Ones and mighty Zeus,
> rescued the Cadmeian's city and
> it did not capsize beneath a flood
> of alien foes, washed away utterly.   (11. 1074–87)

Thus Eteocles' ship of state is still afloat at the end, but the fully developed image brings the themes of siege and curse together and widens their significance by embracing the whole crew of individuals (all destroyed by passion and by destiny) and by changing the helmsmen to Apollo, Zeus, and the blessed gods.

The Tragedy of Eteocles

The trilogy ends with the deaths of Eteocles and Polynices. The fratricide which coincides with the rescue of Thebes demonstrates to the chorus that there is a powerful and just order in the divine cosmos. The family conceived in sin and grown bold by the "prosperity fattened to excess" (1. 771) has been rooted out and the city freed at last from the bloody consequences of its rulers' crimes (11. 922–25).

But the personal tragedy of Eteocles is a more ambiguous matter. Through most of the *Seven Against Thebes* Eteocles appears to be a very different kind of man from Oedipus, Laius, and Polynices. Both the father and grandfather are described as madmen whose egotism has harmed the city. (Oedipus, by the time he curses his sons, is a senile old man). The playwright does not blame him for the siege; rather he stresses the hubris of the invaders.[24] And he presents Eteocles as a rational and heroic leader, a patriot who from the beginning demonstrates his ability to steer his ship to safety. Eteocles dominates the episodes as the general who assumes control of the crisis, able to make decisions, organize his defense, quell the threat of the frightened women, and manipulate the actual combat at the gates.[25] Although the scout expects him to remain safe on the ramparts (1. 68), he valiantly decides to be one of the seven warriors who will defend the city. In fact, like an epic hero, he sticks to his resolve to fight and die with honor. His name, which means "truly renowned," describes his desire for glory (cf. 11. 5–7, 685, 830–31).

But Eteocles' overt behavior as leader suggests to modern psychoanalytic critics a repression of his psychological and emotional kinship with the House of Laius.[26] His overreaction to the chorus's panic provides a rare glimpse into the feelings of the private individual. The chorus's terrified and spontaneous cries so revolt him that he lashes out against women in general (11. 181–200). Of course, his castigation is in part justified by the situation. He recognizes that their passion can weaken the city's defenses. Yet his excessive anger exposes the passionate man beneath the calm leader, to be revealed in greater detail later when he sighs for Amphiaraus, cries out in anguish to the curse, or admits his nightmares about the sharing of the patrimony. It suggests Eteocles' rejection of an element as dangerous to himself as to his family and the state under siege. Eteocles identifies the chorus's passion with their sex, and the enemy outside, but their frenzy, madness, and misery reflect the characteristics of the House of Laius and their hysterical vision of the defeat reflects his own private nightmares. Thus Eteocles, the calm and rational warrior, has vehemently attacked the women because they express the fear and irrationality he has denied in himself.

From his harshness to the women, psychoanalytic critics suspect that he has used misogyny as a defense against his heredity. By avoiding contact with women (11. 187–88), he seems to have separated himself from the family character and history, where the perversion of normal sexual and kinship relations has been the source of madness and the curse. In disdaining marriage and children, however, he has sublimated all his natural desires in his love and protection of Cadmeia. If he should die childless, he could destroy the House of Laius and rescue Thebes, thus fulfilling Apollo's prophecy to his grandfather. But the words of Amphiaraus and Polynices reveal the sexual theme implicit in his defense of the motherland. Significantly, as he arms for battle with his sibling, he turns himself figuratively into a spear by insisting his "sharp purpose" will not be "blunted" (1. 715). Thus, his patriotism derives in part from his psychological inheritance.

His misogyny is part of a larger denial of the feminine or irrational in himself and has resulted in an imbalance of masculine qualities.[27] He is an authoritarian military leader, practical and impersonal. Such a character accounts for his success so far. He maintains order, confidently marshals his troops, and includes himself among the seven champions. But he also undervalues the feminine aspects of life represented by the women's family concerns and their simple religious faith. In the end, he judges the impiety and horror of killing his brother less dishonorable than retreat.

For most of the play, Eteocles avoids all references to his connection with the House of Laius. He is silent about the destiny assigned him and does not mention his own relatives until the moment of recognition. Although Eteocles refers to the curse himself early in the play, he tries to make it an ally by linking it with Zeus, earth, and the city's gods (11. 69–70).[28] Neither he nor anyone else before Amphiaraus ever relates it to the cause of the invasion. His introductions of his other heroes by their patronymics, relatives, or kinship to the Sown Men reveal his consciousness of the importance of family and tradition. Yet, he never even connects the emblem of the Sphinx with the victory of his own father, Oedipus. Moreover, he totally ignores the scout's report of Amphiaraus's charges against Polynices. Instead of acknowledging his brother's presence, he dwells on Amphiaraus. It is obvious that Eteocles has comprehended Amphiaraus's words, for he extends the seer's sexual metaphor about the motherland and fertility and connects it with his own certainty that Loxias's words must bear fruit. But not until he learns that a raging Polynices awaits him at the seventh gate does Eteocles break his silence and release his pent-up anguish. As he proclaims he is a member of a "god-hated race," he reveals himself as a true son of Oedipus: eager, driven by heart-consuming, war-craving folly (11. 686–87), ravenous to kill (1. 692)—like his father and brother, allowing passion to rule his judgment. Again, the sexual connotations of his desire to confront his brother are clear in the chorus's use of terms like *imeros* (1. 692) and *eros* (1. 687).

Thus the play moves from a characterization of Eteocles as confident that he is in control of himself and the crisis to a climax in which he proclaims himself a man controlled by destiny. The most striking example of this pattern can be seen in Eteocles' attitude toward the power of words. In the course of the play, he demonstrates his power over events by manipulating the magical force of his words to effect the action.[29] (Because the ancients believed that words had such force, they used them cautiously and dreaded curses.) In the early scenes, Eteocles is confident that he can use the potential of words, for good or evil, in order to produce the result he desires. He proclaims that the leader must be able to speak the words the crisis demands (1. 1) and knows that a word carelessly uttered can cause disaster. Thus he adds the formula "God forbid" to the articulated possibility of Theban defeat (1. 5) and silences the chorus's description of the imagined catastrophe.

In the shield scene, the physical encounter at the gates is dramatized as a verbal battle in which Eteocles turns the attacker's threats against him. His strategy depends upon his discovery of hidden meanings in the enemy's words, emblem, or motto. By use of word play, he can change the Argive boast into an omen of victory for his chosen Theban opponent. The enemy Hippomedon, for example, threatens with all the power of the monster Typho, but Eteocles confidently matches him wth Hyperbius, a Theban who bears Zeus, the destroyer of Typho, on his own shield. And he discovers in the full moon on Tydeus's shield an omen of his death. In addition, he draws the attention of the gods to the Argive blasphemies, and, in the words of H. D. Cameron, "by exploiting what should be the gods' natural anger, turns the force of the attack and enlists the aid of the insulted divinities."[30]

Eteocles first articulates the limitations of his skill when he hears the scout's report on Amphiaraus. Because the seer has no motto and has accepted the destiny predicted by Apollo, Eteocles can use no word magic against him. Instead he acknowledges the force of Apollo's prophecy and admits that "success comes only from the gods" (1. 615). When he hears that Polynices awaits him at the seventh gate, Eteocles, led to this confrontation by his own word magic, now accepts the efficacy of Oedipus's words:

> Alas, maddened by god and god-abhorred,
> All wretched is mine and Oedipus' race!
> Ah me, now my father's curse is fulfilled!
> (11. 653–5; Dawson, trans.)

In the seventh pairing, he uses the same verbal skill as before, but now he chooses himself as Polynices' most appropriate opponent and thus commits himself to the fulfillment of the curse and prophecy. In predicting his own death, he acknowledges that the final word belongs to the gods and to Phoebus Apollo in particular:

> Since the affair is clearly sped by god,
> On, windborne, to Cocytus' waves, the goal
> set for Phoebus-hated Laius' whole race!
> (11. 689–91; Dawson, trans.)

But we cannot view Eteocles as merely a hero trapped by destiny. Despite the Greeks' belief in gods and *moira*, they did not ascribe human events to external coercion alone. Rather they saw life as a mingling of human and divine causation which scholars have termed "double motivation."[31] In epic and tragedy the hero's behavior depends as much upon his moral character and ability to act as upon the gods' activities. Achilles defeats Hector in the *Iliad*, for example, both because Athena helps him and because he really is the better warrior. In *Seven Against Thebes*, Eteocles' fratricide also results from a fusion of divine and human elements: Apollo's prophecy, Oedipus's curse, luck, and heredity as well as Eteocles' valor, rationality, and skill. Thus Eteocles is an agent as well as a victim of the curse, "simultaneously free and subject to determining powers," in the words of Winnington-Ingram, who judges this "tension between freedom and necessity" to be "essential to the tragic paradox."[32]

Eteocles' recognition of the gods' role in his life does not negate his free will or his responsibility. In the final exchange with the chorus, he chooses his predicted end. To prevent his exit, the women offer alternatives to Eteocles. They insist that he can retreat from the pollution without being judged a coward, and they suggest that the curse may be averted by the proper sacrifice. But Eteocles, warrior and brother, considers fighting to the death his only honorable course. Turning their words against them, he makes himself the offering:

> We have already been abandoned by the gods.
> The grace of our deaths is what they respect
>   as the proper rite,
> So why should we cringe at our fatal destiny?   (11. 702–4)

The final action of the play actually follows the pattern of sacrifice; in the words of Burnett, "the conscious unblemished self-destroying principle, the rejected suggestions that a substitute be found, or that the hero should abandon his resolve, the formal departure for the fateful spot, the lamentation for the victim, and, finally, surrounding all, the public disaster and its swift removal."[33]

His self-sacrifice which is also fratricide summarizes the contradiction in his situation. Although he calls the mutual murder "the proper rite," it is an unspeakable impiety. Yet the destruction of his family saves the city. And his choice coincides with Apollo's prophecy. The chorus expresses the horror of the paradox when they condemn the crime, lament the unfortunate but sinful brothers and yet praise the just resolution.

Epilogue: Speculation on a Political Paradigm

It is possible that the Athenians recognized in the Theban saga a paradigm of their democracy's struggle to separate itself from the internecine rivalries and lust for power of its own ancient clans.[34] The public danger posed by the independent actions of the scions of great houses, such as Megacles, leader of the Alcmeonids, was gradually curbed by the reforms of Solon and Clisthenes. Still the old families tried to maintain their power, allying or squabbling, acting sometimes for and sometimes against the democracy. Even the career of Pericles, a remote descendant of the House of Megacles, was threatened by accusations that he belonged to a cursed family.

Aeschylus's dramatization of the Theban saga clearly traces the relations between an ancient family and the state it rules. *Seven Against Thebes* suggests that there was a progressive development in concern for the common good, from Laius, a reckless individual whose private sin first endangered Thebes, through Oedipus, beloved conqueror of the Sphinx but source of civil war after his unwitting crime, to Eteocles, the public figure divorced from his family and devoted to the state. Whether or not the city was justly punished by the Sphinx and the plague in the first two plays, it is certainly an innocent victim of Polynices and the Argives in the third. The resolution demonstrates the divine will that the city should survive while the House of Laius perishes. Eteocles, the son of Oedipus, must die if Thebes is to prosper, for his family represents the destructive egotism and lust for power that lead to civil war.[35]

But Eteocles is a Janus who represents the contemporary Athenian soldier as well as the ancient hero of myth. Although he engages in hand-to-hand combat like an epic warrior, determined to die "without disgrace" (1. 683), settling for "renown" as a compensation for his "bad luck" (11. 684–85), he also calls himself a "hoplite" (1. 717). Hoplites were heavily armored foot soldiers who fought in ranks, each dependent on the other to maintain the common defense. Eteocles' use of the word implies that he viewed his resignation to the curse in part as a duty to his fellow citizens. Moreover, it indicates that the audience, who fought as hoplites themselves, would approve and perhaps emulate his devotion to the state, if called upon to die in its behalf.

Such a Janus figure would provide a double exemplum of the patriot for a troubled Athens. By 467, Athens's leadership of the Delian League had provoked the hostility of the Spartan confederacy abroad and class conflict and political rivalries at home. The resolution of *Seven Against Thebes* provides a positive statement of the city's most important prerequisite for survival—group solidarity. The death of Eteocles dramatizes the double triumph of the commonweal over private desires. Like Eteocles, the Athenian, as a citizen in a democracy, must be willing to sacrifice personal good for the good of the polis; and as a hoplite he must be willing to sacrifice his life in defense of the motherland.

Chapter Four
Suppliants: Beginnings

Plot and Problems

The unique dramatic form and extraordinary emotional turbulence of Aeschylus's *Suppliants* strike the reader immediately. It soon becomes clear, however, that the drama is difficult to interpret. *Suppliants* is the first play in a connected tetralogy on the myth of the daughters of Danaus. Its text is badly corrupt, and very few fragments remain of the last two tragedies or the satyr play *Amymone*.[1] Courageous attempts have been made to establish a reliable text of *Suppliants*, to explain its form, and to interpret its meaning by reconstructing the following tragedies and assuming a certain relationship between them and the satyr play. Most theories were based on the assumption that *Suppliants* is the earliest of Aeschylus's extant tragedies because of its ostensibly archaic form in which the chorus, not an actor, has the major role. But a papyrus fragment published in 1952 indicates that the tetralogy was produced no earlier than 467 B.C. and could have been composed as late as 456 B.C.[2] Thus there has been almost as much turmoil in the literature about *Suppliants* (in the scramble to readjust theories of Aeschylus's development as an artist, philosopher, citizen, and worshiper of Zeus) as there is in the tragedy itself.[3]

Like the other plays of Aeschylus, the plot of *Suppliants* is simple. It follows the story pattern of "fugitives received" which is also found in *Eumenides*, Sophocles' *Oedipus at Colonus*, and Euripides' *Hikitedes* and *Heracleidae*.[4] Danaus and his daughters, the Danaid chorus, arrive on consecrated ground at the shores of Argos, begging asylum from danger. They have just fled the Egyptians, the sons of their father's brother, Egyptus, who want to force them into marriage and are now pursuing them across the sea. Danaus and the young women have chosen Argos because they claim kinship ties; they are the descendants of the Argive, Io, whom Zeus once loved and led to Egypt before fathering her child (and their ancestor) Epaphus. Thus the family of Danaus can demand sanctuary, not only as kin to the Argives but as kin to Zeus himself, patron of suppliants. After the chorus's agitated parodos explaining the haste of their arrival, Danaus urges his daughters to pray to the proper gods, and appeal to the human authorities for protection. For he has already sighted a troop of armed men approaching from inland.

Pelasgus, the king of Argos, enters with his soldiers to question the women. First he describes his descent, the extent of his realm, and the history of the spot on which they stand. In answer to his questions, the Danaids explain their relation to his ancestress, Io, and the reason for their flight. Their demand for sanctuary puts the king in a difficult position. If he refuses to help them, he risks the punishment of the gods who protect suppliants. But granting asylum would bring war with the Egyptians upon his innocent land and people. He insists that on such an important question he must confer with his citizens, put his opinion to a vote, and abide by their decision. While he ponders his predicament, the Danaids attempt to influence him by citing his pharonic power, the rights of kinship, the horrors captured women face, and wrath of god. When these persuasive devices fail, they add a terrifying threat; they will hang themselves at the very altars of the gods and thus insure dread pollution for his city. Now the king consents to advise his citizens to receive the women. He sends Danaus to lay suppliant branches on the city's altars to gain the sympathy of both gods and citizens. He instructs the women to wait near the consecrated ground until he can return with the assembly's decision.

Left alone, the women appeal to Zeus and sing the entire story of Io's suffering and final peace. When Danaus returns with the report that the Argives have resolved to welcome them as guests and protect them from any harassment, the daughters sing another ode praising the reverent and humane Argive nation. But all is not yet settled. Danaus now sights an armada and warns his daughters to remain calm at the altars while he summons help from the town. Although he assures them that the Argive vote will protect them and that the fleet cannot attack before anchoring their ships, the women sing out their terror (and their hatred

of the suitors) after he leaves. Then a herald approaches from the sea and
threatens violence. But, responding to their cry for help, Pelasgus and
his soldiers come to the rescue. The herald answers the king's questions
insolently and irreverently, and Pelasgus informs him that the Argives
will fight rather than surrender the women. The herald leaves, promising "bonecracking war" to the Argives. Although the chorus now exits
praising its new home and reiterating its hatred of marriage, their
exodus song also suggests that Aphrodite, the powerful goddess of love
and union, must be worshiped as well as the virgin goddess Artemis,
and that they may have to marry. Nevertheless, they leave their
sanctuary for Argos in a grand procession, praying to Zeus for protection and guidance and confident of his aid because of their relation to Io.

Thus the suppliants' story is concluded. The women have gained
asylum, and the danger has been repulsed. For the moment. War with
the Egyptians will almost certainly follow. And there may be trouble
over the question of marriage. The lack of resolution should surprise no
one who is familiar with the *Oresteia*, the only complete Aeschylean
trilogy we possess. The first play *Agamemnon*, ends in an uneasy truce
between the new rulers and the citizens loyal to their murdered king,
with Clytemnestra unpunished for Agamemnon's death. If we had only
the *Agamemnon* or it and the second play, *The Libation Bearers* (which
also ends inconclusively), it would be impossible to predict the content
and resolution of the *Eumenides*, or to comprehend the significance of
the ambiguities and tensions in the *Agamemnon*.

To fathom the difficulty of understanding *Agamemnon* by itself is to
begin to grasp the complexity of discussing *Suppliants*. It is hard to
reconstruct the trilogy from the first play and even harder to comprehend the meaning of the first without the next two. Because the saga
of the Danaids has been transmitted in several versions, most of them
later than Aeschylus, and with many variations in detail, we cannot be
sure what story Aeschylus told. As Garvie has pointed out, the sources
agree on only four elements: (1) Danaus and his brother Egyptus trace
their descent back to Io; (2) the brothers quarreled; (3) the sons of
Egyptus married the daughters of Danaus but were murdered by their
brides on the wedding night at the command of Danaus; (4) but one
bride, Hypermestra, saved her new husband, Lynceus.[5]

Although the saga suggests that a quarrel between Danaus and Egyptus precipitated the flight and murder, the *Suppliants* contains no allusion to a problem between the brothers. Instead, the marriage of their children, which seems to have been a tangential element in the saga, is the center of the conflict in the tragedy. Danaus's daughters have rejected the advances of their cousins and have fled their homes. It is their trouble, not his, that is dramatized, and they, not he, are the spokesmen of the problem. Danaus is present as his daughters' guardian, but, in the first play at least, he has no story or significance of his own.

Only one fragment can be assigned with certainty to *Egyptians*, the second play, but most scholars agree that its content covers the period just before the forced marriage and up to the plotting of the murder. We can only speculate, however, on why the battle between the Argives and the Egyptians ended in the hateful marriage. Nor is there any hint of how the elements were dramatized. It is not even clear who the chorus represented—the husbands, the brides or their handmaidens, or the servants who built the bridal chamber (*"Chamber-builders"* may be a variant title for the second play). Surely neither the war nor the murder was enacted on stage. Perhaps the prologue of the second play explained the events and consequences of the battle whereas the episodes depicted the plot to marry and then murder the Egyptians.[6]

The third play, *The Danaids*, probably began with a description of the actual crime that took place between the plays. The drama must have focused on the result of the murder, but its details also remain obscure. One ten-line fragment is extant, which, according to Athenaeus (who quoted it in *Deipnosophists* 13.73, 600B), was spoken by Aphrodite herself:

The holy heaven yearns to wound the earth, and yearning layeth hold on earth to join in wedlock; the rain fallen from the amorous heaven, impregnates the earth, and it bringeth forth for mankind the fool of flocks and herds and Demeter's gifts; and from that moist marriage-rite the woods put on their bloom. Of all these things, I am the cause.[7]

The saga offers conflicting conclusions to the tale. According to the most persistent versions, either Hypermestra was tried for disobeying

her father and freed by the Argives, or her sisters and father were killed
by Lynceus and punished in the underworld by having to carry water in
pitchers (or sieves) to storage jars filled with holes, or else the sisters
were somehow absolved of murder and given in marriage by Danaus to
the victors in a foot race.

Aeschylus was familiar with the story of Hypermestra. In *Prometheus
Bound* (11. 848–69), the chained hero tells the Danaids' story to Io, who
has visited his lonely crag in her wanderings as a crazed heifer.

> . . . There Zeus shall make you sound of mind
> touching you with a hand that brings no fear
> and through that touch alone shall come your healing.
> You shall bear Epaphos, dark of skin, his name
> recalling Zeus' touch and his begetting. . . .
> This Epaphos shall reap the fruit of all
> the land that is watered by the broad flowing Nile.
> From him five generations, and again
> to Argos they shall come, against their will,
> in number fifty, women, flying from
> a marriage with their kinsfolk; but these kinsfolk
> their hearts with lust aflutter like the hawks
> barely outdistanced by the doves will come
> hunting a marriage that the law forbids:
> the God shall grudge the men these women's bodies,
> and the Pelasgian earth shall welcome them
> in death: for death shall claim them in a fight
> where women strike in the dark, a murderous vigil.
> Each wife shall rob her husband of his life
> dipping in blood her two-edged sword: even so
> may Love come, too, upon my enemies.
> But one among these girls shall love beguile
> from killing her bedfellow, blunting her purpose:
> and she shall make her choice—to bear the name
> of coward and not murder: this girl,
> she shall in Argos bear a race of kings.[8]

Several scholars conjecture from this passage that Hypermestra is the
heroine of the third play and that the fragment quoted is part of a

defense speech by Aphrodite at a trial in which Hypermestra, like Orestes in *Eumenides*, is acquitted. If this were so, one would expect the later importance of Hypermestra to be foreshadowed in *The Suppliants* as Orestes' role is anticipated in the *Agamemnon*. Although there is no overt allusion to Hypermestra in *Suppliants*, Murray finds her importance prefigured in the elaborate analogy between Io's flight and the Danaids'.[9] (In the saga, she alone of the sisters willingly accepted the consummation which Io received from Zeus and became, like Io, mother to a race of kings.) One may also see in the warnings about the danger of offending Aphrodite a disagreement which foreshadows the idiosyncratic behavior of Hypermestra. Perhaps this is enough evidence to support the speculation that Hypermestra was the central figure in the third play.

But it is not necessary to assign the fragment from Aphrodite's speech to a trial in which Hypermestra was charged with disobedience.[10] It is also possible that the sisters were condemned in Hades because their revenge took such a brutal and impious form. (The myth that they carried water in leaky vessels below, however, seems to be later. In the fifth century the water-carriers are the "uninitiated.") Or perhaps the events of the third play absolved the Danaids, without condoning their crime, because of the wrong done them. Maybe Hypermestra's rescue of her husband was linked to the absolution of her sisters. The trilogy might have concluded with their remarriage to new suitors (a resolution to which Pindar, Aeschylus's older contemporary, had alluded in *Pythia* 9.112).[11] Even though this speculation is inconclusive, it is not idle. If Hypermestra is the heroine at the end of the saga, her sisters might be wrong to flee their suitors and, of course, doubly wrong to murder them. Thus our judgment of the Danaids in the first play depends partly on what we think the resolution of the trilogy might have been.

When we look at the *Suppliants* alone, we must face other perplexing questions. If the motive for flight is not their father's quarrel, what precisely is their reason: hatred of men in general? hatred of these particular men? rejection of cousins out of fear of committing incest? or a refusal to be treated as property instead of women? Their emotional explanations are anything but clear and are complicated by uncertainties about the most significant passages of the text. If *Suppliants* was composed late in Aeschylus's career, after he had developed the techniques of two actors conversing together, why does the chorus overshadow Danaus and usurp the functions of an actor in most of the episodes? Moreover, why does Aeschylus seemingly disturb the unity of the play by emphasizing the king's difficult decision, and particularly his appeal to the democratic process? Was Aeschylus commenting on the relations between Athens and Argos at the time of performance? Uncertainties about production also arise. It has been conjectured that the chorus had fifty members, matching the legendary number of Danaids, although we assume Aeschylus's other tragedies used only twelve. And who exactly formed the second chorus at the end: handmaidens whose entrance is unannounced in the text, Argive bodyguards, or half the original chorus?

Unless new papyri establish a better text and fill out the trilogy, we can only speculate about these problems. But it is clear that Aeschylus used the Danaid legend to explore basic questions about human existence. As in the other extant plays, *Suppliants* dramatizes the difficulty of maintaining family unity, political stability, and proper relations with the divine order. These themes are introduced with all their complexity in the first play. One must assume, on the analogy of *Seven Against Thebes* and the *Oresteia*, that they were developed and then resolved in the next two tragedies of the trilogy.

Pattern and Production

The dramatic structure of *Suppliants* is in part determined by the story pattern in which a fugitive arrives in a strange land and asks for asylum.[12] In the two crucial episodes of *Suppliants*, the fugitive maidens must first win acceptance from the host country, which must then keep its promise to defend the guests against their pursuers. The scene is a plot of consecrated ground on the shore of Argos, probably decorated with statues of the gods who protect suppliants.[13] This holy setting would itself underline the cosmic significance of the Danaids' appeal and indict anyone who mistreated the maidens or showed disrespect for the shrines.

Aeschylus introduces the host and then the suitors in two episodes that are parallel in structure but contain significant variations which emphasize the contrasts between the two groups.[14] At the beginning of each episode, Danaus acts as lookout, watching for the approach of some potential danger to his daughters. The preparations for the host and the suitors are similar; their arrivals are anxiously anticipated, described in detail, and then carefully planned for. Because of the size and strength of each group, Danaus advises his daughters to cling to the statues of the gods and remain calm. Pelasgus, the host, probably entered the orchestra with a large retinue of armed men, horses, and chariots. Although the herald's attendants may not have been as impressive as the king's, the might of the Egyptian armada had already been described by Danaus.

Despite the obvious parallelism, however, there are significant differences between the host and the enemy, requiring different responses from the Danaids. In the first episode, Danaus sees the Argives approaching by land from their own city, ready to defend themselves against a possible invasion, and advises his daughters to make their appeal as innocent suppliants protected by the laws of god and man. Because the king understands that his military might cannot help him solve the moral and political dilemma the maidens' presence has caused, he responds rationally to their persuasive arguments. Thus by the end of the episode, his attendants display his power to protect the Danaids.

The confrontation in the second episode is different. The Egyptians' arrival from the sea as invaders manifests the doubtful nature of their pursuit. Because Danaus does not expect them to respect either the shrines of the gods or the laws of Argos, he can advise his daughters only to remain calm until the Argives send help. But the daughters become hysterical with fear. Once the herald enters the orchestra, his threat to drag them from the altars proves that their physical danger is real and comes from godless men.

The king's second arrival, which differs from both earlier entries, displays his commitment to the maidens and his superiority over the suitors.[15] This time he comes unannounced and therefore unexpected, in response to the maidens' cry for help. His quick action confirms that he will assume responsibility for the girls' future safety. The king probably has armed attendants, but he does not threaten the herald with physical harm. Instead even while angrily expelling him, Pelasgus points out the proper procedures for foreigners to claim redress from the state and respects the herald's person, sacred to the god Hermes and therefore protected by the conventions of war and commerce. But the king makes clear that he is not afraid to use force. After the herald leaves, the entrance of an armed bodyguard assigned to protect Danaus (11. 985–87) reaffirms the Argive resolve to fight if necessary.

These three entrance scenes are framed by two contrasting movements which underscore the development of the suppliant pattern. In the parodos, the Danaids, like the Egyptians, arrive from the sea as outsiders. The women are alone and in peril, terrified by the pursuit of their cousins and the strangeness of the new land. By the exodus, however, they move out of the orchestra in the opposite direction, toward the welcoming city, in a calm and stately procession, accompanied by Argive supporters whose presence testifies to the hospitality and courage of Argos.[16]

Aeschylus must have used spectacle to underline the themes implicit in the suppliant pattern. Dark masks and strange costumes would have accentuated the differences between the Egyptian descendants of Io and their Argive kin, for the text frequently refers to the strangeness of the foreigners' dress and physical appearance (11. 234–37, 496–98).[17] In addition, Aeschylus used crowds of extras to increase the tensions which might develop into war or internal dissension.[18] The presence of armed bodyguards and the elaborate entrance processions display each group's power and will to fight. In the exodus, the group of handmaidens and soldiers dramatizes the two-fold success of the suppliants' appeal for asylum. Yet, the fact that some of the group (it does not matter which part) criticize the Danaids' disrespect for Aphrodite foreshadows troubles to come for Argos and for the sisters in the remainder of the trilogy.

In *The Suppliants* the chorus is the main character instead of an eyewitness to or a secondary victim of an actor's tragic plight. Their predominance diminishes the actor's role so that Danaus is used only as a scout, messenger, and advisor and never confronts the king or herald himself. Scholars once associated these features with an earlier style of tragedy where the chorus, from which drama traced its origins, was still the most important element, and the potential of a second actor had not yet been fully explored. Now that a later date for *Suppliants* has been accepted, however, such criticism is no longer applicable. Aeschylus clearly knew how to use the second actor (which he originated), as the shield scene in *Seven Against Thebes* or the episode between Pelasgus and the herald here demonstrates. Therefore, the poet must have had a dramatic reason for letting Danaus dominate the scenes when he is alone with the chorus of his daughters, and then excluding him from the crucial episodes with the other actors, the host Pelasgus and the herald who represents the suitors.

Aeschylus did not want to omit Danaus from the drama. The fact that he is alive and agrees with his daughters' rejection of his nephews indicts the suitors for pressing their claims that the maidens are their property. His daughters' obedience and reliance on Danaus characterize them as young, innocent, and dependent. And Danaus, a male, can move about the strange city performing tasks that the maidens could not do with propriety. Moreover, in the saga, and most probably in the second play, Danaus replaces Pelasgus as leader of Argos and advises the mass murder.

Although Danaus plays a dominant role when alone with his daughters, Aeschylus carefully removes him from the confrontations with the host and the suitors. Having chosen to concentrate on the daughters' desperate situation rather than the brothers' quarrels, he can best dramatize his themes of conflict between force and persuasion or law and lawlessness by letting the females speak for themselves. Perhaps they are the center of interest because women, physically weak and without legal rights in Greece, were always potential victims. Since a society must be judged by the way it treats its defenseless members, the parallel meetings between the women and the two groups of powerful males most effectively underscore the moral issues of the play. If Danaus were to speak for his daughters, his authoritative presence would obscure the conflict between female and male, with all its psychological, political, and metaphysical ramifications.

In using the chorus as main actor in those episodes, Aeschylus has found a true marriage between form and theme. The chorus's traditional role as singers and dancers who respond to events with impassioned lyric matches both their character and situation as terrified maidens.[19] When they share an episode with actors who use a more conversational rhythm and diction, the contrasting modes of expression underscore the differences between the two sexes. The less emotional actors speak in stichic verses with little imagery. The few metaphors of Danaus and Pelasgus are clear and simple comparisons which amplify their ideas. For example, Danaus describes his daughters as tender summer fruit (11. 997–98) or doves chased by hawks (11. 224–26) to define their vulnerability. Pelasgus finds precise metaphors for explaining his predicament to the chorus. He compares his need for clear counsel to a diver's need for clear sight and his own peril to that of a ship caught in treacherous waters, unable to land safely. This last image conforms to his character as leader of "the ship of state."

The men's diction and style reveal their character, age, and interest. As advisor to his daughters, Danaus conveys information precisely and tries to calm their excitement or control their behavior by explaining the reasons for his counsel. Often he caps his words with an epigram which defines him as a man of wisdom and experience (11. 189–90, 201, 732–33, 993–95). Pelasgus's speech is similarly precise but he characteristically alludes to the laws, customs, and procedures of fifth century Athenian society. Danaus also uses these references once he has attended the Argive assembly. There is a possibility that, in contrast to these men, the herald of the Egyptians (or a chorus of his attendants) sang his threats in response to the terrified cries of the maidens (11. 836–45).[20] If so, his use of lyric might indicate his affinity, as foreign, immature, and overemotional, with his female fellow-Egyptians rather than his male elders.

The chorus's lyric mode is by contrast far more metaphorical and suggestive and reflects their emotionalism as females as well as their agitated response to their dangerous situation. The elaborate rhythms of their songs and dances were probably accompanied by excited gestures of suffering. But in the conventional forms of their prayers, the audience would have recognized their own contemporary rites, and would have identified with these foreign-looking and frenzied maidens. In their exchanges with the actors, as well as in their odes, the chorus uses imagery that defines their character and vulnerability as females and simultaneously indicates their uniqueness as Danaids.

The imagery of hunt and flight is the dominant metaphor for the fugitives. As Barbara Fowler points out, it is especially significant because it draws together the major themes of the play (and trilogy):

"Flight-pursuit is also justice-violence, holy-unholy, men-women. Refuge-succor is also Greeks-barbarians, citizens-exiles, and, in another sense, men-women too."[21] There are frequent allusions to the brutal suitors as birds of prey, wolves, or dogs, and the women as doves, calves, or corpses torn apart.[22] Such images also convey the girls' terror of men. In lines 56–62, they compare themselves to the bird-wife, Metis, who killed her own child out of hatred for her hawk husband.

Danaus's comparison of his daughters to tender summer fruit sums up another image pattern which emphasizes the maidens' sexuality and connection with fertility and generation.[23] In addition to numerous references to their softness, there are frequent allusions to the culling of flowers, to gardens or forests, and to rivers that fertilize the land. The Danaids' most extensive metaphor associated with fertility is ironic, however. In lines 104–11, it is hubris, not a blossom, which "starts afresh, the stem which, through desire to marry us, has sprung into bloom with evil and wanton thoughts" (Johanson, trans.).

Another set of images (arising from the suppliants' identification with their ancestress, Io, who was transformed into a cow and seduced by Zeus) reveals the difficulty of their transition from maidenhood.[24] Direct references to Zeus, Io, and their son, Epaphus, are ubiquitous and so are references to the cows, bulls, and pasture associated with the legend. Other elements of the plot, such as the threat of violent seizure by the suitors and the destructive storm the virgins call down upon the men, become associated with the act of consummation between Io and Zeus, which produced Epaphus (Touch) whom they consider Io's blessing and the glory of their race. But the daughters never reconcile the two aspects (Io as victim and mother or Zeus as lover and father). Despite their acceptance of Io and their use of the imagery of fertility and generation, they prefer to remain childless virgins forever.

Fathers and Daughters

The Suppliants is first of all a play about the rejection of a marriage. But the reasons for that rejection are unclear. The daughters of Danaus explain their refusal in the opening lines of the play, but because the text is corrupt, the reasons remain obscure to the modern reader.[25]

We . . . are now fugitives, not because we have been exiled by the people on the score of blood-shed convicted by the citizens' vote, but because we have fled before men by our own act, revolting against marriage with the sons of Aigyptus and their impious (. . .). (11.5–10, Johansen, trans.)

Danaus confirms that he and his daughters consider the suit a sin (1. 230). When Pelasgus asks whether personal hate or an illegal act caused their flight (1. 336), they respond (in another debatable line, 337, which may suggest their resentment at being the means for transferring family property), "Who would love their own masters?" or "buy their relatives as masters/husbands."[26] The girls never really explain whether the Egyptians have a legal claim on them or have committed a criminal act against them. Is the very suit illegal or incestuous? Or has the violent lust of the suitors terrified the virgins? Or are the women man-haters obsessively protective of their virginity and abnormally devoted to their father?

All three answers have been proposed. The question of the legality of marriage between cousins can be easily dismissed. The Greeks permitted marriage to male relatives if the father was willing. Indeed they required it to insure that property remained in the family when the girl's father died without sons.[27] Thus the suit is not impious because it is incentuous. In fact Pelasgus may imply that such a union is beneficial to the family (1. 338).[28] According to contemporary Athenian law, however, a marriage of a daughter to a male relative of her father would only occur if the father was no longer alive to choose her husband himself. But Danaus is manifestly alive and is as unwilling as his daughters to grant his nephews' suit. Thus the sons of Egypt may be acting illegally in usurping their uncle's right to give his daughters away. Whether it is a criminal offense or not, their haste to possess the women (and family property that comes with them) must have been considered presumptuous by the Athenian audience. The fact that they are kin who should protect their own relatives only increases the negative impression. This judgment is confirmed when the herald threatens force against the women and then behaves insolently to a king who has gained the audience's respect. (It is possible, of course, that, in the second play, the Egyptians had the opportunity to defend their claim or to mitigate the dislike for them created in *Suppliants*.)

But Aeschylus has left the rights and wrongs of the flight deliberately vague. As Miss Macurdy has written, the poet "is writing a drama, not about heiresses, but about tragic girls, caught in the net of circumstance and brought by dreadful suffering to commit dreadful deeds."[29] The circumstances both shape and expose the Danaids' character. On the one hand, they are clearly the "weaker sex," victims terrified by the threat of physical violence. They depend on their father for guidance and lose all courage when he must leave their side. Danaus, fully aware of their vulnerability to the appetites of men, warns them of the shame or danger their nubile beauty might provoke. Despite their aversion to the marriage, the maidens themselves are also conscious of their appeal and express their own femininity by identifying with Io and using imagery of fertility.

But Danaus must also advise them to appeal to Pelasgus without bold speech or immodest expression. His tender daughters are willful enough to reject the suitors and resourceful enough to protect themselves by combining clever arguments with suicidal threats. The scene with Pelasgus reveals the aggressive aspect of their collective personality.[30] The conversation begins with a calm exchange of question and answer between the chorus and the king (stichomythia), but develops into a lyric onslaught. When the king demurs, the women insist on his power to act unilaterally, conjure pictures of their helplessness, and call down the wrath of Zeus as Patron of Suppliants and Defender of Kin. Their pressure culminates in a return to the one-line exchange, but this time they dominate, threatening to hang themselves at the altars of the gods, and the king has to submit to prevent the pollution. The Danaids' manipulation of his religious fear and their disdain for his dilemma reveal their potential to inflict injury on others without compunction.

In the first play, one can attribute their conflicting behavior to their desperation. But their boldness is also a natural part of their female response, for it is a verbal rather than a physical courage. Against the Egyptians, they are helpless, but against a king who rules by law and uses reason rather than force to persuade, they can counterpose their feminine rhetorical skills to enlist his aid. They will not explain their grievances in the precise legal terms that Pelasgus requests, however.

As young women in danger, they respond with the emotion that is as appropriate to their character as suppliant maidens as it is to their traditional role as tragic chorus.

In their desperation, they seem to care only about protecting themselves from the lust of their suitors. But their words do not make clear whether they hate only their cousins. Many of their statements refer to their aversion to all men (cf. 11. 10, 30, 40, 142, 150, 230, 330, 392, 790, 805, 820, 1015, 1031, 1057). Since the drama begins at a mid-point in their story, their hatred has already grown too strong for them to make this separation in their own minds; perhaps what was once specific has, under stress, become generalized. By the end, however, it is clear that they would reject all men if they could. In response to their father's warning, they promise that they will remain virgins, "not turning from their former course, unless something new is being plotted by the gods" (11. 1014–17). More bold in the exodus, they appeal to Artemis for protection and threaten grief to anyone who would force the rites of Aphrodite upon them (11. 1030–33). Their statement provokes the warning that Aphrodite must be worshiped too, and that marriage is, in fact, the normal end for women (11. 1034–37).

The maidens' aversion to marriage, coupled with the closeness between father and daughters reflects the young woman's fear of leaving the security of her own home and family for a new and totally different relationship. In ancient Greece, such an anxiety was perfectly realistic since the bride would be a stranger to her husband and would reside with her new mother-in-law in the women's quarters. But such dread is universal. *Suppliants* has many features in common with a fairy tale like "Beauty and the Beast," where the daughter is compelled to leave her father and live with a monster. She longs to return home to the tenderness of her father and sisters where she can remain a child. So Danaus's presence in his daughters' story dramatizes their immaturity and dependence as well as their legal position as wards of a living father.

But, to psychoanalytic critics, the play also dramatizes the fear implicit in the transition from virgins to sexually mature women.[31] In his essay "The Taboo of Virginity," Freud suggested that every woman feels hatred and aggression toward the man who destroyed her virginity, either because the first act is painful or disappointing or because the female remains fixated on her first love object, her father, or because she really hates the male, out of envy of his favored position. Freud conjectured that ancient rites which allowed for defloration and first coitus by persons other than the husband-to-be were a means of deflecting the female's hatred from the man with whom she would share her life.[32] The full Danaid myth parallels this clinical situation (which also appears in other tales: e.g., Judith and Holofernes), for it narrates the revenge women would wreak upon their first conquerors if they followed their unrestrained impulses. In the saga, forty-eight daughters of Danaus decapitate (or symbolically castrate) their husbands on the wedding night. The version of the ending in which they later marry new suitors fits both the clinical situation and the rite; a woman who acts out her aggression on her first mate is perfectly capable of enjoying sex with a second partner.[33]

The women's hatred of the men in *Suppliants* contains the seeds of this pathology. Devereux sees in their nightmare image of the Egyptians as spiders and snakes (11. 885 ff., 895 ff.) elements common in the dreams of women with Oedipal fixations on their fathers.[34] The Danaids do defer to their father and look to him for support. The flight was his idea, and, fully aware of their seductiveness, he encourages his girls to stay away from men. They assure him he has no cause to fear, for they will remain virgins. Such conversations strengthen the sexual overtones of their relation. But we do not know how much Danaus influenced his daughters to hate their suitors. And although legend makes him responsible for their murder, we are not sure how it was presented in the second play. What we might consider signs of his jealousy are also indications of his protectiveness. If he is aware of his daughters' sexuality, so too are the fathers of all growing girls (and boys) who watch their children mature with some regret for the inevitable change in a precious relationship.

Thus the sexual tensions in *Suppliants* dramatize a universal anxiety about one of the most important transitions for both parents and children. But that transition must be made for the individual to become a successful adult. For women this means marriage and motherhood. In "Beauty and the Beast," the heroine navigates the perilous rite of passage; she rushes back from a long-desired visit with her father to save the life of the once-abhorred monster. But, in the Argive saga, the forty-eight Danaids act out their hostility to their animalistic suitors (those hawks, wolves, swarms of bees, spiders, and snakes). Only Hypermestra (and Amymone of the satyr play) makes the transition to full womanhood. Like Io, she accepts mature sexuality and reaps its benefit, a male child.

King and Country

The focus on Pelasgus's decision introduces a new set of themes which are political rather than domestic. When the Argive nation is drawn into the conflict between the cousins, the king realizes that, whatever group he supports, he will risk destroying his kingdom. The seriousness of his dilemma is dramatized in several ways. Most obviously, he articulates it himself, carefully listing his alternatives and despairing of a happy solution. The bodyguard which confirms his strength and authority ironically underlines his helplessness. The maidens at the altar really control the situation. Pious as well as law-abiding, he cannot use his force against them (or the herald) with impunity. If he succumbs to the maidens' persuasion, however, he brings war to his people. The king's behavior changes as he begins to understand this situation.[35] He first approaches the barbarian suppliants with full confidence in his authority, using the verb "I rule" twice in an emphatic position (ll. 255–59) to introduce himself and define his realm. Their demand, however, destroys his self-reliance. He needs support and confirmation of his opinion, fearing to take sole responsibility for the fate of all. Thus his insistence on deferring to his people is a sign of his awareness of his weakness.

But his consultation with his subjects is also a sign that Aeschylus has presented the ancient kingdom of the legend as if it were a democracy like Athens. Considering this an anachronism, several scholars have searched for allusions to specific events or attitudes in Argos or Athens which might help them confirm a definite date for *Suppliants* or draw a conclusion about Aeschylus's opinions of contemporary political problems.[36] There is no specific reference, however, to relations between Athens and Argos (such as appears in *Eumenides* 11. 286–89, 669–73, 762–74).[37] Nor is there any certain proof from the political portrayal either that the play is early in Aeschylus's career or closer in date to the *Oresteia* and *Prometheus Bound*. Yet, if *Suppliants* was produced between 467 and 456, as the papyrus fragment suggests, there is reason to assume that the audience would be well disposed (or at least not hostile) to a character who represented the Argive people. By the early 460s, the Argives may have had a democratic constitution; they did, in fact, ally themselves with Athens against Sparta in 462, only a year after the most widely accepted date for the production of *Suppliants*.[38] Thus, from the point of view of contemporary political events, the Athenians would not have considered Pelasgus's consultation with his people a sign of weakness.[39] In fact, from the first confrontation with the Danaids, he establishes himself firmly as a spokesman for all Hellas, and as a ruler with whom contemporary Athenians would feel a special identification. J. T. Shepphard comments on the significance of Pelasgus's opening speech.

In the first place it makes the appeal of the suppliants to the king as representative of his country far more impressive to Athenian hearers because it makes the king as Pelasgus, son of Palaechthon, stand for the oldest inhabitants of Greece: the appeal is therefore to the Pelasgians, from whom the Athenians, as autochthonous, thought themselves descended. In the second place, the wide extent of his territory makes the king stand for more than a narrow Argive interest: the appeal is to Greece and civilization againt barbarism.[40]

This contrast between Greek and barbarian runs through the drama. Pelasgus is shocked by the Danaids' dark skin and strange dress. He recognizes only their suppliant branches as a sign that they have anything in common with Greeks. The women in turn do not comprehend Greek ideas about kingship and insist that Pelasgus is an autocrat who can act without the approval of his people. The Egyptians offer the greatest contrast. Both Danaus and the king characterize the confrontation by using emblems the audience would associate with Argives and Egyptians. The father assures his daughters that wolves and corn-ears of Argos are stronger than the dogs and the papyrus fruit of Egypt, while Pelasgus implies that the national drink of Egypt, barley-brew, does not produce real men. (The connecting of the mythological Egyptians with Egypt might increase the audience's aversion for the suitors, since Egypt had participated in the Persian invasion of Greece.[41]) Pelasgus articulates his belief that two different civilizations are meeting when he tells the herald, "Foreigner, you insult the Greeks too much" (1. 914).

The audience, like Pelasgus, must have been amazed at first by the difference in appearance between the Argives and the Egyptians, accomplished by the use of masks and costumes. Through the character and diction of the king, however, Aeschylus develops a starker contrast. Before Pelasgus enters, the audience has comprehended the situation from the personal and emotional perspective of Danaus and his daughters. The king, as an outsider and objective arbiter, introduces a new perspective. In this section of stichomythia, he fires off a series of rational and pointed questions to establish the validity of the Danaid claim of Argive kinship, and to determine the legal basis for the Egyptians' claim on them. Unmoved by pity or blood ties, he will not presume the justice of their case. He recognizes that the Egyptians too may be ruled by law and that their legal system might support the hateful marriage. He is, of course, aware of the dangers to himself, but he bases his ultimate judgment on respect for divine law and concern for his people's safety as well as his own self-interest. When he ejects the herald, he speaks for the unanimous vote of the people rather than for himself (11. 942–44).

Thus, Pelasgus functions in the drama more as king than as individual. His lack of personality does not detract from the excitement of the episodes in which he appears, however. In fact the absence of the private perspective is the perfect counterpoint to the personal turmoil of the Danaids. The king and the demos he represents are trapped in a tragic situation because of their kinship with Io, but their response is not presented with the lyric emotionalism associated with tragic anguish. The king's analysis of his dilemma and the Argive assembly's carefully repeated resolution dramatize that their actions result from their adherence to the most important principles of Greek civilization. Their willingness to defend their ideals, with full awareness of the consequences, ennobles the community as a whole.

The fundamental ideals of the Greeks are clearly expressed in the Argive acceptance of the Danaids. Social organization and civilization can develop only if communities value the ties of kinship and protect the rights of strangers. Pelasgus recognizes the foreigners' suppliant branches as a Greek custom and grants the maidens special attention because they claim to be descendents of Io. If he were to deny succor, he would provoke the wrath of Zeus, patron of both relationships. The Egyptians, on the other hand, show their disdain for these customs by coming to remove the girls from sanctuary by force, by attempting to violate their own cousins, and by (so far as we know from *Suppliants*) usurping the right of their living uncle to approve the marriage.

Two further features of Greek society are developed, one the corollary of the other. If the rational and objective king seems to lack a unique personality, it is because Greek institutions are depicted as operating according to procedure and laws which are established by common consent. Impulsive action and expressions of private feeling have no place in matters concerning the common good. The king uses technical terms that refer specifically to Athenian laws and procedures.[42] For example, he expresses surprise that the foreign women have come *aproxenoi* (i.e., without a citizen-host appointed by the state to represent their interest [1. 239]) and later accuses the Egyptians of disregarding the legal requirement that they be represented by an Argive citizen (1. 919). Other statements refer to trial processes, property settlements, and the procedures for passing decrees in the assembly. The asylum the Argives grant is couched in terms which describe the full protection the Athenians accorded strangers who took up permanent residence in Athens (metics). Even Pelasgus's quick response to the women's cry for help follows the customary formulas of prayer and social or legal procedure.[43] Such vocabulary reveals how far the society had developed toward formalizing religious and social ideals so that orderly relations between individuals and nations might be maintained. Nor were these allusions esoteric, for the audience of citizens participated in these aspects of city life as diplomats, judges, lawmakers, and executives.

The attitude of the Danaids toward the Argive system changes in the course of the play. At first they do not appreciate the relationship between the Argive king and his people. They do display, however, a

developed sense of justice and cosmic order. They describe the eternal
system of reward and punishment, even referring to the "third com-
mandment of Dikē," (11. 707–9). Once Danaus has attended the
Argive assembly, he recognizes a relationship between this divine order
and the Greek political organization; he reports that "Zeus added his
final ratification" of the vote (1. 624). Like Pelasgus, he uses technical
terms for procedures and in 11. 609–14 even announces "a metrical
adaptation of the formulas of a contemporary Athenian decree."[44] The
report is all the more effective because a foreigner imitates and praises
the assembly. The daughters include the technical references in their
blessings for Argos (11. 701–3) and perceive the will of Zeus in the good
government of these men (11. 667–76).

The herald also reveals his attitude toward the law in terms the
Athenian audience would recognize. When he first appears, he asserts
the dictum that "possession is nine-tenths of the law" by attempting to
seize the women. This violation of the established sanctities demonstrates the hubris of which the Egyptians have been accused. With
Pelasgus, however, he argues his legal right to carry off his own lost
property. To the protest that he has disregarded proper religious and
legal procedure, he retorts insolently, ironically using Athenian legal
terms to assert the superiority of force to law:

How am I to say that this band of their own female cousins has been taken
from me? Ares most certainly does not hear witnesses when he judges cases
like this, nor does he accept a fee of silver for settling the dispute; no, before
such a case is finished many men fall and shuffle off their lives.

(11. 932–37; Johansen, trans.)

Thus Argos is presented in the first play as a morally superior
civilization, but it is also threatened with terrible war, unless the gods,
patrons of all its codes, written and unwritten, bring deliverance.
Unfortunately, we cannot tell how Aeschylus resolved the problem of
the righteous suffering of Argos and its king. Pelasgus offers the
possibility (11. 940–44) that the Egyptians might return to persuade
rather than fight the Argives. Most reconstructions from the saga,
however, assume that Danaus has somehow become king or at least

master of the palace in the second play. Thus we cannot say whether the
Argives were punished or rewarded for their integrity. Perhaps they
continued to be arbitrators and victims until Aphrodite intervened.[45]
Ultimately in the legend, the community was not only rescued but
blessed. Hypermestra, like Io before her, became the mother of a race of
kings, from whom Heracles, the savior of Greece, descended. Even if
King Pelasgus's heroic defense went unrewarded, the community
which institutionalized divine order would ultimately be vindicated by
its survival. By analogy, Aeschylus's dramatization of the saga would
validate Athens's own ideals.

Zeus and His Daughters

The gods are the ultimate defenders of the defenseless, the patrons of
customs and codes which protect men from each other. Therefore, the
Danaids' flight and the Argives' dilemma affect the just order of the
divine cosmos. *The Suppliants* literally begins and ends with Zeus. The
chorus invokes him as "Zeus Suppliant" in the first line of the parodos
and prays in the last line of the exodus that "right should be with the
righteous through the means of deliverance that come from god." He is
the divine patron of the Argive customs whose sanctity is threatened by
the Egyptians. As Zeus Suppliant (*Aphiktor* or *Ikesios,* ll. 1, 347, 360,
385, 478–79, 616), he protects the defenseless who cling to his altars,
requesting asylum, and his wrath against those who pollute these
shrines is relentless. As "Zeus Guest-Friend" (*Xenios*), he defends the
rights of strangers, both in private homes and in nations, by sanctifying
the relationship between guest and host. In addition, Zeus is the father
of gods and men, and in *Suppliants* he is the Danaids' literal ancestor,
whom they call father (l. 593). Thus, he is the champion of the rights
and obligations of kinship as well.

The customs and relationships of which Zeus is the patron are the
means by which divine justice (personified as Dikē, Zeus's daughter) is
maintained on earth. H. G. Robertson defines Dikē as

the guiding principle of the universe upheld and followed by the supreme
god, and the bond which holds society together, restrains lawless self-

assertiveness, and makes civilized human life possible. Again, *dikē*, as manifested among men, includes the broadest principles of equity and the principles underlying the most detailed provisions of statute law.[46]

Pelasgus, Zeus's human representative, personifies the just ruler. He protects the person of the foreign herald as well as his Danaid kin, and offers both the opportunity for redress through legal means.

When the Egyptians disregard the private rights of their cousins, the law of Argos, and the shrines and customs of local gods, they are also violating the just order of the divine cosmos as a whole. Their impiety is dramatized in various ways. The Danaids and their father often accuse the suitors of hubris or use other terms synonymous with unholiness (e.g., *asebē, disagios, anosios*). Later the herald actually proclaims his disregard for the gods of Argos (1.894) and mocks the women's cries to their Lord (Zeus) with the taunt that they will have many lords in Egypt (1. 906). To Pelasgus, the herald implies that he worships his own gods of the Nile, but in Argos he respects only Hermes, the god of heralds (whom he irreverently calls *masterios,* as if the deity were an Athenian official who searches out the property of exiles [1. 920]). The threat to wrest the maidens from the altars of the gods effectively dramatizes that "lawless self-assertiveness" is also grave impiety.

The Danaids' claim to divine aid stems from the conviction that the obvious hubris of the suitors will not go unpunished by the gods. The maidens are certain of their own innocence because they have not committed any crime themselves and have been unjustly pursued. Equally certain that justice will prevail, Danaus pictures Zeus as a judge of the dead, condemning the outrageous acts of the birds of prey (suitors) even in Hades (11. 228–31). His daughters insist on Zeus's impartiality; as kindred to both sides, he will weigh the wicked and righteous deeds in his scale (11. 402–4).

But Aeschylus has not written a melodrama in which the wicked and the righteous can be easily distinguished or the effects of violence expunged by the punishment of the guilty. Nor are the ways of the gods so clearly understood by men, despite their hope for moral order. The Danaids themselves express their confusion in a hymn to Zeus which is part of their opening prayer.

May Zeus grant that all be well in very truth: Zeus' desire is not easily
tracked: for twisting and shadowed stretch the ways of his mind, beyond our
perception to observe. . . . He hurls men from their high-towering expectation to utter doom, but not with any force does he arm himself: all that the
gods do is effortless. Settled on his sacred throne, he somehow, from that
very place, brings about the object of his thought. (11. 86–103; P. Smith,
trans.)[47]

Driven to desperation by the threat of human force, they employ prayer,
the ritual means of persuasion, to reach "his sacred throne" and make
their safety "the object of his thought."[48] In their frequent use of Zeus's
name (11. 1, 4, 18, 26, 41, 45, 86, 91, 145, 158, 162), they proclaim
their family relationship to him and insist that his causes and theirs
coincide. In much the same manner as they later attempt to persuade
Pelasgus, they threaten Zeus with suicide if their just cause is not
supported. They even blame him for their plight, relating it to Hera's
jealousy against Io, and warn Zeus that he will be judged guilty of
ignoring his kin, if he disregards their pleas.

Yet for all their claim of kinship with Zeus they have only a partial
knowledge of his nature because they refuse to acknowledge his male
sexuality.[49] They base their appeal on the similarity between their
situation and that of Io, both innocent, both exiles driven from home
and tormented by another's passion. They pray that Zeus will release
them from their suffering as he long ago freed Io. In asserting the
similarity, however, they unwittingly distort Zeus's part in the story.
They blame only Hera's jealousy for Io's suffering, but it was Zeus's lust
for the virgin priestess of Hera that provoked his wife. Although the
Danaids do not follow the analogy through, the lust of the suitors has its
divine parallel not in Hera's wrath, but in Zeus's lust for Io. And just as
Zeus's lust first endangered Io, he rescues her not by granting her
perpetual virginity, but rather by impregnating her: "by the force of
painless power and by the God's breath" (11. 576–77) or "by a ballast
which may truly be called Zeus" (11. 584–85) or by the tender act of
touching (1. 313) for which Epaphus, their offspring, was named. Thus
the violent pursuit has been transformed into something different.[50]
The Danaids, however, refuse to accept that a male's fierce desire can
have this gentle and generative consummation.

The Danaids' denial of the positive role of sexuality in human life derives from the real threat to their persons. Paradoxically, however, it leads them to their own "lawless self-assertiveness" against the divine order. Although Zeus has two daughters, Artemis, the virgin protectress of the young, and Aphrodite, the goddess of love and harmony, the maidens show a consistent preference for Artemis at the expense of Aphrodite. They pray to the virgin to keep them pure and unconquered (11. 144–50), referring to Aphrodite only as Ares's bedfellow (11. 664–65), as if she epitomized violence and lust instead of love. Although their father points out that they have reached the season of Cypris (Aphrodite) in line 1001, the girls disregard his implication about Aphrodite's power over them. In the exodus, they beg Artemis's pity and protection so that the rite of Cytherea (Aphrodite) not come upon them: "May this prize be hateful to Cytherea," ends their plea at lines 1030–33. Such a forceful statement provokes the second chorus's warning not to neglect Aphrodite, who with Hera is next to Zeus in power and to whom Desire, Persuasion, and Harmony are related. They conclude their own prayer with a hope for the maidens' marriage, which the Danaids again reject.

To the second chorus, the Danaids' disrespect for Aphrodite reveals a dangerous inflexibility and an obvious affront to the goddess. They warn them to pray for the mean (1. 1060) and not to behave excessively in respect to the gods (1. 1062). Zeus, patron of suppliants and guest-friends, has already answered part of their prayer; the Argives have accepted them and promised to defend them against violence. But the will of Zeus as husband and father may not correspond to their desire for virginity. Although the Danaids were justified in fleeing the violent suitors, they cannot be right to reject marriage and motherhood entirely. The importance attached to Epaphus as the manifestation of Io's divine blessing emphasizes for us, if not for them, the divine sanction of sex, marriage, and the perpetuation of the family. The Danaids' excessive dependence on Artemis is a rejection of the natural order and the norms for womanhood. Their threat to pollute the Argive shrines and their willingness to die or murder rather than marry expose their capability of committing their own hubris which will endanger Argos, the progeny of Zeus and Io, and the principles of Dikē. We suspect that the murder of the Egyptians puts the virgins in the same category as their suitors; the injured become the injurers by the standards of civilized society established in *Suppliants*. If Aphrodite appears as arbitrator in the third play, she supports the values of life-sustaining harmony at all levels, private, political, and cosmic, which are dramatized here through her patronage of marriage and propagation.

Chapter Five
Oresteia: Trilogy Preserved

Overview

After discussing dramas which are fragments, beginnings, or ends to trilogies whose full meaning escapes us without their missing parts, we feel more confident now that we can analyze a trilogy which has been preserved complete.[1] At last we can observe links and changes, trace the development of themes and images, and draw conclusions based on the text rather than on speculation. But the greatness of the trilogy defies complete analysis. It is impossible to convey the beauty and suggestiveness of the poetry in its original Greek or to reconstruct the sights and sounds which we know had a profound effect on the audience. Nor can twentieth-century readers presume to fully comprehend the Greeks' attitude toward the gods and the state or the assumptions about the development of civilization which Aeschylus has dramatized.[2] We can, however, present with some humility, this introduction to the *Oresteia*, with the understanding that no single treatment can hope to capture its magnificent intellectual and artistic complexity.

The *Oresteia* won first prize at the Great Dionysia of 458 B.C., just two years before Aeschylus's death. The three tragedies, *Agamemnon, Libation Bearers (Choephoroi),* and *Eumenides,* were presented in a sequence which concluded with a lost satyr play, *Proteus,* about the wanderings of Agamemnon's brother, Menelaus. Modern readers often study *Agamemnon* alone, although it is extremely difficult to follow and does not resolve the dramatic questions it raises, but the ancient spectators would have considered the drama as a first act in a larger whole. The trilogy is composed so that the *Agamemnon* and *Libation Bearers* define a conflict which can only be resolved by a third and different action. *Agamemnon,* taken alone, seems an obscure play, for the extreme complexity of image, diction, and action is a dramatic device which conveys the moral, emotional, and political confusion of the initial situation. In the second play, where the next generation of characters better understand their positions and motivations, the action is clearer. In *Eumenides,* Aeschylus illuminates the issues underlying the action and resolves them.

Because one must study the parts together to appreciate the whole, the trilogy will be treated as a single play. Although Aeschylus begins his drama *in medias res,* as Agememnon is about to return from Troy, the audience was familiar with the stories concerning the crimes of Agamemnon's father, Atreus. Therefore, it would have suspected with increasing dread some relationship between the events of the present generation and the horrors of the past, which the poet does not mention directly until the last third of the play, when the curse on the House of Atreus becomes a central theme of the trilogy. Atreus was head of the house and ruler of Argos when Thyestes, his brother, raped his wife and attempted to steal his property and power. First Atreus exiled his brother, but judging that penalty inadequate, he invited him home and cooked and served Thyestes' children to him at a feast celebrating the reunion. When Thyestes discovered he had eaten his own sons, he cursed Atreus, promising revenge, and left Argos with his one remaining son, Aegisthus.

The curse arising from this horrible act brought misfortune to the next generation. Atreus's sons, Agamemnon and Menelaus, had married sisters, Clytemnestra and Helen, respectively. Helen, the most beautiful woman in Greece, was seduced and stolen away from the hearth of the House of Atreus by their guest, Paris (Alexander), son of King Priam of Troy. Paris's adultery was a violation of the sacred relationship between guest and host protected by Zeus Xenios ("Guest-Friend"). Therefore, the Argives considered it a serious crime demanding revenge, and launched the Trojan War, subject of the *Iliad* and epic cycle.

The Greek warriors who had sworn to support Menelaus met at Aulis under the leadership of Agamemnon, elder brother of the wronged husband and most powerful king in Greece. When rough seas prevented the fleet's passage to Troy, the priest Calchas informed

Agamemnon that he must sacrifice his daughter, Iphigenia, to the goddess Artemis in order to calm the winds. Agamemnon, confident of the justice of the war and fearful of his restive troops, decided to slaughter Iphigenia so that the expedition could set sail.

Aeschylus begins his drama just as the Argives receive the news that Agamemnon has defeated Troy. The audience would know, however, from such sources as the *Odyssey,* the return stories of the cycle, and the *Oresteia* by the lyric poet Stesichorus, that, during these ten years of war, Clytemnestra had sent her son Orestes away and taken Aegisthus as a lover, and that the Greek soldiers in Troy had committed crimes which were punished on the return voyages. Aeschylus's gradual and sparing presentation of this background increases the mystery surrounding the events of the play itself.

Act I and Act II are both return and revenge stories. In *Agamemnon* several characters in sequence, the watchman, citizen/chorus, Queen Clytemnestra, and the herald, express hope and anxiety about the general's experiences in the Trojan War and his safe victorious return. Tension builds because the expectation of victory as the just punishment of Troy is constantly undercut by suggestions that the general and his men have themselves committed atrocities to insure victory. In fact, the Greek fleet has already been punished, destroyed by a god-sent storm at sea. At the mid-point in the drama, Agamemnon enters in triumph with his war prize, Cassandra, and is welcomed with Eastern pomp by his queen, Clytemnestra, who entices him to enter the palace on a luxurious tapestry. This greeting initiates the revenge story. After Agamemnon's entrance into the palace, Cassandra, the Trojan priestess of Apollo, predicts his murder and hers and relates it to the bloody history of the House of Atreus. Then Clytemnestra murders Agamemnon and his mistress and justifies her deed to the citizens as divine retribution for his sacrifice of their daughter, Iphigenia. Aegisthus, Clytemnestra's lover, later explains that history more precisely, justifying his part in Agamemnon's death as revenge for his uncle Atreus's slaughter of his brothers. Thus, the cycle of revenge as punishment which demands further revenge is clearly established by the end of the play. It is equally clear that Clytemnestra's act of revenge cannot break the cycle. She and her lover plan to replace Agamemnon as rulers of

Argos, but they respond with threats of violence to the chorus's protests
against their tyranny. The *Agamemnon* ends with the chorus cowed for
the moment, but predicting that Orestes, Agamemnon's son, sent
away by Clytemnestra, will someday return to avenge the death of his
father and assume his rightful place as head of the family and ruler of the
state.

Act II, *Libation Bearers,* also exhibits the return and revenge patterns, in dramatizing the murder of Agamemnon's murderers. First
Orestes returns, fulfilling the hopes of his sister, Electra, and the chorus
of household slaves, captives from Troy loyal to their conqueror,
Agamemnon. Orestes later learns that his return has also fulfilled the
nightmares of his mother, Clytemnestra. He enters, not as a conquering
hero like his father, to be warmly welcomed and then duped, but as an
exile in disguise, announcing his own death in order to deceive his
mother and her lover. He has been spurred on by Apollo's demand that
he avenge his father's death or suffer dire punishments, but he also acts
from private motives as son, disinherited heir, and legitimate ruler of
Argos. After praying with his sister and the chorus at the tomb of
Agamemnon to invoke the aid of the gods and the powerful dead, he
tricks Clytemnestra, kills Aegisthus, and then confronts his mother
again. She tries to dissuade him, but he leads her into the house for the
slaughter. When Orestes afterwards proclaims the justice of the matricide to the satisfied chorus, he does not gloat, as his mother before
him did, for he recognizes that his deed was a crime as well as a
necessity. He confesses that his pollution is a danger to himself and his
community and prepares to leave Argos to be purified of blood guilt by
Apollo. As he announces his plans, however, madness overtakes him;
he seems to see the very Furies (Erinyes) from Hell descending on him
to avenge his matricide. The chorus is puzzled that this act has not
ended the chain of reciprocal revenge in the House of Atreus, but sends
him forward to Apollo with prayers for success.

Act III, *Eumenides,* introduces a new story pattern, "suppliant received"; a new setting, the shrines of the gods in Delphi and Athens;
and new characters, the gods themselves—Apollo, the Furies, and
Athena. The play begins at the shrine of Apollo in Delphi, where
Orestes has arrived as a suppliant begging asylum from the Furies and

release from blood guilt. Although Apollo has temporarily drugged the Furies into sleep, he cannot permanently protect Orestes from their vengeance. The god directs the matricide to the shrine of Athena in the Acropolis of Athens, where the goddess will release him from the curse. Once Orestes has fled, the ghost of Clytemnestra angrily arouses the sleeping Furies and sends them to track their prey. Orestes arrives in Athens and clings to the goddess's shrine, but the Furies enter soon after and threaten to destroy him. Athena returns just in time, and after questioning Orestes and the chorus of Furies, she decides the conflict is too important for her to resolve alone. Instead, she establishes a homicide court (modeled on the murder trials of the Court of the Areopagus) where citizen-judges (dicasts) will hear arguments for both sides and decide between them. The two present their cases, with Apollo supporting Orestes' plea. When the jury's vote is equally split, Orestes is set free by Athena's order. Before he returns home, he thanks Apollo, Athena, and the court, promising eternal peace between Argos and Athens and wishing the city prosperity and victory forever. The Furies, incensed by the verdict, call down curses on Athens, but Athena persuades them to become honored participants in the new procedure, ever punishing injustice, but showering blessings on the good as well. When they accept her offer, they exchange their loathsome black garments for the red robes of metics (foreign residents in Athens), a visible sign of their transformation from Furies to Eumenides ("Kindly Ones"). The trilogy ends with a torchlight procession, similar to the Panathenaic Festival, in which the citizens escort the goddesses to their new home, a hallowed cave at the foot of the Acropolis.

It is a long way from the polluted House of Atreus in Argos, whose bloody Furies roost like metics on the roof (*L.B.,* 1. 971) to the clear bright light of Athens, with its court system, public festivals, rites of Apollo, and the patronage of Zeus's daughter, Athena. Aeschylus has chosen a primitive myth about a blood-vendetta which extends for generations and includes cannibalism and child sacrifice. But he has dramatized the saga in a way which makes it relevant to his fifth century audience. In none of the earlier versions of the story (i.e., *Odyssey, Cypria, Nostoi,* Stesichorus's *Oresteia*) was Orestes freed by a verdict of the Court of the Areopagus in Athens. Aeschylus originated this resolution

so that he could trace the development of human justice—from the
blood-vendetta carried out by the family with the support of the Furies
who automatically avenge kindred bloodshed, through the purification
rituals performed at the shrines of Apollo, to its culmination in the state
court system, established by Athena with Zeus's blessing.[3] In
dramatizing the progress of justice from vendetta to trial, he is also
tracing the evolution of social institutions, from family and clan united
by kindred blood, through cult united by ritual and a common patron,
up to its perfection in the democratic polis, exemplified by Athens,
where the families were ruled by law, the gods supported the new
institutions, and the citizens united into a harmonious and effective
whole.[4] No Athenian could sit unmoved while Athena voted like a
citizen according to the procedures established in mythic time, but still
in effect in 458 B.C. Nor could he watch without pride the imitation of
his great Panathenaic Festival and the respectful acceptance of the dread
Furies as metics in his own state. Thus would the contemporary
Athenian recognize the ideals and glory of his city in the resolution of
the myth.

But if this resolution represents the culmination of human progress,
at least two problems disturbed the polis in 458. The Court of the
Areopagus (the aristocratic body of ex-archons which once functioned
as supreme overseer of the laws of the land), had recently been a target of
the democratic reform. In 462, Ephialtes and Pericles carried through
the Assembly an act which removed the court's right to interfere with
democratic legislation and reduced its jurisdiction to cases of premeditated murder. The aristocrats were incensed and Ephialtes himself was
assassinated. Although Aeschylus's own position on this democratic
reform cannot be determined with certainty, in the *Eumenides,* the
court's function as a tribunal for murder is given a divine validation.
Ephialtes and Pericles had also favored challenging Spartan hegemony
in Greece by allying with Argos, Sparta's main rival in the Peloponnese. In 461, the leader of the aristocrats, Cimon, was ostracized and
the alliance with Argos approved. This change, which also produced
fierce debate in the ensuing years, received attention from Aeschylus in
the *Oresteia.* Orestes is clearly a political representative of Argos who
allies himself with Athens, seemingly with Aeschylus's approval.[5]

It is not as important to label Aeschylus an aristocrat or radical as it is to recognize in the entire trilogy a paradigm for necessary compromise between disparate elements in the state.[6] If political vendettas are not controlled, there can be no civil order and consequently no peace and prosperity. Traditional groups like the Furies must be reconciled to the new system, treated with honor, and allowed to serve the state so that they can preserve for themselves and the community whichever of their principles remain valuable. Athena, establishing the Court of the Areopagus, defines its functions in words which echo the Furies' defense of their grim penalties:

> Here the reverence
> of citizens, their fear and kindred do-no-wrong
> shall hold by day and in the blessing of night alike
> all while the people do not muddy their own laws
> with foul infusions. But if bright water you stain
> with mud, you nevermore will find it fit to drink.
> No anarchy, no rule of a single master. Thus
> I advise my citizens to govern and to grace,
> and not to cast fear utterly from your city. What
> man who fears nothing at all is ever righteous? Such
> be your just terrors, and you may deserve and have
> salvation for your citadel, your land's defence
> such as is nowhere else found among men . . .
>   (*Eumenides*, 11. 690–702)[7]

Her admonitions provide not only an eternal definition of good government, but also a timely warning to a population recently embroiled in civil strife.

Aeschylus dramatizes the conflict between blood vendetta and newer attempts to insure justice so that it embodies other significant conflicts. On one level, he defines the opposing forces through the tradition of a transition from the rule of largely underground or chthonic goddesses to that of sky gods like Zeus, Apollo, and the asexual Athena, a change which was accompanied by increasing male domination and the victory of reason over intuitive savagery. Aeschylus uses this fundamental opposition to symbolize other significant polarities in human life: male and female, parent and child, old and new, individual and common good, peace and war, anarchy and tyranny. Thus the situation is not simple; each new action explores the struggle for psychological and social balance and the dangers threatening its achievement. The balance is finally reached but the nature of the trial, the equal vote, and the unmistakable allusions to contemporary problems suggest that the balance is tenuous at best, perhaps because the forces in opposition are eternal and irreconcilable without some superhuman effort.

Act I. *Agamemnon:* Confusion

Return and Revenge.   The anxieties of the different characters who await Agamemnon's return in the first half of the play create an atmosphere of tension and doubt that gradually indicts him and presages his murder. As each character presents his own viewpoint or news, the war is exposed as an ambiguous event: a just punishment of Trojan hubris, but also an opportunity for further injustice by the Argive avengers. Seen through different eyes and in various situations, the victorious general becomes transformed into a slaughterer or sacker of cities and his regal wife into an unnatural, masculine woman. Thus the expected return also portends a necessary but hideously unjust act of vengeance. This increasing tension is underlined by the frequent alternation of confidence and doubt, of good news and bad, expressed both consciously and ironically, through word and action.

The watchman who speaks the prologue is the first witness who combines the joy of the news of victory with anxiety about its ultimate cost. He sits atop the palace of the House of Atreus in Argos, looking for a beacon flash that will signal Agamemnon's victory at Troy. This loyal servant hopes for his king's safe return but is full of anxiety because the house is now ruled by a "man-counseling woman" (1. 11). His jubilation at the sight of the torch signal trails off into silence; he knows more about the house than he dares to say. He has, however, introduced us to the major characters, King Agamemnon, whom he respects, Queen Clytemnestra, whom he suspects, and the House of Atreus itself, family and property, past and future, shrouded in mystery.

The chorus of Argive elders who come to the palace in response to the news of the victory is one of the poet's major means of conveying information, defining the significance of the facts, and increasing the tension. In the parodos, they explain the most important reasons for the watchman's anxiety. The chorus describes Agamemnon's momentous decision to sacrifice Iphigenia to insure passage to Troy but ends with the hope that all will turn out well now that victory has been achieved. But the chorus's own character and situation belie their prayer. As experienced citizens too old to fight, they recall the launching of the expedition and yet have been present as eyewitnesses to events in Argos during the war. Until Agamemnon returns, they expound on the way in which the foreign war destroys civilian life and endangers the political stability of Argos. Once Agamemnon, their legitimate king, has been murdered, they represent the endangered citizens, threatened by the new tyrants, but openly hostile.

As good citizens, the chorus provide the bridge through which the citizen audience can understand the meaning of Agamemnon's return. In conversations with the herald, the queen, Agamemnon, and Aegis-thus, the old men display attitudes with which the citizens of Athens would identify (patriotism, loyalty, fear of tyranny). Their treatment by other characters exposes in turn the rulers' political intentions. For example, the contrast between Agamemnon's respectful response to their advice and Aegisthus's angry threats dramatizes how far the political situation in Argos has degenerated.

As chorus, the Argive elders must describe events and attitudes in the imagistic language and logic of lyric. Since the dreadful events and vain hopes are expressed in vivid pictures of pathos, sung and danced in rhythms which stir emotion, the chorus can arouse the audience to share its pity and fear for the participants in the tragedy. They can convey, as no dialogue can, the emotional turbulence and moral confusion implicit in Agamemnon's victory and death. In their first three odes, they introduce the important images of animals hunted and trapped, of sacrifices that are also savage murders, of sacred things trampled, of generations tainted and tainting, which will be repeated and developed in lyric and action until the culmination in the exodus of *Eumenides*. The structure of their odes underscores the confusion: the elders begin by commenting on the events of the previous episode, concluding that justice has been done. But each ode ends by suggesting that Agamem-non, as yet unpunished, is subject to the same order of justice.

But the chorus does more than present the political or psychological perspective on events. Before Agamemnon arrives, the elders' odes shift constantly from the description of specific human events and psychological states to the general cosmic law which their story illustrates. In clear and direct statements, they present the precepts about the dangers of too much wealth, the certainty of punishment for those who defy the divine order by committing violent acts, and the relation between suffering and wisdom. Here too the form of the lyric contributes to its effect, for they couch their ideas in the diction, structure, and hymns familiar to Athenians from their own worship.[8] Their prayers that good prevail seem vain at the end of *Agamemnon* when they are silenced by Aegisthus's armed guard. Yet even as evil piles upon evil in the first play, they offer the hope that a cosmic order exists where a supreme and impartial ruler (Zeus) sits above the fray dispensing justice.

A detailed analysis of the parodos illustrates how Aeschylus uses the chorus to establish both the facts and their ambiguous implications.[9] In lines 40–62, the chorus states the cause of the war: ten years ago the sons of Atreus set out to punish Troy and Alexander for the theft of Helen which was a violation of Zeus's law of hospitality. The elaborate simile which introduces Agamemnon and Menelaus as birds defending their nest reinforces the idea of the justice of their cause. But in the next strophe, their actions are described as having been undertaken not for their chicks but for a promiscuous woman. Moreover, the young for whom the war has been initiated are associated with images of sacrifice and feasting which allude both to the horrible feast of Thyestes and Agamemnon's sacrifice of Iphigenia.

The chorus's questions to Clytemnestra about the sacrifices she has ordered reveal their anxiety about the next fact they must relate: the omen at Aulis. The birds from the simile reappear as royal eagles who rip apart a pregnant hare and devour her unborn young. Calchas the priest interprets the portent and predicts the anger of Artemis, patroness of all helpless cubs and specifically of savage lions (the heraldic symbol of the House of Atreus). On the most literal level, the hare, natural prey of eagles and vultures, is Troy, clear transgressor of Zeus Xenios. But the birds' savage meal is in itself a crime. The language which connects it with feasts, hunts, sacrifice, and lions suggests that Artemis's anger in anticipation of the Trojan slaughter is also a punishment in kind for past deaths of innocent young in the Argive family. The omen exposes the nexus of justice and injustice. The choral refrain "Sorrow, sorrow, but good win out in the end" (11. 129, 139, 159) expresses their moral confusion.

In despair, they turn for reassurance to Zeus, who, as supreme ruler, must be the ultimate cause of these distressing events, and find a reason for his tolerance of so much crime and suffering.

> Zeus who guided men to think,
> who has laid it down that wisdom
> comes alone through suffering. . . , against
> our pleasure we are temperate.
> From the gods who sit in grandeur
> grace comes somehow violent.
> (11. 176–83; Lattimore, trans.)

The passage is difficult to interpret. In the phrase "wisdom through suffering" (*pathei mathos:* Lattimore's "alone" is not in the Greek), the chorus is alluding to an old saying which implies that fools must learn from bitter experience what others already know. In the context of the parodos, these words confirm that this much violence is necessary as Zeus's means of punishing the transgressions of deluded fools. Thus the elders gain the courage to narrate the remaining facts: Agamemnon's terrible decision (to sacrifice his daughter rather than abandon the war), his subsequent reckless behavior, and the death of his innocent child. Again the imagery of feasts and young animals connects Iphigenia to Thyestes' sons and the charges of Artemis. The chorus, after relating potentially disillusioning events, concludes by repeating the hope that all will be well and the maxim that "Justice allots learning to those who suffer" (11. 250–51). But in the course of their painful narration, Agamemnon has become the agent as well as the victim of violence, the one who also must experience evil because he has not been wise.

The first episode, between the chorus and Clytemnestra, adds both information and anxiety. When Clytemnestra emerges from the palace doors to confirm the rumors of victory, she declaims two long speeches, the first explaining the geographical details of the beacon system she established and the second picturing the grim emotional and physical reactions of both sides to the war. She then prays that the victors beware of wreaking too much vengeance, and offending the gods of the defeated land, for she knows conquerors can be conquered in turn by love of gain and that offenses against the gods and the dead are inevitably punished. The episode establishes several things at once. It introduces Clytemnestra as a powerful, imaginative, articulate woman fully capable of forethought and bold action. But her brief dialogue with the chorus, in which they exchange disparagements of the female sex, adds tension because it suggests that her behavior is somehow aberrant. Worse, the good news of victory is tainted by the anticipation of disaster if the men take too great advantage of their success.

But the chorus begins their first stasimon by rejoicing; the Greek victory at Troy has confirmed that Zeus indeed punishes transgressors who "trample on things inviolable" (11. 371–72). To them, Paris's crime illustrates a general truth. Excess wealth makes men proud and exposes them to *Peitho* ("Persuasion" or "Flattery") and *Atē* ("Infatuation," "Madness," and "Ruin"), which tempt them to "kick the great altar of Dikē out of sight" (11. 384–85). Paris, so tempted, has revealed his imperfection, like a cheap bronze tested by use. He chased after Helen as a child chases after a bird and brought destruction to his city. As the chorus describes Menelaus's loss, however, they are overcome by anguish at the loss of their own loved ones who went to war, and blame not the Trojans but the Atreidae, from whom they demand retribution. Their closing words asserting that justice will surely overtake "those who have killed many" (1. 462) and "plunderers of cities" (1. 471) apply to Agamemnon as well as to Paris.

In the next episode, a herald enters to announce Agamemnon's success and imminent return. An audience that had just heard Clytemnestra's warning and the chorus's pronouncements would recognize the irony of his enthusiasm.

Salute him [Agamemnon] with good favor, as he well deserves,
the man who has wrecked Ilium with the spade of Zeus

vindictive, whereby all their plain has been laid waste.
Gone are their altars, the sacred places of the gods
are gone, and scattered all the seed within the ground.
With such a yoke as this gripped to the neck of Troy
he comes, the king, Atreus' elder son, a man
fortunate to be honored far above all men
alive; not Paris nor the city tied to him
can boast he did more than was done him in return . . .
Twice over the sons of Paris have atoned their sins.
                    (11. 524–33, 537; Lattimore, trans.)

The herald's episode also advances the story of return and revenge.
Most important, good news is immediately followed by bad. Asked
about Menelaus, the herald reluctantly reports that the entire fleet,
except for Agamemnon's ship, has been destroyed by a storm raised by
the gods (11. 649–53). Thus, it is clear to the audience, if not to him,
that most of the Argive fleet had already received its punishment. They
would surely understand the folly of his statement that Agamemnon's
ship was guided to safety by a god (1. 663) or "life-saving Fortune" (1.
664). But they would also identify with the herald, a simple, reverent,
patriotic soldier whose account of the suffering of ordinary soldiers
would correspond to their own experiences in modern warfare. This
deglamorized presentation of an epic battle undercuts the assumption
that the Trojan War was a glorious crusade led by heroic men.[10] The
herald scene also increases the mystery surrounding Clytemnestra.
When she asks him to convey her welcome to the king, her jubilant
speech, full of endearing references to Agamemnon and assurances of
her fidelity, provokes an enigmatic comment from the chorus: "Thus
has she spoken to you, and well you understand/words that impress
interpreters, whose thought is clear" (11. 615–16; Lattimore, trans.),
which renders her sincerity as a wife suspect and engenders further
tension about the welcome she is preparing.

The chorus's second stasimon is pivotal, pointing backward to the
Trojan War and forward to the general's entrance. Overwhelmed by the
bad news of the fleet's destruction, the elders begin by blaming Helen
for the multiple disasters, comparing her to a lion cub treated as a pet,

who, when mature, shows its true nature and turns against its nurturers. So she has become a Fury, punishing the Trojans whose great prosperity has tempted them to commit hubris. But the parable of the lion cub has wider implications, reminding us of all the innocent lion cubs referred to in the parodos and now clearly connected to the House of Atreus—those family members who were once soft and tender, but then reverted to their parents' nature and turned savage.[11] As such, it applies most obviously to Agamemnon's sacrifice of his beloved daughter, but it also alludes to those nurtured in the house who will turn against its inhabitants (i.e., Clytemnestra, Aegisthus, and Orestes). Although the chorus indicts the House of Priam in Troy, the lion parable has led us to think of Helen in the light of the wealth and power of the House of Atreus which has already bred hubris through two generations. The descriptions of Helen's luxury have implications for the Argive halls as well, for they too are perilously "gold stained by reeking hands" (1. 776), as Agamemnon's triumphal return and Clytemnestra's extravagant welcome will demonstrate.

The long-awaited entrance of the mighty hero is the turning point of the drama. All of the suspicion of his excess wealth, his hubris, and his delusion that he can act with impunity are confirmed by his behavior. He enters in triumph, borne by a horse-drawn chariot, his concubine Cassandra by his side, and followed by a troop of warriors.[12] After a confident prayer of gratitude to the gods for helping him to his just victory, he boasts of Troy's punishment in words that recall the chorus's grim assessments of the war and its participants:

> The storm clouds of their ruin live; the ash that dies
> upon them gushes still in smoke their pride of wealth.
> For all this we must thank the gods with grace of much
> high praise of memory, we who fenced within our toils
> of wrath the city; and, because one woman strayed,
> the beast of Argos broke them, the fierce young within
> the horse, the armored people who marked out their leap
> against the setting of the Pleiades. A wild
> and bloody lion swarmed above the towers of Troy
> to glut its hunger lapping at the blood of kings.
>   (11. 819–28; Lattimore, trans.)

He seems fully confident that he can overcome the citizens' resentment
and duplicity the chorus warns him about. Nor does he anticipate any
danger from Clytemnestra, although he has sacrificed their daughter to
become a "sacker of cities." His trampling on the purple carpet
symbolizes his actions, past and present. Although he knows that such
honor befits only gods and that his footsteps would destroy the delicate
fabrics that are the wealth of the House, he nevertheless gives in to
Clytemnestra's flattery and persistence.[13]

The welcoming scene also shifts the attention from Agamemnon's
guilt and return to Clytemnestra and her act of revenge. Her hypocrisy,
her aberrant behavior, and her own hubris are apparent from the way
she greets him. First she addresses the Argive citizens about the return
of her husband. To gain their sympathy, she proclaims a hyperbolic list
of flattering metaphors for the joy with which she now receives him.
Then she addresses Agamemnon directly and, like Peitho in the first
stasimon, begins to cajole him into placing "his foot which captured
Troy," too good for mere earth, upon the delicate tapestries. Her
manipulation of the proud warrior demonstrates not only her insincer-
ity but her unnaturally masculine behavior. Agamemnon protests her
aggressive attempts to persuade him: "It is not the character of a woman
to desire battle" (1. 940). This masculinity is a sign of her proud
self-confidence as the real possessor of the palace. In her magnificent
speech that accompanies his entry, she displays her own pride arising
from her faith in the unlimited wealth of the House of Atreus and in the
unlimited favor of the gods. Her ironic prayer, "Zeus, Zeus accom-
plisher, accomplish these my prayers" (1. 973), foreshadows her revenge against her husband, but it also portends punishment for her own
sins.

Now that Agamemnon and Clytemnestra have been indicted by
innuendo and actual behavior, Aeschylus spells out the story of the
House of Atreus in order to show the influence of the past on the present
actions of the characters. The sad tale of the adultery of Atreus's wife
and the death of Thyestes' children, slain by their vengeful uncle and
eaten by their father, is the origin of the blood vendetta that has trapped
Agamemnon and Clytemnestra. The special significance of the information about the curse is indicated by the unusual way in which it is

conveyed by Cassandra, the Trojan priestess of Apollo. Her silence
while she stands in Agamemnon's chariot as the husband and wife
converse and her later refusal to speak to Clytemnestra draw attention to
the importance of her words.[14] When she finally does speak to the
chorus, Aeschylus makes her tell her story twice, first in frenzied,
enigmatic lyrics which express the horror of the House and then in
calmer dialogue, which clarifies the most important details. Cassandra
also predicts that Clytemnestra, "this lion-wife" (1. 1258), and Aegisthus, the craven "wolf" (1. 1259), will murder her and Agamemnon
but foresees that the son will return to slay the mother, avenging his
father and herself. Thus, the powerful and unending cycle of the blood
vendetta is made clear before Clytemnestra murders Agamemnon in his
bath.

The chorus is at a loss when they hear Agamemnon's cries from
within. As they debate the best course of action, Clytemnestra emerges
from the palace to announce that she has murdered their king and his
mistress. With the two corpses lying beneath her on the ekkyklema,
she joyously relates the details of her deed: how she trapped him in a
coverlet, struck him thrice, and delighted in his blood spurting upon
her. She proclaims herself an avenging Fury for her dead daughter and
insists the murder is a just offering to Zeus for Agamemnon's sins
against the family. The chorus protests, fully aware that another act of
revenge cannot end the cycle, for Zeus has ordained that "he who does
shall suffer," and so the race is "still bound fast in the net of Atē" (11.
1562–65).

The appearance of Aegisthus dramatizes the depth of Clytemnestra's
delusion. Aegisthus also claims that he is the just avenger of Atreus's
crime against Thyestes. His grim description of the cannibalism makes
it unlikely that the vendetta will stop here, for Agamemnon, like
Thyestes, has left a son behind. Although Clytemnestra can control the
quarrel between her lover and the hostile citizens, there is little hope
that her wealth will enable her to rule in peace. The uneasy truce at the
end and the prediction about Orestes signal that the avenging Fury will
return.

Character and Responsibility. Two-thirds of the way through
Agamemnon it is clear that the king and queen are trapped in a system of

justice that necessitates that the avenger of a crime become a criminal himself. But the playwright does not excuse individuals by making them victims of the curse of a blood-vendetta. Rather he explores the extent of their responsibility, dramatizing the choices and personalities which have helped to shape events. The chorus expresses its awareness of the double motivation of external compulsion and personal will when it asks Clytemnestra,

> What man shall testify
> Your hands are clean of this murder?
> How? How? Yet from his father's blood
> might swarm some fiend to guide you.
>   (11. 1505–1508; Lattimore, trans.)

Before Agamemnon enters the orchestra, or Cassandra alludes to Atreus and Thyestes, Agamemnon's own responsibility for the sins against Troy, Argos, and the gods has been established.[15] It is true that Zeus Xenios sent forth the expedition and that Artemis demanded the sacrifice of Iphigenia. But Agamemnon's situation is more complicated than this. As a leader of a great and wealthy house, he has the feeling of unlimited power and the responsibility to exercise that power under crucial and sometimes intolerable conditions. Moreover, Agamemnon is more vulnerable because, as an heir to the curse as well as the property of Atreus, he has inherited the potential to beget further impiety. His position as general of the Argive army places him in a situation where he is tempted to commit an act which in other circumstances would be unthinkable. Although external forces impose a terrible choice on Agamemnon, he never mentions these compulsions. In the chorus's report of his own words, he moves from horror at the conflicting demands placed on him to an analysis of the equally disastrous alternatives, struggling between two different personal and human feelings—a father's love for his daughter and a general's responsibility to his troops. And he chooses for a personal reason, his fear of abandoning his duty and exposing himself to disgrace.

Thus the sacrifice has a human as well as a divine cause. Another man in similar circumstances might have chosen differently, but Agamemnon, when tempted by his ambition, decides to sacrifice his daughter to calm the storm. The chorus's description of the characteristics exposed in Agamemnon contains all the key words for moral imperfection: boldness, reckless daring, infatuation. Their account of the sacrifice, with its references to other crimes in the House, suggests that the son of Atreus has become like his father and is fully capable of begetting further crime—the savage slaughter at Troy and the destruction of the Trojan altars.

Agamemnon seems deluded into believing he can act with impunity. Once he has decided to sacrifice Iphigenia, Agamemnon prays that "it may all be for the best" (l. 217), and he returns from Troy convinced that everything has succeeded as planned. His first speech, which thanks the gods as his partners in the destruction of Troy, displays his ignorance of the fact that he has committed crimes that must be counted against him. His consciousness of his own righteousness is inconsistent with all precepts, signs, and dangers that everyone else—chorus, wife, and herald—at least dimly comprehends. He is clearly among the "sackers of cities" and "those who have blood on their hands" from whom punishment must be exacted. Indeed, that punishment has already begun with the storm at sea. He also believes that, as a wise and experienced leader, he is immune to the conspiracies of his subjects. This delusion is exposed immediately when he is so easily deceived by his wife, a woman whom everyone else suspects. A man who has murdered his daughter and brought home a mistress should at least expect some ill-feeling from his wife.

His glorious entry characterizes him as one whom extreme good fortune has tempted to extreme behavior. As if expecting protection from his wealth, he "trample[s] on things inviolable" (the chorus's metaphoric definition of hubris [ll. 371–72, 382–84]). Because Aeschylus can only report indirectly on Agamemnon's behavior during the war, the general's words and actions as he enters take on tremendous significance.[16] The pomp with which he arrives displays his excess wealth. The way in which he compromised the Argive victory is rendered doubly damning because he and his herald gloat over the slaughter of innocents and the destruction of shrines. The silent presence of Cassandra is a further sign of his presumption; the virgin priestess of Apollo who rejected that god's sexual advances at her peril has been forced to share the bed of Agamemnon. Thus when he enters his palace by "trampling" on a fabric he knows is too good for ordinary men and too expensive to waste, he literally demonstrates a hubris that must be punished.

Although his punishers, Clytemnestra and Aegisthus, are instruments of the curse and just avengers of Iphigenia, they are no less guilty than Agamemnon. Clytemnestra's sexual jealousy of Agamemnon's mistress, Cassandra, whom she calls "the public harlot of the sailors' benches" (11. 1422–43), falsifies her claim to be only an avenging Fury for the House of Atreus. She gloats that Cassandra's dead body lying above Agamemnon's has "added relish to her own [adulterous] marriage bed" (1. 1446). The fact that she keeps a lover exposes her unnatural desire to usurp a male privilege and assert her equality with Agamemnon, who, like all warriors, keeps a concubine. But, because Aegisthus is judged less than a man, a coward who has allowed his woman to commit the manly act of slaughter, her choice of him confirms what her earlier pride and plotting have implied: her own ambition to control the House and state. Her lust for power has already disrupted the family and the citizens; Orestes has been sent away and the legitimate king displaced from his throne.

Her choice of Aegisthus is both a consequence of her ambition and a cause of her doom. With a weakling as partner, Clytemnestra expects to remain in control. She understands that she has now become a murderer herself, but hopes that by giving up some wealth and ruling with moderation, she can bribe the evil daemon and go unpunished, thus ridding the House of further bloodshed (11. 1566–76). Yet Aegisthus's very cowardice necessitates a degeneration in the family and the state. His inferiority to Agamemnon, pointed out by Cassandra and the chorus, is demonstrated by his need for an armed bodyguard to control the citizens. His fear of vengeance from Agamemnon's children or the restive Argives must lead the couple to increase their oppression in order to maintain their power.

Helen, Paris, and the Trojans also fit the pattern Agamemnon and Clytemnestra exemplify. Great wealth leads them to believe they are entitled to whatever they desire. All except Cassandra and the chorus suffer from the same delusion and remain ignorant of their own accountability. This generation does not possess wisdom, and so the House of Atreus has sunk even lower by the end of *Agamemnon*.

Disorder and Sorrow. In *Agamemnon*, Aeschylus dramatizes the way in which the moral confusion affects personal relations, family life, and the community's health. The relationship between male and female, so important to a stable society, is in total disorder in the *Agamemnon*. The watchman's phrase, "man-counseling woman," introduces one important theme which is traced through the generations to its resolution in the *Eumenides*: confusion of sex roles. Clytemnestra, defensive about her femininity even when she uses it to achieve her aims, is an unnatural woman who, in Agamemnon's absence, has usurped the powers and prerogatives which belong by nature (in the Greek world view) to males.[17] She has misused her position as queen and abused her natural role as mother (as we shall see more clearly in *Libation Bearers*) to accomplish selfish ends. In all the episodes she appears cleverer than her male interlocutors. According to Cassandra, she is "the lion," stronger than her lover. But Agamemnon is neither craven nor female like Aegisthus. Clytemnestra reveals the full perversity of her behavior when she defeats even Agamemnon, first by a persuasive argument and then by a physical attack.

Although Clytemnestra is by far the strongest character in the play, others exhibit the same deviation from normal sex roles. Cassandra's refusal to share Apollo's bed and bear his children is also a denial of the proper role of women. Aegisthus's womanish nature is condemned by Cassandra and the chorus, but Menelaus, too, exhibits signs of weakness and an uxoriousness toward Helen that has in part caused the war.[18]

Disorder in the male-female relationship is also reflected in the treatment of women as property—symbols of men's wealth or prestige.[19] Adultery, which dominates the history of the House of Atreus, is the illicit seizure of someone else's property, a grabbing of more than one's portion, and thus a sign of hubris. Adultery in *Agamemnon* is an important manifestation of moral confusion. The Trojan War was begun to avenge Paris's theft of Helen, who is always described in terms of the luxury that surrounds her. But the chorus condemn the war as madness because it is fought for an adulterous woman. The members of the House of Atreus are involved in adulteries that enhance their status. The quarrel between Atreus and Thyestes started with the "trampling of a brother's marriage bed" (1. 1193), but Thyestes tried to seize Atreus's property and power along with his wife. Cassandra, Agamemnon's war prize, is all the more valuable because she is his "flower, chosen out of much wealth" (1. 954–55). Aegisthus becomes tyrant of Argos by sharing Clytemnestra's bed.

Adultery and the male perception of women as wealth to be forcibly conquered are only the most obvious signs of the perversion of family life in the House of Atreus.[20] Ambition for power and glory replace the concern for stable family relationships that leads to prosperity. Agamemnon has neglected his wife for many years in favor of the war in Troy. When he finally does face Clytemnestra, his first words are "Daughter of Leda, Guard of my house, your speech was like my absence, for you drew it out too long" (11. 914–15). Nor does his plea for kindness to Cassandra indicate sensitivity to his wife's feelings. Clytemnestra's hatred for him is clear from the way she glories in his death, refuses him a decent burial, and mutilates his body (in part a magical means of preventing revenge). Helen, of course, has simply abandoned all her responsibilities to husband and home. But the real proof that male interests outside the home have destroyed the family lies in the fact that Agamemnon has chosen the war in Troy over the life of his daughter. The play's first sacrifice is described from the daughter's viewpoint to emphasize the father's denial of her value as his child, member of his household, and potential breeder of his descendants. The disillusioned chorus weighs Iphigenia's worth as virgin and innocent against the worth of Helen the adulteress. But from the earliest days of the House of Atreus, children have been the victims of their male parents, used by the adults as means to achieve dubious ends. Tantalus, the first father of the house (1. 1469), served his own son, Pelops (1. 1600), to Zeus at a banquet he prepared for the gods. Aegisthus's brothers were destroyed by the quarrel between Atreus and Thyestes, whereas Orestes, Iphigenia's brother, has been exiled and deprived of his inheritance by his kingly mother. In fact the perversion of family values is expressed by the chorus's metaphor of generations; hubris

committed by those with great prosperity gives birth not to children
but to further hubris, insatiable woe, and the spirit Atē, reckless and
unholy (ll. 751–56).

Everyone in Argos falls victim to the disorder in the royal family.
Men young enough to fight must bleed and die in a foreign land because
of Menelaus's grief and the need to avenge Paris's crime. It is clear that
the wealthy House of Priam earned its punishment for accepting
Helen, but there is no reason to believe that the Trojan land and gods
deserved to be obliterated or that the youth of Argos should die fighting
in Troy. Those who are not warriors, Clytemnestra and the chorus,
sympathize with the agonies of the common soldier. Clytemnestra's
account of her lonely vigil may not be completely sincere, but it does
describe the anguish of the waiting wives. The chorus, too, reports its
agony when ash-filled urns return home in place of live sons and
husbands and fathers. So in Argos grief has turned to anger and
resentment, and rebellion is smoldering by the time Agamemnon
returns. As the legitimate king, he respects his subjects and appears
ready to re-establish good government. But his death signals a new and
worse political situation. Unable to claim legitimate authority or build
support, Aegisthus and Clytemnestra will rule by force and oppress the
citizens, establishing a tyranny that will engender new resentment and
finally necessitate tyrannicide. Thus the characters' failures, coupled
with the vendetta, have spread disorder which threatens to destroy the
individual, the family, and the state.

   Disorder in the Cosmos?   There seems to be as much confusion
in the cosmos as there is on earth. From the divine perspective, the war
against Troy is just; Zeus Xenios sends his eagles forth to punish Paris's
desecration of Menelaus's hearth. But Artemis is also divine and she
demands that Agamemnon sacrifice his daughter in order to reach Troy.
Her motive is never explicitly stated. In the saga, Agamemnon of-
fended her by either killing her stag or boasting that he was the better
hunter. Here, however, Calchas's interpretation of the omen of the
pregnant hare implies that Artemis, protectress of all the helpless
young, demands payment in anticipation of the slaughter of the
innocents in Troy. Her demand threatens the expedition and conflicts
with Zeus's support. Agamemnon's decision to accommodate Artemis
by sacrificing his daughter brings down upon him the Furies who have
hovered over the House of Atreus since the first kindred murder. Yet the

allusion to lion cubs suggests Artemis is also punishing him for the crimes of his father, and her demand only perpetuates the cycle of violence she hates. The Furies do not always confine themselves to avenging the murder of kin; they also destroy those whose wealth and power lead them to commit such injustice as violating the guest-friend relationship. Thus Helen is the avenging Fury to Troy just as Clytemnestra is to Agamemnon. But the sons of Atreus too are described as Furies sent against the Trojan transgressors by Apollo, Pan, or Zeus (11. 54–59). By lines 461–63, however, they have become the "killers of many men" whom the black Furies (Erinyes) in time consign to darkness. Thus the Furies, Artemis, and Zeus seem to have conflicting purposes. But all punish by demanding a repetition of the act they are punishing.

On one level, the divine disorder is a reflection of the ambiguities and insoluable problems of human life. War, even when just in principle, outstrips the idea by the grimness of its reality. It destroys the innocent with the guilty, corrupts the righteous defenders of the principle, and hardly seems worth the cost in the end. The opposition between the male divinities who send forth the expedition and the goddesses Artemis and the Furies of Iphigenia reflects the conflict between martial, imperialistic drives and the feminine values of home and family. In war, these two are incompatible; Agamemnon cannot in fact be both husband and general.[21] Even in peacetime, however, individuals have difficulty satisfying their own needs without trespassing on the needs of others. When powerful people attempt to get more than their portion, they often drag down those who rely on their judgement and protection. So the picture of anarchy and disorder in the cosmos caused by each divinity jealously protecting his own prerogatives validates the reality of instability in human life.

But the chorus's prayers, hymns, and speculations present a picture of a divine order superior to the one suggested by the turmoil of the situation. The gods are partners with human beings and keep a watchful eye on events as patrons of those parts of society that need protection. The elders know that danger comes from too much good fortune which leads the prosperous to discount the gods and suppose that they can commit forbidden acts with impunity. But the gods are certain to punish any impious deed, no matter how important the agent is. Their divine violence is in fact a favor, for the suffering of those who trample on justice teaches wisdom (or knowledge of limitations and certainty of punishment).

No one in the first play has learned anything from the grim cycle of bloody crime, but progress is possible. The allusion to Zeus as the third and final ruler suggests the possibility of overcoming the failures of the past and establishing a new and better order. After two earlier generations of violence, this Zeus is now in firm control, dispensing reward and punishment, having established the law that "wisdom comes through suffering." In the hymn presenting this precept and Zeus's genealogy, the elders refer to him as "Whoever Zeus may be, if this name is pleasing to him" (11. 160–61) or, later, "Zeus, the cause of all, doer of all" (1. 1485). In avoiding the formula for one specific patron, they invoke the supreme deity who keeps the balance between all patrons, or all the disparate forces who have their own functions to perform as separate elements of the cosmic order.[22] The hymn makes it possible to hope that the apparent disorder is a reflection of the characters' failure to perceive their own limitations. In fact, the divine order, by punishing transgression in the present generation, will engender in the next the wisdom that can lead to a new procedure for effecting justice and a higher level of civilization.

Image and Action.   Throughout the trilogy, Aeschylus develops his imagery in an unusual way; he begins by impressing a picture on the audience's imagination and then he gives that picture life by reproducing it in the action. By this device, the poet can describe violent behavior or explore complex ideas that can't be staged and then charge the action he does stage with a fuller range of meaning by making the metaphor real.[23] For example, in *Agamemnon,* the general's entry into the palace has a strong intellectual and emotional impact precisely because his act of trampling on the delicate tapestry corresponds exactly to the chorus' metaphorical description of hubris as "trampling on things that should be inviolable" (a metaphor extended by the frequent association of moral transgression with kicking, overstepping, or treading [11. 383–84, 885, 1193, 1357, 1601]). His trampling here confirms visually the reports that he has desecrated the shrines of Troy and annihilated the city. Other more complex image patterns expand and change in order to convey the moral ambiguity and the circularity of the blood vendetta. For example, the poet develops ubiquitous imagery of hunting and trapping animals so that it expresses both the idea that the avengers of crime become entrapped by committing a crime in turn and the judgment that rational men are potentially animals who kill instinctively in response to injury. The paradox that an atonement for crime is a crime in itself is embodied in the identification of forms of worship, like sacrifice or libations, with bloody slaughter and hunting or eating prey raw.[24] After these patterns of hunting and blood sacrifice have been developed to describe all the crimes in the House of Atreus, in *Eumenides,* they take on a visual reality when the Furies, the "hounds of Clytemnestra," actually chase Orestes, "the hare," into the orchestra, trap him at the altar of Athena, and try to sacrifice him. Thus, just before the code is transformed, the action summarizes its paradoxically bestial, circular, and yet religious aspects. Such correspondences between image and action occur in each play, but the four major patterns—hunting and trapping, bloodshed as sacrifice and murder, allusions to legal process, and contrasts between light and dark—appear throughout the first two plays and then reach their culmination as climactic action in *Eumenides,* where the new developments in the patterns symbolize the resolution.

From the parodos of *Agamemnon* on, the metaphors of hunting which emphasize enclosure are extended in order to underline the fact that the stalkers are eventually caught in their own traps.[25] Agamemnon and his men "fence" and "net" their victims only to become ensnared in turn. The chorus imagines the general not only as "casting his yoke about the neck of Troy" (11. 358–60), but also as "fastening the yoke strap of necessity upon himself" (1. 218). Later Agamemnon is described as a spider trapped in a web (11. 1492, 1516). The general who walked on a tapestry is himself trapped in one, when Clytemnestra entangles him in a coverlet which is called "a net of Hades" (1. 1115), a net for fish and "evil wealth of raiment" (11. 1382–83). The spectacle reinforces the image and the idea. After his death Clytemnestra and Aegisthus stand over his slaughtered body, pointing to the bloody coverlet in which she trapped him.

The pattern of entanglement contains a rich store of animal imagery which accumulates from play to play in such a way that it expresses the play's major themes: circularity, savagery, disorder in nature, and the paradox of punishment. On its most obvious level the metaphor conveys the idea that the vendetta is futile and unending. In *Agamemnon*, animals appear first as victims or prey and then become stalkers themselves, only to be described, in the two later plays, as victims once again. For example, early in the parodos, Agamemnon and Menelaus are vultures bewailing the theft of their fledgling, Helen, from the nest. But these birds, now eagles, soon stalk and destroy a pregnant hare and devour her unborn offspring. After his murder, however, Agamemnon will again be the bird (eagle) whose fledglings—this time Orestes and Electra—are in danger.

Because the lion is the symbol of the ruling house in Argos, references to tender cubs (whether victims or pets) who when grown cannot conceal their savage nature express not only the idea of futility, but also the particular savagery of the House of Atreus which turns its violence against its own. Yet Helen the cub matures into a Fury, an instrument of barbaric but just revenge for Troy. The application of the image to Agamemnon, "the ravening lion who licked the blood of Troy," and to Clytemnestra, the aberrant lioness awaiting his return, reinforces the ambiguity of their positions. The disorder of their marriage relationship is underlined by the unnatural act of a female lion killing her mate (with cow and bull variations in 11. 1125 ff.) and the lioness's choice of a wolf to replace him. But even a lion or bitch (1. 1228) is an insufficient metaphor for the monstrosity of Clytemnestra. She is more like an amphisbaena, a snaky creature from myth, or Scylla, the woman transformed into a beast with barking dogs emerging from her middle (1. 1233).

Such animal imagery will be developed in the next play where the children are compared to hares and nestlings when viewed as victims of Clytemnestra, but, when seen as avengers, are described as lion cubs, dogs, or snakes. Because of the identification of all these animals with so many equivocal situations, Electra and Orestes seem paradoxically just by association with Apollo and the Furies, and yet savage and monstrous by association with their mother. The confusion is increased by the double source of the animal imagery. The similes and metaphors come from the poetry spoken by the characters or chorus, but the gods send the omen about the eagle who is the royal bird of Zeus and Clytemnestra's dream of the snake, Apollo's sacred animal. This connection underscores the double motivation for human deeds and the relation between the human and divine vendetta. In *Eumenides* the literal appearance of the Furies (which combines all previous animal imagery, e.g., flying hounds, snake-haired, barking, following a scent) dramatizes the savagery, futility, and moral ambiguity of that code.

Because each death in *Agamemnon* can be seen as a holy offering to the divine patrons of justice as well as a bloody murder of a human being, the descriptions of death are couched in the imagery and language of ritual sacrifice and libation.[26] The chorus recalls that Iphigenia was led to the altar like a goat, Troy's destruction is pictured as an offering to Ate, and Cassandra, after Clytemnestra has ironically invited her inside to share the sacrifice at the hearth, goes like a cow to the altar. In *Agamemnon*, the sacrifice imagery reaches its climax when Clytemnestra, standing over her bloody victims, describes Agamemnon's falling blood as a libation to Zeus of the Underworld and the murders as sacrifices to Ate and the Furies, by which she thinks she has fertilized the land. But the blood of sacrifice grows more patently demonic and poisonous as the facts about the curse of kindred slaughter come to light.

In *Agamemnon*, the picture of the House, splattered by blood spilled in sacrifice or murder, becomes a reality in the spectacle of Agamemnon's entry.[27] The purplish brown tapestry, the color of dried blood, symbolizes the blood licked at Troy as well as the new blood about to be shed. The blood-colored tapestry also represents the past of the palace that reeks with slaughter. The image of bloodshed will expand in the *Libation Bearers* and reach its climax in the *Eumenides*, where the Furies, wearing bloody black robes and dripping blood, will demand the blood-spattered Orestes as the last sacrifice.

Because the question of justice is central to the play, the acts of revenge are also described in the language and imagery of legal procedure. Aside from the numerous references to *Dike*, justice which is both cosmic and human, Aeschylus uses specific terms borrowed from fifth-century law courts to define characters and actions.[28] For example, Agamemnon and Menelaus are introduced as Priam's "opponents

AESCHYLUS

at law" (*antidikos*, 11. 40–42), the Atreidae are called "principals in a suit" (1. 451), the herald summarizes the war as if it were a legal recovery of stolen property (11. 534–37), and Agamemnon imagines the gods voting against Trojan acquittal like a jury (11. 810–17). These allusions reinforce the idea that the war is an instrument for punishing injustice. After the murders, both Clytemnestra and her lover stand before the citizens to defend themselves, arguing the justice of their cases. Like the other devices, the imagery from the legal system begins in *Agamemnon,* develops in *Libation Bearers,* and comes to fruition in *Eumenides,* where the dispute is settled by a real trial, with dicasts voting after hearing the arguments of a technical plaintiff and defendant.

In *Agamemnon,* the alternation between light and dark, in spectacle and imagery, underscores the reversal from joy to sorrow and gradually creates an atmosphere of overwhelming gloom.[29] The play may have literally begun in brilliance; if it started as early as dawn, Aeschylus could have used the rising sun to represent the beacon which announces victory. Then the real light would be amplified by imagined torches when Clytemnestra describes the beacons flashed across the sea and orders sacrifices that light up the city. But as victory and sacrifice become morally ambiguous, light and images of light fade, to be replaced by the darkness associated with Night and her daughters, the Furies, so that pictures of the obscurity of Hades, and black blood spilled on the black earth predominate by the end of *Agamemnon.* In *Libation Bearers,* this initial movement from light to dark takes on a greater significance because light becomes associated with Phoebus Apollo, bright god of purification who commands Orestes to avenge his father's death and seems to promise an end to the vendetta. After that delusion is destroyed, however, the contrasting metaphors of the light and dark become real characters in conflict in *Eumenides,* when Apollo and the black-robed Furies appear and fight against each other, first at Delphi and then at Athens. The exodus in which the Furies are escorted out of the orchestra by torchlight dramatizes the compromise of both the gods' conflict and the two metaphors. Thus, this pattern, like the others, is first developed to express contradictory ideas about justice and then transferred from metaphor to character in action to explicate the full meaning of the opposition and the brilliance of the resolution.

Act II. *Libation Bearers*: Return and Revenge Again

Plot. *Agamemnon* concludes with the hope that Orestes will come back to avenge the death of the king. *Choephoroi* [Libation Bearers], the second act of the *Oresteia,* opens with the king's son, now full-grown, approaching his father's tomb to mourn and beg assistance for his revenge. Accompanied by his Phocian friend Pylades, Orestes first prays to the gods of the Underworld and Agamemnon, and then leaves two locks of his hair as a token of his mourning. When the young men see a company of black-robed women approaching, they hide in order to discover the reason for the procession to the tomb.

The band of women are the Libation Bearers, household slaves brought back by Agamemnon, the chorus of the second play. Their parodos tells us that Clytemnestra, having had a terrifying nightmare, has ordered them to make an offering in an attempt to appease the spirit of the unavenged Agamemnon. They doubt their libation can have any effect, however, because there can be no atonement for blood spilled on the ground. Their lyric, which repeats the iambic rhythms of the great odes of *Agamemnon,* connects this new action to the earlier cycle of bloodshed and inevitable punishment.

Electra, Orestes' sister, has been sent out with them to make the libation, but she doubts whether she can pray for her father's murderer at his tomb. The chorus advises her to request good things for the loyal and revenge for the guilty. These words disturb Electra, because she questions the righteousness of the code they express—the doctrine of reciprocity, the basis of the blood-vendetta. Yet she pours the offering, praying to be better than her mother.

After the chorus sings a brief lament, a "paean or song of honor" for the dead king, and asks for a deliverer of the House, Electra discovers the hair on the tomb, and then footprints. When the women react to these strange signs, Orestes comes out of hiding. Brother and sister are overwhelmed with joy; they see in their reunion a rebirth for their family. After praying to Zeus not to forsake Agamemnon's orphans, Orestes reveals that Loxias (Apollo, God of Prophecy, Healing, Light, Purification, and Law) has ordered him to avenge Agamemnon's death and has threatened mental and physical torture from the Furies of Agamemnon if he does not kill the murderers. Orestes also summarizes

his own reasons for the revenge: the god's command, sorrow for his
father, desire for his rightful legacy, and the need to free the citizens of
Argos from the tyranny of "two women" (11. 269–305).

In order to accomplish the dangerous deed, Electra, Orestes, and the
chorus appeal for aid to Agamemnon's spirit. Together they perform a
kommos, or song of mourning, in which they tear their hair, rend their
clothes, and beat the tomb, as they sing alternating stanzas, reminding
Agamemnon and the gods of the dead of the horror of Clytemnestra's
crimes and their own grief and anger. This is the lyric zenith of the play.
The characters have already presented their reasons for the act in a
rational, straightforward manner. Now the rhythm, vivid language,
gesture, and dance of the extended lyric express their powerful emotions.[30] The chorus begins by calling on Zeus and the Fates to accomplish justice, assuring Agamemnon, his children, themselves, and the
audience at large that the forthcoming murder will embody the fundamental principle that "the doer must suffer." Each participant then
mourns the dead hero in a formal dirge, recounting dishonors to him,
and cruelties to themselves, and interspersing prayers and cries of
lamentation. The chorus stimulates the resolve of the children by
predicting good fortune and repeating the ancient code of the blood-
vendetta:

> It is but law that when the red drops have been spilled
> upon the ground they cry aloud for fresh
> blood. For the death act calls out on Fury
> to bring out of those who were slain before
> new ruin on ruin accomplished.
>   (11. 400–404; Lattimore, trans.)

These words should be ominous for the audience, but the characters
have clearly benefited from singing the kommos. They have given their
dead father his long-deserved honor and found release for their own
pent-up anger and grief. They have also conjured real help from the
realm of the dead. The powerful spirit of the unavenged Agamemnon
and his divine champions now literally enthuses them so that they are
spiritually and emotionally prepared for the matricide.

Once the physical and psychological situation that demands redress has been explicated, the poet moves the revenge plot forward quickly. Orestes learns the dream that terrified his mother: she bore a snake who suckled a curd of blood. Recognizing himself and his matricide in the prodigy, Orestes outlines his plan. He and Pylades, disguised as Phocian strangers, will announce the accidental death of Orestes and be welcomed into the house where they expect to find Aegisthus. Electra is to keep watch inside while the chorus remains without to act as the situation demands. Nothing works out as planned, however.[31] After the chorus sings an ode about monstrous women who killed their own male kin, Clytemnestra unexpectedly answers Orestes' knocks on the palace door and informs him that Aegisthus is not at home. She hears his news with an inscrutable exclamation of grief, but recovers quickly and offers him hospitality while she sends for the king. The chorus affects the action when the nurse, Cilissa, who has raised Orestes from infancy and truly loves him, rushes out of the palace sincerely lamenting his death. Although she has been sent to fetch Aegisthus with an armed guard, the women persuade her to change the message so that the tyrant will return without protection. The next stasimon is a formal prayer for the House's deliverance from suffering. Aegisthus then rushes toward the palace, announcing the news of Orestes' death as unwelcome, but eager to confirm its truth. As the chorus visualizes the murder, the tyrant's death cries are heard. A slave runs out of the palace shouting, but does not try to protect the queen, for he judges her impending murder a "stroke of justice" (1. 884).

Orestes' confrontation with Clytemnestra is startlingly swift. Instead of long, persuasive speeches of defense or remorse, the queen cries out for a "man-slaying axe" so she can kill her son, and, at the sight of Aegisthus dead, bewails her lover. Then she cleverly appeals to Orestes as his mother, bearing the breast with which she says she suckled him. Orestes now turns to Pylades, a silent actor, and asks, "Shall I respect my mother?" Pylades' reply, the only time he speaks in the play, "Count all men your enemy rather than the gods" (1. 902), would startle the audience, underline the gravity of the act, and reaffirm its necessity. Resolved, Orestes directs his mother to the palace. She continues to argue, but Orestes meets her pleas and threats so firmly that she finally acknowledges him as the unavoidable serpent of her dream.

Although the chorus regrets the death of even these two tyrants, they sing a hymn of triumph to Orestes and praise the gods who have brought joy and have at last cleansed the House. Orestes reenters, holding up the torn and bloodied robe which trapped Agamemnon in his bath and the chains which bound him in death. As he stands over the slain couple, he defends his act as justice for an adulterer and vengeance for a husband-killer. Although he can point to law and the gods to support his innocence, he knows that he, too, is now polluted by kindred bloodshed. As he announces that he must go into exile and seek purification from Apollo, he suddenly becomes mad and imagines he sees the blood-dripping, snake-haired Furies of his mother's wrath swooping down to avenge her. He escapes in haste while the bewildered chorus summarizes the history of the House and wonders whether there will ever be an end to the destruction.

Variations on a Theme.   There are so many similarities in construction between *Libation Bearers* and *Agamemnon* that it seems to be both a repetition and an extension of the action of the first play. In each play the main character's return is expected with hope and trepidation. The first parts of the two plays, through lyric and characterization, develop the emotions and expectations that charge the homecomings with significance.[32] Once the explication is complete, the return and revenge plots coalesce in the confrontation between Clytemnestra and the man who has arrived.

The alternation between good news and bad, hope and fear, in *Agamemnon* is repeated in the *Libation Bearers*. Electra moves from joy to dread after finding the hair and footprints, and the nurse's wails are calmed by hope. Orestes tricks the murderers by pretending to announce bad news (of his death) which is ironically good news to the royal pair. The reversal to bad news, which is good news to the other characters, comes at the moment Clytemnestra recognizes that the messenger of her son's death is Orestes himself. But the play contains a further reversal that leaves the ending just as incomplete as that of *Agamemnon*. The chorus has expected Orestes' action to bring release from the curse and the return of the rightful heirs to Agamemnon's throne and property. Orestes' appearance with a suppliant's branch and his announcement of exile are shocking. The poet's delay of this part of Apollo's command until after Clytemnestra's murder increases the impact of the reversal and amplifies the shattering of the delusion that further bloodshed can break the cycle of the vendetta.

But there are significant contrasts which suggest that *Libation Bearers* dramatizes a deterioration of the situation in *Agamemnon* and yet is a step forward toward a resolution. The plight of the citizens and family is manifested by the new site and characters of the first part of the play.[33] The action takes place at the tomb of Agamemnon and is performed by slaves rather than citizens and by a royal pair who have been made a slave and exile by the death of their father. The family has been driven out of the palace, and the state has been subdued by tyrants. The elders of Argos who in *Agamemnon* were courageous enough to criticize their leaders openly are nowhere in sight. Instead, there are only foreign women who are war captives from Troy, fiercely loyal to Agamemnon and his children and passionately committed to the principles of the blood-vendetta, but cowed by the tyranny of Clytemnestra and Aegisthus.

Orestes' return is different from his father's. The son of Agamemnon arrives not as a victorious general in a chariot, but as an exile on foot who must disguise himself and lie about his death to be welcomed into his own palace. Clytemnestra still controls the House of Atreus and her lover, Aegisthus. Yet when the scene moves from the tomb to the palace and Orestes gets himself invited inside, he literally begins the long procession toward his restoration. His own act of revenge is the reverse of his mother's. As Clytemnestra herself says, the tricker has been tricked (1. 888). He drives her out of the house, and she cannot persuade him to spare her, as she was so easily able to persuade her husband to expose his hubris. When Clytemnestra is forced into the palace to meet her death, there is no delusion on either side; both son and mother know what must be done. As in *Agamemnon,* the avenger controls the entrance to the palace and emerges, with the corpses in tableau on the ekkyklema to explain his act. Unlike Clytemnestra and Aegisthus, however, Orestes does not exult in the deed or boast of his own righteousness. Nor is he so deluded that he can remain at the hearth and throne he has polluted. His branch and wreath signify his intent to seek purification at Delphi according to Apollo's instructions. His hasty escape from the scene of the murder leaves the palace empty of citizens and ruler, but his destination builds the hope of a divine solution to the political and moral chaos.

Changes in the House of Atreus.   The setting at the tomb of Agamemnon also underscores the new interest in the House of Atreus as an endangered family and household. The foreign war and the dangers arising from men's ambition for conquest and glory have already been presented in the first play, in the character of Agamemnon. In *Libation Bearers,* Agamemnon is reevaluated as the beloved father and successful protector unjustly slain by ambitious and greedy tyrants, and the drama concentrates on the presentation of the household, emphasized by the predominance of women characters (chorus, daughter, nurse, mother), the real managers of the domestic system.

The years have not transformed Clytemnestra or Aegisthus. The amphisbaena of *Agamemnon* is still as monstrous to the chorus of *Libation Bearers.* The murder of Agamemnon was not sufficient to mollify her hatred. She mutilated and fettered his body before casting him into a dishonored grave (partly to render his unavenged spirit impotent to harm her). She never shows regret for the act, but only anxiety at a dream which portends punishment. Clearly she has enjoyed taking over his property and his power. The chorus and Electra complain of the extravagance with which she and her lover surround themselves while robbing the state and her own children.

The relationship between Clytemnestra and Aegisthus still exemplifies moral and social disorder. Her passion for her lover seems to have grown; the only pure emotion she expresses is sadness at the sight of his dead body. But Orestes describes the couple as "two women," and the playwright gives the lover no opportunity to establish his manhood. In his only scene, Aegisthus appears both nervous and deluded as he questions the chorus about the message and boasts that he can detect any plot. Nor is his murder dignified as an act of vengeance. He is dismissed as an adulterer who has received his lawful punishment. It is Clytemnestra who appears fighting for her life, physically as well as verbally. Aeschylus, of course, must intensify the drama of the matricide, but the resulting diminishment of Aegisthus only confirms the perversion of male and female roles in *Agamemnon*.

But Clytemnestra, the outraged wife and mistress of Aegisthus, belongs primarily to *Agamemnon*. There her evident sexual passion and ambition cast doubt on her claim to have slain her husband only to avenge her daughter. Here in *Libation Bearers*, where her role as "Mother" predominates, her treatment of her remaining children demonstrates conclusively that she has perverted the duties of motherhood. She has traded Electra and Orestes for Aegisthus, depriving them not only of their father but also of their birthright. Her lament at the false report of Orestes' death may express some genuine feeling, but she would kill him with an axe to save herself. And Aeschylus introduces a dramatic foil, Cilissa, Orestes' nurse, who cannot restrain her tears at the bad news, who lovingly recalls Orestes as an infant, who remembers all the mothering she herself provided, and who bitterly exposes Clytemnestra's joy and relief behind the pretense of grieving.

Such a scene demonstrates that Clytemnestra has been an unnatural mother to Orestes, just as she was an unnatural wife to Agamemnon. In fact the two are probably related. Her dream of giving birth to a snake which suckled her blood predicts her matricide by Orestes at the command of Apollo, whose symbol is frequently a snake. But, according to Devereux, a psychoanalytic critic, the dream also shows Clytemnestra as a bad mother, a masculine woman who views the fetus as a parasite, dreads nursing as if it were cannibalization, and fears the baby's bite as both castrative and sexually exciting. Although Clytemnestra performs all the right maternal acts as if making up for her failure to love in life, her unconscious guilt feelings (symbolized by the transformation of her child into a snake) insure her punishment.[34]

Orestes fulfills the corresponding mythic and psychological archetype. He is the son who must kill the killer of his father. It is his sacrificial duty to kill the old king when his power wanes, a mythic pattern familiar from the story of Uranus, Cronus, and Zeus (referred to in *Agamamnon*) as well as Hamlet.[35] Because, as in the other tales, the wife of the killed king has been an accomplice of the slayer, the story has psychological overtones. It is significant that Orestes punishes Aegisthus only as an adulterer, for Aegisthus has acted out his own latent

Oedipal fantasies by killing Agamemnon and bedding Clytemnestra. But Orestes can satisfy his fantasies by killing his father-surrogate, Aegisthus, without guilt and replacing him on the throne, while still revering Agamemnon, his real father. Although he must kill his mother instead of realizing the other half of his Oedipal fantasy, his stabbing her is an act of symbolic incest which reveals his repressed desires and contributes to his madness.[36]

But Aeschylus is not primarily interested in these archetypal aspects of Orestes' act. He concentrates instead on the differences between this generation and the earlier two. Both Electra and Orestes can articulate clearly their legitimate reasons for murdering their mother. Electra's strong feelings of hatred for her mother and Aegisthus do not prevent her from doubting the piety of asking the gods to support a murder (1. 122). She includes in her prayer to her father:

> . . . Grant that I be more temperate
> of heart than my mother; that I act with purer hand.
> (11. 140–41; Lattimore, trans.)

Nor is Orestes as deluded as his predecessors, who were so eager to reap the benefits of their acts that they failed to recognize their own criminality. The son drags his mother into the palace with the words, "You committed a wrong; Now suffer a wrong" (1. 930). Their own righteousness is reinforced by the fact that their personal motives coincide instead of conflict with the preservation of the House and the public good. Although Orestes himself must suffer, his twin acts of murder and self-exile free the state, the House, and his sister from pollution and tyranny. The House is threatened by the loss of its last male leader, but the public situation is improved by this act of bloodshed.

The third generation also restores the importance and proper functioning of the family. Orestes and Electra are brother and sister rather than lovers, so that their claims of just revenge are not distorted by the multiple adulteries which marked the moral confusion in *Agamemnon.* They represent for each other the mother, father, and sibling lost to them through kindred slaughter. Their behavior reestablishes the bonds of family love so disturbed by Agamemnon's adventurism and Clytemnestra's ambition. Moreover, each child accepts his or her proper sex role. Electra refuses to become an aggressive woman like her mother. Having done her part by praying for Orestes' return and singing the kommos, she goes inside the palace and remains in the background (as Aegisthus once did) while the murder is committed. Orestes then proves himself the ruler of the family by defeating the pseudomale, Clytemnestra, at her own game of trickery and assassination.

The purity of the planners, however, does not assure the purity of the plan. Now, after three generations, the issue lies bare and undistorted by delusion, ambition, or perversion. The system of the blood-vendetta cannot be just if a son must become a matricide to avenge his father and then must be killed in turn to satisfy his mother's unavenged spirit. This extreme example proves the inadequacy both of the moral concept and the procedure. Yet because Apollo has demanded Clytemnestra's death, and the Furies insist on Orestes', the question of justice now implicates the gods.

Image and Idea.   The futility of the vendetta is underlined by the hunt imagery continued from *Agamemnon*. The descriptions of entanglement in net, curb, and web refer to Clytemnestra's robe, the chains that trapped Agamemnon, and to the snare of Orestes' plot. In fact, the chorus names the curse itself "a great curb" (1. 961). The circularity, savagery, and moral ambiguity of blood guilt are most vivid in the animal imagery associated with trapping prey. Agamemnon is again the eagle, now called upon to help his own nestlings, Electra and Orestes, as he once fought for Helen. Clytemnestra is again a dread viper (11. 248, 994, 1047), but Orestes, too, has become a snake (similar both to Apollo and his mother) in her dream and in fact will be pursued in turn by the Furies, whose snaky locks he can see at the end of *Libation Bearers*. The transformation from fledgling victim to Fury and savage criminal is underlined by the association of the avenging children with lions, dogs, and ravening wolves. Here, too, the circle continues, for the Furies are referred to as the "hounds" of Clytemnestra who will literally track the scent of Orestes, the hare, in the next play.

Two other motifs prominent in *Agamemnon* remain major images in the *Libation Bearers*. The first half of the play is a literal libation, the pouring of a liquid offering upon the tomb to honor the unavenged spirit of Agamemnon. The murder of Clytemnestra is offered as an atonement for his slaying. Thus all the imagery of libation and sacrifice so important to the claims of justice in *Agamemnon* is further dramatized here. The frequent images of blood spilled on the ground, most often imagined as clotted, frozen, or congealed, re-create the picture of the blood-red tapestry of *Agamemnon,* as if it were still visible in the orchestra. Although Orestes offers "the third potation of unmixed gore to the Fury" (11. 576–77, 1073), the libation which should be final, the imagery of sacrifice remains incomplete after the murder. The chorus notes that the blood is still fresh on Orestes' hands and the murderer sees the Furies dripping "that hateful stream" from their eyes, Furies who will try to suck out his blood in payment for spilling his mother's.

The blood, and the libations spilled on the ground, are demanded by the age-old chthonic powers who live in the darkness beneath the earth. These deities of the underworld and the black night which engulfs them predominate in the imagery and prayers of the first half of *Libation Bearers.* The female goddesses, the Furies, Mother Earth, and Night, all represent the code of the vendetta which is supposed to preserve the family. Even the male gods appealed to at the beginning of the play are chthonic—Hermes who watches over the dead (11.1, 165), Zeus below the earth or Hades, and Agamemnon's spirit. Apollo himself holds a chthonic—Hermes who watches over the dead (11. 1, 165), Zeus below the earth or Hades, and Agamemnon's spirit. Apollo himself holds a cavern below Parnassus. The House, too, is sunless and shrouded in cally in the figure of Orestes, the supposed deliverer (1. 131). Although the matricide is committed in the evening (1. 660), the chorus's hopeful prayers are now directed to the male gods of the upper realms, Zeus as father of the Olympians (11. 783–84), Apollo, who will bring the light of freedom to a house that can raise its eyes (11. 808–10), and Hermes, who shall illuminate the darkness (1. 815). The chorus is sure it can see the light (11. 808, 863, 961), and Orestes calls on the sun to witness the justice of his matricide (11. 985–86), but the black-robed Furies return at the end of the play. Apollo's command to murder the woman on behalf of the man brings no light after all. His protection of the suppliant and his purification may represent an advance over the savagery of the Furies, yet he cannot prevent them from exerting their claims to kill the murderer. Thus, the imagery of light and darkness is also incomplete at the end of *Libation Bearers*.

Other image patterns from *Agamemnon* are repeated in the second play. Words that relate to trampling and technical terms which refer to earthly as well as cosmic justice recur. The sounds and images of mourning, which alternated with those of joy and triumph in *Agamemnon*, reach their climax in the kommos for the slain king and the prayers of joy after Orestes' act of revenge. The survival of the House of Atreus is represented by the physical presence of Orestes and Electra, who call themselves "orphans" and "seed," extending the metaphors of generation from *Agamemnon*. But the seed so nearly destroyed is also tainted, for the hubris that keeps giving birth to new hubris is literally dramatized when the son murders his mother, replicating the unnatural relationship prefigured in Clytemnestra's dream.

Two ideas expressed in a minor key in *Agamemnon* are amplified in the second play. The storm introduced as a reality which destroyed the fleet becomes a metaphor to define the danger to Agamemnon's children and his house. The chorus's prayer comparing the expected release from the curse to a storm-free journey where "our ship goes well" (11. 819–24) recalls the elders' song in *Agamemnon* about the wealthy house which by jettisoning its cargo might escape reefs and sinking (11. 1005–13). But as "black-blood spilled" destroys any hope for safety, the libation bearers soon realize that the matricide has been yet another tempest (1. 1066). Similarly, the imagery of disease and cure in *Agamemnon* becomes prominent in *Libation Bearers,* where the remedy for the clear-cut sins of murder and tyranny looks so simple at first and where Apollo, God of Healing and Purification, demands new murders. But although Orestes is threatened with terrible disease if he fails to kill Clytemnestra, that cure produces further infection instead of health; Orestes' madness is the physical manifestation of his moral pollution. Hope remains, however, that the God of Healing will be able to cleanse him.

Act III. *Eumenides:* Conclusion by Compromise

New Beginning.   The action of the third play arises directly out of the ending of the second. Orestes has just fled Argos, seeking purification at Delphi, his departure hastened by his vision of the pursuing Furies. *Eumenides* opens at Delphi with the priestess of Apollo praying to the gods of the shrine. After entering the temple, however, she dashes out, terrified by the sight of Orestes seated within as a suppliant and surrounded by the sleeping but monstrous Furies. When she leaves, Apollo exits from the shrine with Orestes and instructs his charge to flee the tracking Furies until he reaches Athens and can finally be released by Athena and the judges chosen to hear his case. Apollo sends Hermes as an escort and promises his own and Zeus's protection. After these two exit, the ghost of Clytemnestra appears (on the ek-kyklema rolled out from within the shrine), bloodied by her wounds and furious at her unavenged murder, to rouse the sleeping Furies who have been drugged by Apollo. Slowly they wake, whining and moaning at the sting of Clytemnestra's reproaches, and then finally appear in the orchestra to sing and dance an angry parodos (in emotional dochmiac rhythm from the kommos of *Libation Bearers*) because Apollo, son of Zeus, has stolen Orestes, their rightful prey, polluted and deserving of gruesome death. When Apollo returns to drive them from his shrine, the Furies insist on their ancient dispensation to punish matricide. Apollo argues that their justice is inadequate because it does not protect husbands from murderous wives. The argument cannot be resolved at Delphi, and the Furies rush out after Orestes while Apollo vows to protect the suppliant.

Like the first two plays, *Eumenides* begins with a prayer that defines the setting, but now the place is different, Delphi instead of Argos, and the events after the prayer are structually and visually shocking.[37] The priestess's exit after her prologue is followed not by the expected parodos, as in *Agamemnon* or *Libation Bearers,* but by the return of the priestess herself, now distraught. The ensuing series of brief scenes underlines the unexpected turn of events. Each section, even the delayed parodos, is marked by the exit of the participants to another destination, Athens. As Apollo says, the matricide will have to wander further in time and space, enduring the Furies' pursuit, until he can win his release. These strange scenes manifest the reality of the chase, only imagined before by a mad Orestes, and visually destroy the hope of Orestes, the chorus, and the audience that Delphi can provide a final solution.

At Delphi, however, the characters do move further away from the curse on the House in action as well as in scene. Whereas the earlier two plays were constructed as return and revenge dramas, *Eumenides* follows the pattern of the "suppliant received" in which the question of Orestes' protection becomes the focus for expressing the inadequacies of the concept of justice developed so far. The drama begins by emphasizing the loathsome qualities of the demons of the blood-vendetta who as representatives of automatic and unequivocal revenge, refuse to acknowledge any criminal's right to asylum. The priestess's description of the Gorgon-like monsters illustrates how alien the Furies are to the shrines of the Olympians who protect the defenseless. After Apollo reiterates the inhumanity and isolation of the Furies, the spectacle of the ghost of Clytemnestra, bloody, enraged, and shrieking for vengeance against her son, confirms their monstrosity. The Furies finally appear in the orchestra in person, perhaps one by one, black-robed and bloody, with masks surrounded by snaky hair, dripping blood from eyes to cheeks. (According to the *Life of Aeschylus* this spectacle was so terrifying that pregnant women in the audience aborted at the sight.)

Once their horror has been fully established, however, they introduce the important principles they represent and initiate the first phase of the central debate of the play. They are angry at Apollo because this new god has encroached on the ancient prerogatives and responsibilities assigned to them by Destiny. They have been given the power to impose savage punishment as a means of deterring crime and injustice. Apollo's protection of the suppliant criminal will produce social chaos and disrespect for law. Apollo argues, however, that the enforcement of the Furies' justice contains a serious weakness. By avenging only kindred blood transmitted through the mother, they permit the murder of husbands by wives and thus do not protect the marriage relationship sanctified by Hera, Zeus, and Aphrodite. But even Apollo, in justifying Clytemnestra's murder, is unable to rise above the principle of revenge. Yet his substitution of purification ritual and exile for death as a punishment for matricide is a step toward the revolution in the system of criminal justice ultimately proposed by Athena.

By the end of the prologue, the debate has become cosmic as well as human, a clash between divine interests which can be resolved only by another impartial divinity, Athena, who must decide whether the new gods will replace the old.

From Image to Action.   The central action of *Eumenides* is the trial of Orestes before Athena and the judges of the Court of the Areopagus. Orestes, purified by ritual as well as by long travel and travail, arrives at the temple of Athena in Athens and clings to the image of the goddess for protection. Then the Furies enter, tracking the scent of his blood "like hounds after a wounded fawn" (1. 246), ready to suck him dry even at the altar. Although Orestes protests that he is now free from pollution, and calls on Athena for help, the Furies know that nothing but the murderer's own blood will atone for matricide. They dance around him, singing a binding song, a magic means of preparing him for the loathsome death they intend, but their stately lyrics (in new rhythms) also enumerate the principles of justice behind their horrible punishment. Athena arrives just in time and questions the characters, showing respect both for the Furies and the suppliant. She recognizes the difficulty of resolving the conflict: the killer now seems pure, but the Furies have great power to punish the host country; she must, like Pelasgus in *Suppliants,* choose between two evils (11. 480–81). Instead of deciding by herself, she offers to establish a court of the best citizens to hear the evidence and judge the case. After Orestes and Athena exit to prepare for the trial, the chorus sings a second stasimon in the same rhythms as the first, again proclaiming their justification for demanding their dreadful price:

> There are times when fear is good.
> It must keep its watchful place
> at the heart's controls. There is
> advantage
> in the wisdom won from pain.
> Should the city, should the man
> rear a heart that no where goes
> in fear, how shall such a one
> any more respect the right?
> (11. 516–25; Lattimore, trans.)

Many of the major images and themes of *Agamemnon* and *Libation Bearers* culminate in the action at the temple of Athena and the Areopagus. The imagery of the hunter tracking its prey reaches its climax when the Furies literally pursue Orestes from Delphi to Athens and then surround and entrap him. Their odes, like Clytemnestra's invocation, extend the animal imagery from earlier plays—lions, serpents (visible in the Furies' hair), hounds, and even the hare (Orestes as victim), which recalls the omen at Aulis from the parodos of *Agamemnon*. The Furies are following the trail of blood left by the polluted Orestes, whereas they themselves drip blood from their mouths and eyes, so that the earlier metaphor of blood spilled on the ground becomes a reality in their chase, visible in their costumes and on Orestes' robe, hands, and sword. Because Orestes, as bloody prey, is also an atonement offered to the unavenged spirit of Clytemnestra, the Furies use the imagery of libation and sacrifice as they literally prepare their victim for death at the altar of Athena. The darkness in which the House of Atreus has been engulfed is in *Eumenides* the darkness of the Furies themselves, dressed in black, daughters of Night (11. 321–22, 416), confined to sunless gloom (11. 387, 396), and spreaders of dark pollution and murky mist over sinners. Other image patterns such as disease/cure, the storm that destroys, and particularly the trampling on justice recur. Although the Furies' savagery achieves some respectability, their dance and dance imagery associate them with earlier tramplers. At those who kick the altar of justice with an impious foot, the Furies "leap" with heavy fall and bring down their own feet (11. 540–41, 370–75). Thus, in image as in fact, the Furies trample in turn, and perpetuate the cycle of violence.

The resolution comes from the new procedure of trial by jury established by Athena on the hill of Ares, the Areopagus. Again the change of setting, marked by the words of Athena, indicates an important new development. The resolution takes place not in the palace, home of the family, and not in the temple, home of a god, but in the state, home of a body of citizens (1. 685). Although the goddess introduces and then participates in the first murder trial, the human jury casts its own votes and will later take over the process. The legal terminology and the instinctive attempts to argue guilt and innocence in the earlier plays suggest that mortals were groping toward a new procedure which the gods as partners have now helped them to institute.[38] The process described by Athena, with its oaths, witnesses, and proofs (11. 482–87), systematizes the justifying speeches of Clytemnestra and Orestes in the earlier plays. Although the text is corrupt, the trial itself is probably a prototype of all the future trials in the Areopagus, imitating the herald's opening proclamatory speeches, interrogation, voting by ballots cast in two different urns (foreshadowed in *Agamemnon* 11. 814–17), and the traditional "vote of Athena" in favor of the defendant when the votes are equal.[39] The commonplaces used in Orestes' trial reflect the rhetorical devices of fifth-century speeches. The chorus refers to Zeus's treatment of his own father, imitating the historians' and rhetoricians' strategic use of myth, whereas Apollo alludes to the scientific and philosophical theories of Aeschylus's own time to prove that the male is the true parent.[40] Thus the trial is both the culmination of all the legal imagery for the first two plays and the paradigm for all future resolutions of conflict.

Behind the process of the trial lies an examination of conflicting principles of justice and an attempt at resolution. Although Athena's speech to the first jurors claims that the values and goals of the Areopagus are simply extensions of those of the Furies (11. 690–99), the trial itself introduces ideas that transcend the Furies' code. Mercy for the accused (reflected in Apollo's protection of the suppliant) is joined to the idea that gods can free humans from the sentence of death. Twice the characters refer to Ixion, the first suppliant, a murderer whom Zeus himself protected (11. 441, 718). Apollo acted in a similar way, first releasing Admetus from his fate and then saving his wife, Alcestis, who had volunteered to die in his place (11. 723–24). Now Athena promises Orestes that same protection, at least until the trial is over. Although the Furies' arguments are so powerful that half the jury votes to condemn Orestes to death, the principle of mercy wins the day. Athena has already declared that if the vote is equal, the defendant must be acquitted.

The trial also introduces the idea that particular circumstances of the murder may in themselves exonerate the murderer. The question arises here for the first time because Orestes possesses more wisdom about his motives and the magnitude of his crime than his parents or grandparents did. The trial itself is established as a procedure for learning and weighing all the facts before imposing a penalty as irrevocable as death. Once Orestes' dilemma is understood, reciprocity must be tempered with mercy. The Furies too, once they express the ideals behind their monstrosity, can be venerated as Eumenides (Kindly Ones) instead of hated and shunned by all who see the light. Thus, Athena, Goddess of

Wisdom, by examining all sides of the question, can point the way to compromise as a resolution.

Other features of the new system of justice arise directly from the mythic conflict. Once Orestes confesses to the deed, he and Apollo must persuade the jury that he has committed a lesser crime, deserving of a lesser penalty. Therefore, they argue that the death of Agamemnon had to be avenged because he was a husband, protector, and breadwinner whose murder was a serious crime. In contrast, Clytemnestra's death was warranted by her shameful behavior. Apollo's distinction between the kinds of murders was a reality in the legal processes and codes of historical Athens. The plea that Orestes committed an unlawful homicide lawfully could have been made in the Athens of Aeschylus's day (at the Delphinian Court associated with Apollo). The penalty Orestes ultimately pays, limited exile and purification, corresponds to the Athenian punishment for unintentional homicide.[41] On the other hand, although the end of the vendetta will produce less severe punishments, traditionally "just" crimes of revenge, such as Orestes' matricide, will for the first time become unlawful. Athena's new procedure insures that the killer will be judged and punished by the state's legal system, freeing the family from the vendetta while preserving the family's rights and responsibility to prosecute those who harm it.[42]

Apollo's argument that Agamemnon was more important than Clytemnestra resolves the disorder in the relationship between the sexes by defining the proper relations between husband and wife and making women subordinate to men. Apollo reminds us that Clytemnestra was an aberration, a monstrously cunning, lustful, and ambitious woman, whose behavior has demonstrated, by contrast, what a wife and mother should be. Athena's reason for voting for Orestes' acquittal confirms the superiority of males; she herself has no mother, belongs altogether to Zeus, and approves the male in all things (11. 736–40). The establishment by scientific argument that kindred blood is transmitted through the male rather than the female gives marriage divine sanction as the bond that cements the family. The proof that the male is the true parent restores responsibility for the family to the father who earlier pursued his outside responsibilities at the expense of the household.

Whatever the source of Aeschylus's (and fifth-century Athens's) belief in male superiority, it is obvious that the trilogy connects the most primitive aspects of human life with the instinctive savagery of females.[43] Clytemnestra and the Furies appear together in this play in all their monstrousness, in opposition to Orestes and Apollo. The transfer of power from female to male is part of the mythic background of the play. The priestess of Delphi, for example, describes how Phoebus received the shrine from Phoebe as a birthday present. Now Clytemnestra and the Furies must yield to Zeus—father, king, and husband—who together with his children Apollo and Athena represents the merciful, cognitive, and civilizing male leadership promised in the hymn to Zeus by the elders of *Agamemnon*. The asexual Athena, who solves the conflict by inviting the Furies to join the new order, symbolizes the possibility of true harmony between the two sexes, but only because she subordinates her female instincts.

Grand Finale: Wisdom at Last.   The trial has sprung Orestes from his trap. After thanking the gods and promising an eternal alliance between Argos and Athens, the mortal defendant can return home, restored to his possessions and power. The impartial citizens of Athens have also fulfilled their duty as jurors. But the restoration of the cosmic order is more difficult. The vote has been equal because both sides have been right and wrong. A murderer still lives whose death would be both a just and an unmerciful act. The decision by the jury is a new means of attempting to resolve the unresolvable. The solution depends not so much on the discovery of the right answer (which may be impossible) as on the acceptance by all parties of the court's verdict. Before the trial Athena made the Furies and Apollo agree that they would entrust the settlement of the conflict to her. Now the goddesses refuse to acquiesce to the acquittal of Orestes and want to retaliate against Athens itself because it did not properly punish Orestes.

In the scene which follows Orestes' exit the Furies threaten to blast Athens with their poisonous breath. Athena calmly responds, however, with patient reasoning, to persuade them that the jurors' equal vote proves the people's continuing reverence for their principles. She herself, respecting their age and power, offers them dwellings, worship, and honor in Athens if they will remain and send forth benefits instead of curses. But her gentle persuasion is backed by force; she possesses the power to discharge Zeus's lightning against them. The Furies finally demonstrate their acceptance by replacing threats with blessings—health instead of disease, prosperous regeneration in place of sterility or tainted progeny, warm breezes that nurture instead of hot, stormy blasts, and fury against foreign enemies, not brothers/citizens. But, as Athena makes clear, their beneficence will depend on how well the citizens of Athens obey the right:

> In the terror upon the faces of these
> I see great good for our citizens.
> While with good will you hold in high honor
> these spirits, their will shall be good, as you steer
> your city, your land
> on an upright course clear through to the end.
> (11. 990–95; Lattimore, trans.)

This represents a transformation of the ancient doctrine of reciprocity. Now the principle which demanded punishment for evil also promises reward for good (which, as the other side of the *quid pro quo,* is implicit in the doctrine; cf. *Libation Bearers,* 1. 109). As Apollo had once released the House of Admetus from evil ("Is it not right [*dikaion*] to do good for the one who honors you, especially when he needs you" [11. 725–26]), so too has he protected Orestes, who worshipped him, obeyed his orders, and performed the rituals demanded by his cult. Now Athena applies this interpretation of the principle to the Furies themselves. She changes only slightly the traditional definition of justice, "he who does wrong must suffer," when she offers the Furies the chance "to do good and experience good" (1. 868). By recognizing the power for good in offering rewards as well as penalties, Athena is able to bring together Apollo and the Furies, once divided by misunderstanding and hatred. The Furies learn that they can remain true to themselves as enforcers of justice and deterrents of crime while working with rather than against the new gods represented by Apollo. The words of the chthonic goddesses prophesy new harmony: ". . . the blessings/that make life prosperous/may be made to burgeon from beneath the earth/ by the sun's radiant beam" (11. 922–26).

When the Furies receive their just rewards in the exodus, the metaphors of light and dark, and blood or worship become part of the literal action to symbolize the new and harmonious order. The goddesses will remain chthonic deities, but, as the citizens escort them to their new home beneath the Acropolis, the Furies (now *Semnai* or Holy Ones) put on the red robes of metics (foreign residents protected by law) as tokens of their new honored status. The state's hospitality to the Furies reverses the earlier distortions of guest-friendship, whereas the change of dress makes visual the transformation of justice from the savagery of blood spilled on the ground to the more civilized reciprocity supervised by the state. The torches their escorts carry symbolize not only the Furies' new harmony with Apollo, but also their progress from the obscurity of Hades to the clear light of law and reason. This ending fulfills the promise of the prologue of *Agamemnon*. The torches of the red-robed processional are the first beacons to signal lasting victory over savage forces, as the chorus promises:

> There shall be peace forever between these people
> of Pallas [Athena] and their guests. Zeus the all seeing
> met with Destiny to confirm it.
> (ll. 1044–46; Lattimore, trans.)

This grand finale may seem overly optimistic, but it was probably meant to be a paradigm for the settlement of all conflicts which threaten to destroy society. Even when each side can rightly claim justice, a compromise must be reached. It will be accepted and lasting only if it allows both parties some measure of honor and redress. The means of achieving a final compromise is the ballot (as in the law court or assembly of Athens), influenced by reasoned argument and deliberation rather than by force or dishonest flattery. Athena, Goddess of Athens and masculine female, symbolizes the new balance that the compromise achieves. She is the female enforcer, the warlike dispenser of Zeus's punishment, but she does not resort to force because her lips and tongue are sufficient to persuade. This superior skill also has a male source, Zeus Agoraios, who, as patron of the popular assembly and artful public speaker, supports the democratic processes. The Furies themselves recognize the dangers of intransigence and divisiveness, and the value of civic unity:

> This is my prayer: Civil War
> fattening on men's ruin shall
> not thunder in our city. Let
> not the dry dust that drinks
> the black blood of citizens
> through passion for revenge
> and bloodshed for bloodshed
> be given our state to prey upon.
> Let them render grace for grace.
> Let love be their common will;
> let them hate with single heart.
> Much wrong in the world thereby is healed.
>   (11. 976–87; Lattimore, trans.)

The Athenians of 458 B.C. watching the actors and chorus march out bearing the torches and wearing the red ceremonial robes so closely associated with their own public festival would surely recognize a message for themselves in Aeschylus's conclusion to the myth.

In fact, when the chorus of Athenian citizens refers to itself as "learning moderation in time" (1. 1000), it draws together past and present, bloody myth and bloody history, under Zeus's rubric *pathei mathos* ("learning through suffering," *Agamemnon*, 11. 176–78, 250–51).[44]

But in *Agamemnon* wisdom is inhibited by fear and pride. Characters like the watchman, herald, and chorus hesitate to tell what they know or accept the full meaning of what is told them, whereas the major characters are fools who assume they can remain unpunished for their own crimes. The sign of their error is their overreaction to injury— Atreus's banquet for Thyestes, Agamemnon's two-fold punishment of Troy, Clytemnestra's slaughter of Cassandra, and Aegisthus's tyranny. But their mistakes warn others, like Orestes and Electra, to examine their own motives and deeds beforehand. Orestes tells Athena he has been literally "schooled by miseries" (1. 276). The elders of Argos have suffered too, not only as witnesses to the effects of the curse on the

House of Atreus, but as citizens whose lives have been endangered by the actions of the ruling family, most tragically in the Trojan war, which they have learned has been bloody and pointless as well as heroic. It is this dual perception of truth that constitutes wisdom and leads to a recognition that motives and circumstances must be evaluated before acts are performed. This concept achieves its actualization in the trial itself, which systematizes the procedure for learning as much as possible before imposing a penalty so that the punishment will not exceed the crime.

Aeschylus's audience, watching the whole familiar story culminate in an unexpected resolution at Athens by means of a unique Athenian procedure, must have participated vicariously both in the suffering of the characters and the wisdom of the compromise. In fact, the playwright compels his spectators to connect the conflicts in the myth with contemporary problems by using the Court of the Areopagus, focus of so much civil dissension, as the site and means of the resolution and by alluding to the hotly debated issue of the Athenian alliance with Argos. He keeps them aware of their own anguish over foreign affairs and democratic reforms, while at the same time, through the exchange between Athena and the Furies, emphasizing the terrible dangers of civil war and anarchy. Aeschylus greatly honors the Areopagus, which, like the Furies, has just had its powers reduced in the name of progress. In the Furies' gradual conversion, he gives the historical court a cosmic precedent for accepting its limited function. Whether Aeschylus approved of the reforms or not is unimportant. He clearly supported the process of persuasion by careful debate, decision by the vote, and the idea that all parties must accept the verdict as final. Thus he speaks against political vendetta and for honorable compromise both in the House of Atreus and in Athens.

Zeus and the Cosmic Paradigm.   By the end of *Eumenides,* "Zeus, causer of all, doer of all," without whom nothing can be accomplished among mortals (11. 1485–88), has fulfilled the expectations of the elders of Argos. This conception of Zeus as "all-seeing" and "all-powerful," the source of wisdom, father of Justice, and equal of fate, suggests a monotheistic ideal behind the polytheistic cosmos. But the Zeus who reigns from Olympus is very different from the one God of the Judeo-Christian tradition. As an anthropomorphic deity, Zeus, by definition, embodies the qualities and imperfections of men, and supervises a cosmos very similar to the human microcosm. Zeus is not a transcendental deity who sits outside time observing his creation. Rather, like men, he has his own genealogy and life history in a universe which existed before his birth. Zeus has come to power after two generations of rebellion. First his father, Cronus, overthrew his grandfather Uranus, who was "swelling with Martial boldness" (*Agamemnon,* 1. 167–68) and then he in his turn, "like a wrestler overthrowing his opponent thrice" (*Agamemnon,* 172–73), defeated his father, Cronus. He has emerged, like Orestes, from a faulty and violent past. The chorus of *Agamemnon* is certain, however, that his own reign will be everlasting and that his precepts are just and gracious because violence and suffering have led to wisdom.[45]

Zeus oversees a world much like that of men, in which there are different generations, different sexes, and a multiplicity of interests and duties assigned to divinities as their portion (*moira*). Each god has his own territory and clients—Hermes, guide and lord of the dead, Pan of the flocks, Artemis, protectress of the young of all living things. Such diversity engenders dissension. The conflict of personalities and functions, reflected in all three plays, is dramatized most vividly by the opposition between the Furies, the old, female, chthonic, infectious, and savage representatives of the vendetta, and Apollo, young, male, bright, lawgiver, healer, protector of suppliants, and purifier. Both the Furies and Apollo understand their duties and the limits imposed on them by Destiny (*Eumenides* 11. 171–72, 313–15, 332–40, 347–52, 715). In the case of Orestes, however, their allotments clash so that neither can fulfill his responsibility unless the other yields.

Zeus, even more than the other gods and like the human characters in the trilogy, has diverse and conflicting interests. In *Agamemnon,* he appears as Zeus Xenios, defender of the guest–friend relationship, connected to Night, Goddess of the Underworld, and the chthonic deities: "This law stays forever on the throne of Zeus eternal: the doer must suffer" (*Agamemnon,* 11. 1563–64). Yet, in *Eumenides,* he is Zeus Ikesios, who protects outlaws and has released Ixion from the death penalty. Like Agamemnon, the general, Zeus the ruler also has responsibilities as the head of a family. As father, son, and husband, he upholds the authority of males. Yet, as husband, he also must support the special interests of his wife, Hera, patroness of marriage. Moreover, it is he who stands behind the diverse functions of his children— Aphrodite, goddess of love, and Artemis, virgin protectress of the young.

Because the gods retaliate with violence to threats against their prerogatives, this conflict of interests contributes to the indiscriminate slaughter of the Trojan War and the cycle of revenge in the House of Atreus. The male gods, Zeus, Apollo, or Pan, send war (Ares) to Troy to punish the violation of the guest-friend relationship. But Artemis, female protector of innocents, demands a bloody price for the slaughter of the young. The Furies instigate their instruments, Helen, Clytemnestra, and Aegisthus, to spill more blood for blood spilled. Apollo, too, on the instruction of Zeus, demands the murder of the female for the death of the male. By the time of the trial, even the gods recognize how inadequate the doctrine of reciprocity and automatic defense of interest has become; the gods' instrument, Orestes, becomes a matricide to avenge his father, and Zeus's responsibilities to punish and protect clash directly.

From this new understanding comes a new procedure: deliberation and persuasion sponsored by Athena and inspired by Zeus Agorios, patron of the assembly and public speaking. Force becomes a last resort, a punishment and deterrent to those who disobey the laws which have been voted by the majority and are the means of effecting the principles of cosmic justice on earth.

Thus the divine paradigm validates the human struggle and the possibility of progress.[46] The new, but now eternal, ruler of the universe has learned to control the disparate elements of his world by a judicious blend of persuasion and force. The picture of the whole composed of separate and competing parts reflects the Greeks' own social and political history of conflict between city-states, classes, and sexes. It also contains the eternally significant polarities of competition and cooperation. The anthropomorphic deities who represent special interests, who have their own skills, personalities, and sexes, reaffirm the importance of the individual and his need to fulfill his potential. So

Zeus, as the archetype for all important roles and relationships, represents man, a whole himself composed of disparate elements. But Zeus
has attained full potency as the one ruler and has instituted cooperation
and compromise as the means of achieving order. As such he is a potent
prototype for the democracy itself, composed of individuals who must
come together into a unified state in order to survive. Zeus's development into a wise and powerful ruler after three generations of violence
provides the most reassuring model for the House of Atreus and the
polis of Athens. If this exemplar for individuals and society has himself
"learned wisdom from suffering," then there is hope that man, too, can
outgrow his savagery and achieve a harmony in himself, his family, and
his state.

Chapter Six
Prometheus Bound:
Interpretation by Analogy

Plot

Prometheus Bound is probably Aeschylus's most famous play because it bears the name of one of the most provocative archetypes of Greek myth. Prometheus, whose name means "Forethought," stole fire from the gods and gave intelligence and technology to man. In later times, his suffering (he was condemned by Zeus to be chained to a rock) has symbolized heroic sacrifice in the struggle for justice and man's salvation. To the Church Fathers, Prometheus represented the suffering Christ while to a writer like Shelley he exemplified the human rebellion against an unjust God.[1]

The tragedy presents many problems for the modern critic. Some questions we have faced before: an unknown date of composition, an insufficient understanding of the devices of production, only scant remains of the rest of the trilogy. These uncertainties are dwarfed by a question that has not come up in our earlier discussions. Despite the fact that Alexandrian critics assigned the play to Aeschylus, many modern scholars doubt that he is the author of *Prometheus Bound*. Nineteenth-century readers denied that the same poet could conceive of Zeus both as the just, omnipotent god of the *Oresteia* and the cruel tyrant of *Prometheus Bound*. Contemporary critics, while recognizing that this is not a crucial objection, have nevertheless amassed a body of evidence suggesting that Aeschylus did not compose the play.[2] We will consider this possibility at some length later on, but first we must summarize the plot.

The play begins as Might and Force, the servants of Zeus, lead Prometheus to a lonely Scythian cliff, accompanied by Hephestus, the divine smith and god of fire, who has been ordered to nail and chain the rebel. Hephestus, as Prometheus's kin, pities him and regrets his cruel punishment, while Might pitilessly drives Hephestus on, threatening the wrath of Zeus if he should slacken.

Once the enslavers exit, Prometheus breaks his silence and calls out to nature, sky, waters, earth, and sun to witness his unjust suffering.[3] In a blend of lyric and dialogue rhythms, he proclaims his anger and pain, but explains the reason for his punishment, which he has foreseen: he gave to man "fire which has been the teacher of every art and a great resource" (11. 110–11). Suddenly he hears the noise of wings approaching and cries out in terror, anticipating further humiliation and torture from Zeus. This opening monologue reveals a two-sided Prometheus—strong in mind and spirit, but also physically weak and fearful.[4]

The sounds are those of the approaching chorus, the daughters of Oceanus, who have come in a winged chariot to commiserate with Prometheus. In response to their lyrics, Prometheus chants his anguish, but also predicts that Zeus will eventually release him in order to preserve the throne from a danger only Prometheus can foresee. Then the god explains to the chorus why he was punished: he and his mother, Themis/Earth, helped Zeus overthrow his father, the former ruler, Cronus, by guile. When Zeus, having consolidated his power, planned to destroy the human race, Prometheus alone defied him. Pitying men, Prometheus gave them blind hope, which kept off fore-knowledge of their fate, and then fire, "from which they will learn many arts" (1. 270). The chorus urges him to save himself, but he promises to tell them more of the future instead.

Now Oceanus, their father, arrives to offer help, also drawn to Prometheus by pity, kinship, and respect. His plan is simple; Prometheus should humble himself and curb his angry speech so that Oceanus can go to Zeus and request his pardon and release. Prometheus dissuades Oceanus from an intervention which might incur Zeus's wrath. He recalls Atlas, whom Zeus forced to hold up earth and heaven, and Typho, the fire-breathing monster, whom Zeus reduced to ash and buried beneath Mt. Aetna. Intimidated by these examples, Oceanus hurries away, convinced that Zeus is still too angry to be assuaged.

Next the chorus sings a stasimon lamenting the fate of Prometheus and blaming Zeus for his disrespect for the older generation of gods. They assure Prometheus his suffering is universally lamented by the people of the world, the waters above and below the earth, and even Hades. Prometheus at first expresses anger at the ingratitude of the new gods whose honors he himself designated, but then, in a long speech, the god of forethought describes how he rescued men from their primitive state ("like the shapes of dreams they dragged through their long lives and handled all things in bewilderment and confusion" [11. 448–50]) by teaching them all the arts: calculation of the stars, mathematics and language, the domestication of animals, naval science, medicine, mining, seercraft, and sacrifice. The chorus is impressed but urges him to make his peace with Zeus. Although Prometheus predicts that he will suffer further agonies, he hints that he knows something about Zeus's fate that he cannot reveal too soon, for this foreknowledge will be the instrument of his escape. The chorus, appalled at his sufferings, prays that they may never offend Zeus. They blame Prometheus's fearless, independent mind and too great love of man for his fate; he should not have overstepped the balance established by Zeus.

After the chorus's words about man's weakness and their memories of Prometheus's marriage, Io, the only mortal in the play, enters, a half-cow, half-maiden, driven to this lonely site by a gadfly. As Io chants out her agony in lyric frenzy, Prometheus recognizes her as the victim of Zeus's lust, now cruelly tormented by Hera's jealousy. The episode consists of three long speeches. First Io relates how Zeus, through dreams and oracles, made known his passion and forced her father, Inachus, to abandon her. Suddenly her shape was changed and she was driven away, first by the hundred-eyed monster, Argus, and then by the gadfly. Next Prometheus describes her future wanderings through inhospitable places of Scythia and the Caucasus until she crosses from Europe into Asia at the channel to be later named for her, the Bosphorus or Cow's Ford. To comfort his fellow victim, Prometheus tells Io that Zeus will someday fall from power if he marries a woman whose son is fated to be mightier than his father. Only Prometheus's release will save Zeus. He adds that Io's descendant is fated to release him. The two stories are brought together in the third speech in which Prometheus predicts that Io will wander through hostile Asia until she reaches Egypt, where Zeus will impregnate her with a touch and she shall bear Epaphus ("Touch"), ruler of the Nile. In the fifth generation, the daughters of Danaus will return to Io's home, Argos, fleeing a forced marriage with their cousins. The only Danaid to marry rather than murder her husband will bear a race of kings from whom Prometheus's liberator, a great archer, shall come. Although Prometheus never reveals their names in the play, we know from myth that the goddess was Thetis, her son Achilles, and the liberator Heracles. Stung by the gadfly again, Io departs from the orchestra in a frenzy.

After the chorus of women, horrified by the danger of Zeus's lust, prays to avoid his eye and marry safely, and Prometheus expounds on the threat that marriage holds for Zeus himself, Hermes enters, sent by Zeus to force Prometheus to reveal the name of the goddess who will be the instrument of his downfall. But Prometheus, having foreseen and accepted further torture, refuses to give up his secret before time teaches Zeus to suffer, too. Hermes taunts Prometheus and lists the punishments that he will have to endure—an earthquake, a confinement in Hades, and then a return to light long after so that Zeus's eagle will pluck at his liver every day—until some god is willing to take on his tortures and go down to Hades in his place (as Chiron may have done in the myth). The chorus urges Prometheus to give up, but refuses to desert him when Hermes summons the earthquake. The last fifty lines are chanted as a lyric finale expressing the crescendo of emotional tension and physical terror, as Prometheus describes how thunder and lightning are confounding all nature, and cries out to earth and sky to witness his unjust agony.

Authorship and the *Prometheia*

What reasons exist for believing that Aeschylus did not write the play we have just summarized? Some critics judge that *Prometheus Bound* is not as dramatic as the other six plays we have because it contains a monotonous succession of long speeches and uses empty spectacle to alleviate its wordiness.[5] But analysis according to less subjective criteria, such as the poet's use of meter and language and the production techniques indicated by the text, shows that the play is in fact different from the other plays of Aeschylus.

The meters of the lyrics and dialogue exhibit characteristics that have more in common with the techniques found in Sophocles' or Euripides' plays. Most striking is the domination of the episodes over the lyric parts. Choral odes comprise only 13 percent of *Prometheus Bound,* which corresponds to the proportion in a typical play by the later playwrights rather than to the other plays by Aeschylus, where the lyric parts range from a third to more than half.[6] Moreover, some rhythms in *Prometheus Bound* appear nowhere else in Aeschylus (e.g., dactylo-epitrites), whereas rhythms common in his other plays have a different usage in this one (e.g., lyric iambs, recitative anapests, and the iambic trimeters of dialogue).[7]

The diction, syntax, and style of *Prometheus Bound* also correspond to those of the later tragedians. Where one may trace a historical process in the development of a construction, phrase, or idea, as in the use of prepositions with certain cases, *Prometheus Bound* indicates a later stage in the language.[8] Features of style, such as the "emphasis on the brevity and clarity of speech, the artificial introduction of *gnomai,* and signpost formulae, which all suggest an unusually self-conscious and rhetorical arrangement of words and speeches," point to the influence of the Sophist teachers of rhetoric who were active in Athens in the second half of the fifth century.[9]

Many ideas expressed in the play reflect the philosophic interest in man's mind and nature associated with the enlightenment in Athens in the age of Pericles. In fact, the primary theme of the play, man's progress from savagery to civilization, is usually traced back to Protagoras the Sophist, whose influence has also been recognized in Sophocles' *Antigone* (ca. 442 B.C.).[10]

The text itself seems to demand a more sophisticated production than was probably possible in Aeschylus's day.[11] The words indicate that the chorus flies in on a winged chariot or chariots and that Oceanus arrives shortly after them on a flying sea horse. Ancient commentators thought the crane was used for both entrances, but it is doubtful that the machine (which we are not certain even existed in 456 B.C.) could carry the whole chorus together or singly through the air, deposit them, and then fly in Oceanus. Some critics suggest that the words and maybe even the chorus's dance motions imitating flight supplied enough description for the audience's imaginations. Oceanus, too, might have entered the orchestra on foot, having disembarked out of sight of the orchestra.

But it is hard to believe that nobody flies in when the text is so insistent on the spectacle. Moreover, the two flying entrances explain away some peculiar features of the play. The chorus's parodos is a lyric dialogue rather than an ode (unique in Aeschylus but found in later tragedy). Prometheus asks them to "come down" so they can hear his tale (11. 271–73), to which they respond that they will leave their chariots and descend to earth (11. 278–80). In the intervening episode, Oceanus ignores his daughters completely. These details make no sense unless the chorus flies in on one or more cranes, sings the parodos ode from the air without dancing, and then disembarks from their cranes offstage while Oceanus enters and talks to Prometheus. After he is flown out, the women come into the orchestra on foot. But such a spectacle requires an elaborate pulley system and a scene building large enough to hide it.

These arguments lead most scholars to conclude that *Prometheus Bound* was written after 456, the year of Aeschylus's death. A reference to *Prometheus Unbound,* part of the original trilogy, in Cratinus's comedy *Ploutoi* of 429, indicates the *Prometheia* was written before 430.[12] West dates the play between 445 and 435, when the developing conditions of the Theater of Dionysus in Athens would have allowed for the elaborate production he conjectures.[13] But those who argue for so late a date must explain Prometheus's prediction of an eruption of Aetna that occurred in 479 or 477 (perhaps the poet was imitating an earlier passage by Pindar).[14] More important, they must account for the facts that Aeschylus was given credit for the drama by scholars of the third century B.C. and that the play we have fits into a trilogy which has several extant fragments also assigned to Aeschylus by the ancient sources. Answers to these questions have been suggested by various modern critics, who show how errors might have been made in the tradition, speculate on the identity of the unknown poet, or argue against the assumption that there ever was a trilogy about Prometheus.[15]

Other scholars defend Aeschylean authorship in various ways. The "un-Aeschylean" clarity of the language can be interpreted as a bold device to personify Forethought through his precise speech. If *Prometheus Bound* was written in Sicily, where Aeschylus died and where in his lifetime science, ethics, and rhetoric were already developing (e.g., Pythagoreanism, Empedoclean and Heraclitean physics, Alcmaeon's medicine, and the oratory of Corax and Tisias), one may assume that many of the ideas of the enlightenment were already known to him. The references to the eruption of Aetna and the peculiarities of his diction can be considered "Sicilianisms" pleasing to his audience, whereas the unusual features of structure are said to have resulted from the less sophisticated level of production in Sicily.[16] Furthermore, those distressed by the short lyrics and absence of metaphorical language advance the theory that Aeschylus died before he could complete *Prometheus Bound* or the rest of the trilogy and that a later poet finished the composition. This helps explain why only one other play of the assumed trilogy, *Prometheus Unbound,* was frequently cited by the ancients.[17]

Despite the lack of positive proof on either side, the arguments against total Aeschylean authorship are too strong to be ignored. The best working hypothesis seems to be the one summarized by Taplin:

> It may be entirely by a follower and admirer; but it is my suspicion that the play was left unfinished, perhaps less than half-finished, at Aeschylus' death, and that it was completed later and on the model of the celebrated *Prom Lyomenos* [*Unbound*].[18]

Such an admission does not make *Prometheus Bound* a bad or less interesting play. If it is an imitation, it shows how great the influence of Aeschylus, particularly of his *Oresteia,* was.

Prometheus Bound, focusing on Prometheus's challenge to Zeus's authority, may be seen as one part of a lost trilogy which dramatizes the development of Zeus into a wise, omnipotent ruler.[19] As the *Oresteia* presents a historical process through which the old and young gods compromise on a new alignment of powers, so too the *Prometheia* presumably traces a similar process and ends when Zeus has learned to temper his power with forethought and pity, stabilizing a divine order more just to gods and men. Fear engendered by Prometheus's secret, like the conflict provoked by Orestes' matricide, would be the catalyst for the transformation.

This analogy with the *Oresteia* is not at all fanciful. Enough fragments of *Prometheus Unbound* remain to support the conjecture that these two plays dovetail like the first two plays of the *Oresteia* to suggest both a continuation and a step forward toward the resolution.[20] Like *Libation Bearers, Prometheus Unbound* has the same plot construction as its preceding play. Prometheus is again chained to his lonely rock and is visited by various characters to whom he explicates his situation. Heracles, in a clear parallel to Io, wanders by and learns of his past and future travel. But there are significant changes. Much time having passed, Prometheus has emerged from Hades and is suffering the additional torture of the eagle. Now Prometheus's will seems to be weakening. Moreover, Zeus's hostility to his subjects seems to have diminished. The chorus of the next play consists of the Titans, once imprisoned by Zeus (*Prometheus Bound* 11. 219–21) but now released and free to visit Prometheus. In Prometheus's tale of Heracles' wanderings, Zeus "pities" his endangered son enough to provide him with weapons for his defense. It is not clear what happens in the play, but probably Heracles shot the eagle with his bow without Zeus's permission and Gē [Earth], Prometheus's mother, a figure parallel to Oceanus, interceded with Zeus.[21]

There is not much evidence for further speculation. We know the name of a third play, *Prometheus Pyrphorus* [Fire Carrier], which many scholars consider the first play in the trilogy, dramatizing the theft of fire from Olympus.[22] But because the epithet Fire Carrier also alludes to the Athenian festival honoring Prometheus, Athena, and Hephestus as the divine sources of fire, other critics argue that the *Pyrphorus* was the third play celebrating the divine compromise. It is possible that the last play (whether *Pyrphorus* or *Lyomenus*) dramatized the initiation of the festival to celebrate Prometheus's welcome back to Olympus (validating his gift of fire to man) and the reconciliation of the old gods with the new. Perhaps the ending even confirmed Zeus's kinship with man by his acceptance of the mortal Heracles in exchange for the divine

Chiron and the solemnizing of a marriage between a god and a mortal
(Heracles and Hebe? or Peleus and Thetis, the goddess fated to have a
son stronger than his father?). We can imagine, on the analogy with
Eumenides, a patriotic imitation of an Athenian torchlight procession,
probably presided over by Athena herself, inviting Prometheus to share
her glory as the ultimate manifestation of the new Olympian compromise. An inspiring model for an Athenian audience, but only a
fantasy until some new discovery proves the existence and content of the
Prometheia.

Action, Sound, and Spectacle

Whatever the original staging, *Prometheus Bound* has been judged as a
plotless, wordy play which used "mechanical sensations" as a compensation to "win the attention of the uneducated majority."[23] But, in
fact, the play has a striking plot, complex enough in Aristotelian terms
to contain both a reversal and a recognition. At the beginning, Prometheus is isolated and vulnerable, but, by the end, his spiritual condition has radically changed despite the increase in physical punishment.
By the unique strength of his mind and will, Prometheus has transformed himself from a victim into a powerful rival of Zeus. The further
punishments Zeus threatens indicate his recognition of Prometheus's
power over him, whereas Prometheus's defiant acceptance of new
pain underscores the futility of Zeus's attempt to impose his will on
Prometheus.

The spectacular devices, and particularly the use of flying, are
integral to the development of this plot. The threat of danger from the
air hangs over the play because the audience, from its knowledge of the
myth, is expecting the entrance of Zeus's eagle to torment further the
helpless Prometheus.[24] Thus the entrances of the chorus and Oceanus
in flight, so carefully described, intensify the initial sense of Prometheus's immobility and impotence and emphasize Zeus's power. But,
ironically, the entrances of sympathizers in place of the eagle not only
dissipate the danger, but cast doubt on the efficacy of Zeus's punishment. More important, the motion of the characters underlines their
own bondage to Zeus's violence and power. Oceanus hurries away from

Prometheus in fear of Zeus's wrath. Io's agony of uncontrollable frenzy, in stark contrast to Prometheus's immobility, makes visible the error of equating freedom with physical movement. Thus, the spectacular entrances, which first increase anxiety for Prometheus, gradually modify the perception of his bondage. It is his last visitor, Hermes, who is called Zeus's slave, and Prometheus's refusal to be moved by Hermes' threats indicates his own spiritual freedom.

Similarly, the device of the marriage secret is not a "mechanical sensation" to keep the audience in a state of artificial excitement. The secret is the dramatic proof of Prometheus's power as "Foreknowledge" and Zeus's own bondage to Necessity. Bit by bit, Prometheus reveals the secret to his visitors as he responds to questions, predicts a reconciliation, argues that time is needed for any resolution, or angrily promises Zeus's defeat. This gradual revelation stimulates tension because Prometheus is eager to speak but knows he must not. The other characters increase this tension by chiding the hero for letting his rebellious tongue get him in trouble, yet Prometheus knows the unique power of the word which will finally free him from his enemy if he waits and keeps silent. This power to speak or not to speak transforms him into Zeus's equal. By himself, Prometheus has set in motion the historical process of further punishment and reconciliation. By the end Hermes' threats and the audience's fears about new punishments are outweighed by the mysteries of Prometheus's prophecies: who is the goddess? who is the liberator? who is the divine substitute, etc.?[25] Now the delayed mention of the eagle is anticlimactic. The storm at the end of the play no longer symbolizes Zeus's strength, but rather his weakness against Prometheus's silence. In passively accepting the violence of the storm, Prometheus is stubbornly refusing to change his position. Thus his immobility, as a visible complement to his silence, has now become a sign of his own power.

Zeus himself never appears. Instead the playwright dramatizes the god's superior power and his limitations through the devices of character, scene, spectacle, and imagery. The presence of his representatives Might and Force, personifications of abstractions, implies that Zeus controls the universe by brute force alone. (Hephestus's verse, "Your tongue cries out like to your appearance," l. 78, suggests that the two

emissaries wore masks or costumes that emphasized their inhumanity.)
Zeus's cruel use of force is further demonstrated by the characters' fear of
his wrath, which in itself deters Hephestus and Oceanus from their
altruistic intentions. The harsh punishments of Prometheus, Atlas, and
Typho prove how mercilessly he treats his enemies, whereas the agony
of the innocent Io compounds the impression of his pitiless and selfish
misuse of his power. The final earthquake demonstrates the destructiveness of his might.

His use of force displays his desire to enslave the environment and
turn it into the instrument for satisfying himself. Prometheus, bound
and chained before the audience, is the prime example. The imagery of
the horse harnessed, or the animal yoked to the plow, frequently
describes his punishment.[26] This metaphor also embodies Zeus's attitude toward his subjects as beasts of burden to be tamed to his
purposes. Io has been literally reduced to an animal by Zeus's lust,
appearing before the spectators as both maiden and cow with a bovine
mask displaying Zeus's abuse of her beauty. But Zeus also thwarts the
positive potential of others and turns them into instruments of destruction. Hephestus, the divine smith, must nail and chain his kin. With
fire and its technology, which Prometheus has used to free man, Zeus
reduces Typho to ash, burns Io with his passion, and initiates the
earthquake that turns all nature to chaos.

But there is an ironic limitation to Zeus's power: he cannot control
the mind by enslaving the body. Fear of him does not prevent his
subjects from feeling pity for Prometheus, nor can his treatment of Io
destroy her will to survive or her courage to face her future. The earth,
the sea, the sky, and even Hades, Zeus's instruments of new torture,
remain sympathetic observers of Prometheus's plight. Zeus's subjects
demonstrate a freedom to think, feel, and judge which challenges the
initial impression of Zeus's absolute power.

The setting provides an effective background for the exploration of
the relative powers of Zeus and Prometheus. To isolate and silence
Prometheus, Zeus has ordered him chained to a lonely rock in a distant
mountain range. After his binding, the three characters who represent
Zeus abandon Prometheus so that he is visibly alone as he cries out to
inanimate nature. The fact that his visitors obviously come from distant

places emphasizes his isolation from civilization. Ironically, however, the number of entrances emphasizes that Prometheus is not really alone, physically or spiritually. The ending is a reversal of the prologue. Hermes exits alone, making Zeus appear the isolated and vulnerable deity. The Oceanids remain with Prometheus, even to endure the earthquake, and the earth and sky he invokes at the end are, as we now know, sympathetic witnesses.

The poet also uses sound and the imagery of sound to contrast Zeus and Prometheus. The remote cliff is silent as well as lonely, and Prometheus himself utters no word at all while Hephestus and Might bicker, and the smith hammers away. Might urges Hephestus to increase the force of his hammering, and the resulting noise has been loud enough to disturb the Oceanids in their far-off cavern. This cacophony becomes associated with Zeus's might. He is responsible for the cruel beat of the hammer, the irritating drone of Argus's pipes, the shattering noise of the thunderbolt, the deep-bellowing thunder of the earthquake, and the final terrifying sounds of the storm. Whether there were sound effects or not, the words alone conjure a noisy spectacle which symbolizes Zeus's destructiveness.

Prometheus, in contrast, moves from proud and angry silence, through groan and lamentation, to a full display of the power of the word, in the rational persuasion of Oceanus, the long speeches of exposition to Io and the chorus, and even in the heated argument with Hermes. The precision of his language and the wordiness of the play dramatize the intelligence and spiritual power with which he opposes Zeus's use of brute force. Prometheus lists language or "the arrangement of letters" (1. 460) as one of his gifts to mortals. It is the gift which underlies all the others and the one the playwright can most easily exhibit as proof of Prometheus's power to civilize.

But there is another sound midway between cacophony and rational speech—groaning—which becomes symbolic of feelings of pain and pity for another's pain. The various characters' cries, dirges sung and danced, the numerous allusions to lament, all call attention to this different aspect of Prometheus's power, his ability to feel for others and act altruistically on behalf of them. The sympathy Prometheus felt for suffering humanity is returned to him by man. Such pity is a bond which eases the sufferer's burden, as Prometheus tells Io. Zeus does not yet possess this kind of knowledge. When Prometheus sighs, "Alas!" Hermes boasts that Zeus does not know the word, but Prometheus is certain that Zeus will learn it in time (11. 980–81). He too will know how it feels to be a slave (1. 927), like a beast of burden, bearing hard labors on his neck (1. 931). This extension of the yoke image suggests that Prometheus offers an alternative to Zeus's harness as a means to bind men—pity learned through suffering. The word "Friendship," which defines Prometheus's motive for helping man and the shared feelings of his sympathizers, is the same word Prometheus chooses to describe his future reconciliation with Zeus (11. 188–92).

Drama of Abstractions

The characters of *Prometheus Bound* behave as much like allegorical figures as live personalities.[27] The names of the first participants signify the central conflict: Might and Force enslave Forethought. The action exposes the conflict between Intelligence and Tyrannical Power and its effect on themselves, their community, and their environment. Because the brutal Zeus Aeschylus presents is so shockingly different from the majestic Zeus of epic, cult, and art, Aeschylus does not show him to the audience. (In fact, there may have been a taboo against showing Zeus on stage.) Thus, although Zeus is omnipotent in the drama, he remains transcendent. His absence amplifies the abstraction and makes him an even more terrifying and oppressive personification of brute force.

Zeus, as the personification of force, is repeatedly called "tyrant" by the other characters and displays many of the qualities which would have typified the tyrant for a fifth-century Athenian audience.[28] Having overthrown the legitimate ruler, Cronus, he has rejected the traditional rules and become a law unto himself. He uses lackeys like Might, Force, and Hermes and imposes his lust on unwilling women. Moreover, he shows no gratitude to his friends (Prometheus helped him defeat Cronus) and is merciless to his enemies, or the many he suspects of being potential enemies. Like all tyrants, he is alone, surrounded by servants instead of friends, while Prometheus on his lonely rock possesses the sympathy of Zeus's disgruntled subjects.

The opposition of Prometheus to Zeus defines other features of the allegory. Zeus the Tyrant can permit no disobedience. Prometheus, who thwarts Zeus's plan to destroy men, thus represents the Rebel in conflict with Authority. But Prometheus also stands for the Individual Will asserting its Freedom against the Community. (Prometheus's theft of fire has been an injustice to the other gods, according to Hephestus as well as Might [11. 11, 29–30].) The conflict further symbolizes the separation between god and man. Prometheus's identification with humanity is the source of his heroism but exposes him as Man to the tortures of a malevolent God.

Brute Force, however, is an insufficient instrument for controlling the Rebel, the Individual, or Man. The ashes of Typho smoulder still, destined to erupt into flame one day, and the Tyrant is doomed to repeat the failures of the past and be overthrown in his turn by a stronger son because he lacks the vision to use force for any purpose beyond maintaining himself. Forethought is the necessary complement of Force. Zeus needed it to defeat his own father and will not be able to survive the threat to his throne without it.

To characterize Forethought, Aeschylus has redefined the traditional culture hero familiar from Hesiod's *Theogony* and *Works and Days*.[29] From the son of a minor Titan and unimportant nymph, a trickster who cheated Zeus and was rightfully punished, Prometheus has become the source of intelligence and technology. Aeschylus emphasized the primacy of intelligence by changing Prometheus's parentage so that his mother is Earth/Themis, the mother of all and the source of all knowledge in the universe. Prometheus has been her partner in putting Zeus on the throne and shares her knowledge of the secret. Mother and son belong to the older generation, but they represent stability and justice based on intelligence, which all the Titans except Zeus rejected in favor of force. Now, however, Zeus is the upstart who has destroyed that former order and redefined justice in his own terms, relying on force himself.

Prometheus also possesses the qualities symbolized by the fire he stole: forethought, intelligence, wisdom, craft, technology. Prometheus displays them in his conversations with his visitors. He is first and foremost a teacher of wisdom, delivering precise, carefully or-

ganized lectures on the past, present, and future. The chorus and Io
often address him as teacher; although Oceanus comes as schoolmaster
to Prometheus (1. 322) he leaves schooled himself by Prometheus's
miseries (1. 391).[30] Prometheus's verses contain many *gnomai* (brief
phrases which express traditional wisdom), some introduced by first-
person verbs or phrases implying his own authorship. In addition,
words referring to knowing, thinking, teaching, learning, and speaking recur throughout the play to emphasize his didactic function.

Prometheus's meaning as Forethought or Intelligence is further
underlined by the many puns on his name or references to him as *sophos*
("wise" or "clever"). Some of these are ironic, however, since Prometheus has been unable to "forethink" his way out of his personal
disaster. This paradox points to the future. By the end of the play, time
has emerged as the ultimate teacher. If Zeus will have to learn to suffer
in time, so too must Prometheus learn wise discretion, as Hermes
warns (1. 1000). And Prometheus himself says, "Time as it grows old
teaches all things" (1. 981).

To characterize Prometheus as Intelligence, Aeschylus displays the
ideas of the philosophers, scientists, rhetoricians, and historians of what
has been termed the Greek Enlightenment in the language, metaphor,
and content of *Prometheus Bound*.[31] The most sophisticated members of
the fifth-century audience might have recognized references to a theory
of the elements, the belief that fire is the prime matter of the universe,
and the concept that some eternal principle of intelligence governs the
universe. The depiction of a world in chaos because Might and Intelligence are at war corresponds to the opinion of many early philosophers
(e.g., Pythagoras, Heraclitus, and Empedocles) that cosmic order is
achieved by a harmony of opposites.[32] More central to *Prometheus Bound*
and the conjectured *Prometheia* (as well as the *Oresteia*), however, is the
new theory of human progress expressed in Prometheus's catalogue of
his gifts.[33] According to Hesiod (*Works and Days,* 11. 109–211), man
had degenerated from an ideal state, termed the Golden Age, down
through the silver, bronze, and his own iron age. Prometheus, however,
echoing Xenophanes and Anaximander, as well as Protagoras, reverses
the process, describing how man began as a mindless creature but
gradually learned how to control his environment by using Prometheus's gifts. As we shall see, Aeschylus presents the entire trilogy as a
mythic paradigm that validates this human evolution.

In his catalogue, Prometheus is careful to show how the various branches of science, astronomy, grammar, mathematics, seacraft, farming, and medicine have been used to improve human life. The conversations themselves exhibit how far the Greeks' comprehension of their world had actually progressed. This is most obvious in Prometheus's accounts of the wanderings of Io and Heracles, which cover so much territory, describe so many peoples, and may actually trace the fifth-century map of the world.[34] The contemporary Greeks' interest in human history is also evident in the careful linear account of Io's family and the way in which Io's descent connects Greece to Egypt, considered the mother of all civilization by the ancients.[35] The accusation that Zeus is a tyrant, supported by the accumulation of the same characteristics found in Herodotus's *Histories*, Book 3, Chapter 8, suggests that citizens were beginning to analyze political behavior and define types of leadership.[36] In fact, the interest in language itself, exhibited by the wordplay, etymologies, and devices of rhetoric (as well as the relation of "words" to Prometheus's glory and plight), illustrates the contemporary recognition of the power of human thought and communication.

Medicine is the gift of Prometheus that is most frequently alluded to, probably because it was the least esoteric art, based on careful observation of household occurrences and intentionally formulated in the language of ordinary patients.[37] The science of medicine was a new development of the early fifth century. In contrast to the earlier belief that the gods inflicted disease to punish transgression, Alcmaeon of Croton (and the later writers of the Hippocratic Corpus) located the source of disease in nature:

. . . The bond of health is the "equal balance" of the powers, moist and dry, cold and hot, bitter and sweet, and the rest, while the supremacy of one of them is the cause of disease; for the supremacy of either is destructive. Illness comes about directly through excess of heat or cold, indirectly through surfeit or deficiency of nourishment. . . . Health on the other hand is the proportionate admixture of the qualities.[38]

New methods of treatment accompanied the new perception: careful observation of the course of a disease to determine changes in balance and techniques to restore balance by removing the excess or increasing the defect. Although the playwright is dramatizing a myth about the gods, where the divine Prometheus presents medicine to man, and Zeus is the source of Io's and Prometheus's illnesses, Prometheus's description of the art emphasizes man "falling sick" in nature and using nature to help himself. Moreover, the precise terminology of the medical passages displays the growing awareness of the need for observation and exact recording of symptoms. Io's frenzy is actually described in the terms associated in the Hippocratic Corpus with epilepsy.[39]

Aeschylus uses the science of medicine for more than a display of Prometheus's gift, however. He develops the theory of health as a balance of powers into an illuminating analogue of the cosmological and political situation. Through the use of disease and cure as metaphors for states of mind, the poet explicates the crisis of the first play as a cosmic state of illness or disproportion.[40] Zeus has too much power, punishes too harshly, is deficient in justice, pity, and trust, and will soon suffer literal pain. Prometheus, in incurable agony now, is too humanitarian, too rebellious, too angry. The use of familiar medical terms describes the present disharmony in a concrete way. For example, the dialogue between Prometheus and Oceanus illustrates how the poet uses the imagery to clarify Zeus's excess and its treatment:

P.   This cup I shall drain myself till the high mind of Zeus shall cease from anger.
O.   Do you not know, Prometheus, that words are healers of the sick temper?
P.   Yes, if in due season one soothes the heart with them, not tries violently to reduce the swelling anger.

                                                    (11. 375–80; Grene, trans.)

Prometheus's insistence that the disease must run its course and receive the right treatment at the proper time alludes to contemporary practice in order to clarify the need for time in the reconciliation between him and Zeus. But the analogy implies the cure: the abstract ideal of cosmic and political health is the "proportionate admixture of qualities": forethought and might; independence and submission to authority; will and obedience.[41]

But all the characters point out the paradox that Prometheus, the source of medicine, cannot yet heal himself. They recognize disease in Io and Zeus as well, but none can render effective treatment. Ironically, Prometheus's too great concern for man has spread disease to all who now inhabit an unhealthy or disproportionate universe where there can be no progress without a restoration of the balance. Nature, once organized into distinct elements, has returned at the end to chaos, with air and the sea confounded by Zeus's earthquake. Io's fate reveals how inadequate Prometheus's arts have been so far; the natural world is still full of horrible monsters such as Gorgons and griffins and the one-eyed daughters of Phorces who threaten the wandering maiden. Worse, in a world where there is no trust between gods, men cannot trust each other. Io must avoid numerous hostile peoples who use Prometheus's technology to forge weapons of destruction. Only the Amazons, haters of men, pity the wretched girl. Even Prometheus's gift of divination leads to suffering; Inachus and Io learn the cruel demands of Zeus from the interpretation of dreams and oracles.

But Prometheus foresees the time when he will be released and Zeus will be free from danger:

that will of his shall melt to softness yet when he is broken in the way I know, and though his temper now is oaken hard it shall be softened: hastily he'll come to meet my haste, to join in amity and union with me—one day he shall come.

(11. 190–95; Grene, trans.)

When Zeus's anguish compels him to release Prometheus in exchange for the goddess's name, Zeus will literally possess the forethought and intelligence that his initial victory through guile presaged. But the words "amity and union" imply he will gain human feelings as well. Prometheus's account of Io's future hints that in time Zeus will change his attitude toward his subjects. He will cure and impregnate Io, his worst victim, by his gentle touch. Bound to the human race by Epaphus, their son, he will protect the Danaids, his progeny, from their cousins' lust: "God will begrudge them the bodies" (1. 859), where the passage implies just punishment for unjust behavior. The fact that the races that once endangered Io's life will one day commemorate her journey with the names Bosphorus and Ionian Sea suggests a concomitant change in human attitudes and relationships. The prediction that "Pelasgia will receive the daughters of Danaus" (1. 860) hints at the development of obligations toward guests or hosts, and strangers or suppliants, of which Zeus was divine patron.

Such progress is only glimpsed in *Prometheus Bound,* but is further developed in the fragments of *Prometheus Unbound.* Thirteen generations later, Zeus has freed his former enemies, the Titans, and has felt such "pity" for his son, Heracles, that he has sent him a stormcloud of rocks as a defense against his fierce enemies. Although Prometheus warns Heracles, like Io, of dangers from nature and hostile men, he also describes political progress; Heracles will visit a "just community, more just than any other and friendlier"; and the Scythians are called "well-governed."[42]

If time has taught Zeus intelligence and altruism, what will it teach Prometheus? Will he recognize that his own behavior and condemnation of Zeus have been excessive? Perhaps Prometheus will come to accept Zeus's force as the necessary complement of his own intelligence and altruism, having learned that too much "pity" can prevent stability and progress. In fact, Prometheus has already used force himself, in order to establish a better world for men. Ironically, Prometheus's description of the domestication of animals on earth corresponds exactly to the major imagery associated with Zeus's misuse of power.[43] The yoke and harness, with all their trappings, describe how Zeus compels and enslaves his subjects, as if they were animals. For example, Prometheus cries out, "Wretched me, I am yoked in these tortures" (l. 108), whereas Zeus's bit and goad force Io and Inachus to submit. But Prometheus himself boasts:

It was I who first yoked beasts for them in the yokes and made of those beasts slaves of trace chain and pack saddle that they might be man's substitute in the hardest tasks; and I harnessed to the carriage, so that they loved the rein, horses, the crowning pride of the rich man's luxury.

(11. 461–66; Grene, trans.)

His statement rests on a belief in hierarchy where animals must be used to serve the higher purposes of man. Man in turn is a lesser being than the gods and must be taught by Prometheus how to appease them. Yet all the characters but Prometheus recognize a cosmic hierarchy and accept their positions in it. Oceanus advises Prometheus not to kick against Zeus's goad, and Hermes' words echo Prometheus's own description of his conquest of horses:

> You are a colt new broken, with the bit clenched in its teeth, fighting against the reins, and bolting.
>
> (ll. 1009–10; Grene, trans.)

Prometheus's ability to make correct distinctions (i.e., risings from settings of the stars, the ordering of numbers, the arrangement of letters) and to control nature is responsible for initiating progress among men. But a parallel process is taking place in the cosmos as a whole. Prometheus has already experienced two generations of rulers, and Zeus's accession by guile rather than force should begin a new stage. The quarrel between Zeus and Prometheus is a point of crisis in a long process of the gradual refinement and harnessing of the potential of the universe. Zeus may lack intelligence at first, but he cannot abandon force if he is to persuade recalcitrant elements to bow to necessity. In this context, Prometheus's pity for Atlas and Typho is misplaced. Atlas's burden is the mythic representation of the separation of earth and heaven from the primeval waters, whereas Typho's defeat is one aspect of Zeus's victory over the monstrous and destructive elements in nature, and Typho's confinement is another part of the increasing separation of realms, i.e., the establishment of Hades.[44] In *Prometheus Bound,* the rebel foresees that Zeus's force will work on him, too, that he must one day bend his own knee to necessity and curb his excessive will, independence, pity, and altruism, so that he, too, serves the highest authority, a Zeus who, once he rules with forethought, rules for the good of all and is equal to necessity.

Thus, the poet is dramatizing one moment in mythic time, before the just and anthropomorphic order of Zeus was firmly established. But the father of gods and men, the dispenser of rewards and punishments according to the principles familiar from Homer up to the *Oresteia,* is neither seen nor clearly anticipated in *Prometheus Bound.* And the conflict between young Zeus, so arbitrary and unfeeling, and Prometheus, the son of Earth, subservient with her to Zeus, is so intense that it seems unresolvable. The primeval power of intelligence, accompanied by altruism and the impulse to progress, must always struggle against brute force, which destroys indiscriminately. Other fundamental polarities—man against the mysterious cosmos, gentleness versus cruelty, group versus individual, reason versus passion—underline the eternal opposition from which progress emerges. [45]

Archetype for Human Life

Prometheus Bound also gives to the allegorical gods human qualities that relate them to the Athenian audience. All the characters but Io are immortals, but, as anthropomorphic deities, they obviously must think, talk, and behave like men. In fact, each embodies a particular character type. Zeus resembles contemporary descriptions of the Tyrant. Prometheus himself behaves like other tragic heroes, in self-imposed isolation, proud and strong, respected for his principles but misunderstood, suffering through choice, self-dramatizing, rebellious, and presumptuous. [46] Oceanus is the moderate man whose mediocrity exposes the excess and grandeur of the hero, whereas Hermes is the brash youth unable to argue against experience. Io and the female chorus represent women with their own blend of passivity, passion, and interest centered on the family. [47]

All these anthropomorphic deities are drawn together by the very important human bond of kinship. Family ties, which incur responsibilities as well as good feelings in Greek society, generate sympathy and attempts to help from Hephestus, Oceanus, and the Oceanids. The primary emotion expressed by all, even nature, is pity, a quality Zeus lacks, but will learn in time. Presumably it is one's own pain which enables him to sympathize with the pain of another, and even try to alleviate his suffering (altruism).

Aeschylus's gods, like men, have limited powers and are vulnerable to suffering and pity. [48] None of the familiar divinities possesses his full potency in *Prometheus Bound*. Hephestus is not master of his own craft, Oceanus appears weak and ineffectual, and Hermes the Messenger is a petulant lackey whose orders are ignored. Although those gods are subject to Zeus's whim, Zeus and Prometheus are themselves subject to necessity. Prometheus's impotence is the focal point of the drama, whereas Zeus's own weakness unfolds gradually as the marriage secret is divulged. Humiliated by his treatment, Prometheus grows so full of hatred and anger that his passion vitiates his forethought. The might and force of Zeus, on the other hand, when exemplified by the earthquake and pitted against Prometheus's defiance, seem weak and blustering. The developing conflict thus reveals gods who, like men, are paradoxical mixtures of contradictory passion and powers—whose lives are at best a mixed blessing.

From this perspective, Prometheus appears to be the archetype for man himself, particularly as perceived by fifth-century Greece.[49] He is rational and pragmatic, able to use his knowledge to control his environment for his own purposes. Proud of his accomplishments, he is eager to teach others. Fifth-century Athenians, who had developed the democracy, defeated the Persians, and materially improved their lives, would justly feel this pride in themselves as rational men who had produced technological, moral, and social progress. Yet, Prometheus's intellectual pride has its negative aspects. He, too, acts selfishly to accomplish his goal, stealing fire from his peers and becoming so irrational in defense of reason that he prefers to see a new upheaval rather than secure the throne for his hated enemy. His pride and anger, which lead him to boast of his foreknowledge, are signs of the internal limitations of the perfectibility of rational man. But there is also an external limitation, represented by Zeus, nature, and necessity. There are destructive forces in the universe which man cannot overcome and must simply endure.[50] Perhaps the earthquake and volcano exemplify the indifference of the natural universe and the ever-imminent danger of a return to chaos. Moreover, man's portion is inevitably limited by his mortality, and he is, by definition, a lesser creature than the gods he emulates, unable to fathom or control the mysterious forces outside himself that govern life. The best man can ultimately achieve is the self-knowledge that enables him to accept the limits of his portion. Here we reach an essential element of tragedy; man's grandeur is most evident when, like Prometheus, he rebels against the limits, defying forces he cannot ultimately defeat for the sake of his principles or his integrity.

But human beings live in society. The additional characters of Zeus, Io, Themis, and Inachus provide archetypes for the complications of family life. Together Prometheus, Zeus, and Themis form an Oedipal triangle with its conflict between father and son, or old generation and new.[51] By Aeschylus's account, this opposition threatens to repeat itself perpetually and prevent stability and progress. Zeus is the son who has just overthrown his father Cronus with the help of Prometheus and his mother. But, instead of the progress anticipated in his victory by guile, the drama focuses on Zeus as the authority to be overthrown in turn, and Prometheus the elder is the new rebel, who, with his mother again, asserts the necessity of a still newer order. In his dual role, Zeus manifests the constant strife between the generations. His fear of the marriage secret indicates that he recognizes that he will become a victim of still another mother and son (Thetis and Achilles). *Prometheus Bound* hints at an alternative to this destructive cycle, however. If Zeus avoids the wrong partner he can produce children who are not threats to his reign. Perhaps Hermes' obedience to Zeus presages the positive progress toward stability that Zeus's other Olympian children (e.g., Athena, Apollo, Aphrodite) achieve. *Prometheus Bound* itself, however, presents the human reality of generational strife, while only faintly denying its necessity.

Zeus's victimization of Io also dramatizes the mysterious power of human sexuality. Io's dreams, her fears of leaving her father, and her father's hesitant but final expulsion of Io suggest the strong, but taboo, Oedipal feelings.[52] Lust then literally turns the virgin into a frenzied animal, driven from civilized places into the wilds of nature, the site of the Dionysiac, pursued by a hundred-eyed monster and a gadfly, whose name, *oistros,* means "lust." But sexuality is a positive force as well. The intercourse between Zeus and Io that produces progeny is a blessing, a gentle touch. And the succession of generations brings progress with it. Zeus does not permit the cousins of the Danaids to satisfy their lust as he once did. In addition, the one Danaid whom "desire softens" (1. 865) becomes the ancestress of Heracles. *Prometheus Bound* describes a civilizing of the male-female relationship—from Zeus's violence against a reluctant Io to the Danaid Hypermestra's willing submission to her husband's desire. The marriage rite solemnizes their lust and blunts natural sexual antagonism and fear with the promise of offspring.

This perspective on marriage which connects the destinies of Io, Zeus, and Prometheus also serves as a commonplace image for expressing the important moral ideas of portion, limit, and hierarchy. The chorus's response to Io's experience relates the myth directly to the concept in a way the audience could comprehend.[53]

> A wise man indeed he was
> that first in judgment weighed this word
> and gave it tongue: the best by far
> it is to marry in one's rank and station:
> let no one working with her hands aspire
> to marriage with those lifted high in pride
> because of wealth, or of ancestral glory.
> (11. 887–93; Grene, trans.)

For them, as women, safety lies in securing a suitable match. Io's life proves the danger of attracting too great a partner. But Prometheus's secret is a symbol of a broader truth: all men must learn to know themselves and accept their portion. Even Zeus's choice is limited by necessity, and, if he contracts the wrong marriage, he, too, can become a slave.

The two extremes of slave and tyrant emphasize the social and political aspects of the drama. Zeus and Prometheus represent all rivals for power in the state, but the allegory gave their strife a special meaning for the Athenian democracy. The harsh, autocratic Zeus would resemble the popular memory of Hipparchus, the deposed son of Pisistratus, Xerxes, the Persian emperor, and perhaps Heiron, the tyrant of Syracuse.[54] Prometheus represents not only the revolutionary who envisions a better world and becomes a benefactor to the powerless, but also the new democracy itself, struggling against internal aristocracy and foreign invasion. Oceanus, in attempting to bring Prometheus and Zeus together by advocating concessions from Prometheus, behaves like the peacemakers who, from fear of disorder and violence, advise accommodation to the enemy.[55] Prometheus knows, however, that necessity demands struggle as much as reconciliation. Zeus cannot overlook Prometheus's disobedience and Prometheus must accept the consequences of his rebellious act or compromise his purposes. So

Prometheus forces the conflict to a more desperate stage, which paradoxically brings him closer to victory. Thus *Prometheus Bound* validates the need to fight for principles despite the danger involved. If *Prometheus Bound* suggests past struggles in which Athens was successful, it also includes all present and still unresolved ones, for in life, if not myth, each new advance brings its own set of oppositions, as the Athenians who witnessed the rivalry of Cimon and Pericles following the formation of the Delian League knew well. In the words of David Konstan,

The myth gives shape and meaning to the conflicts of the present. The greatness of *Prometheus Bound* is to convey this vision of the whole in unblinking recognition of the necessity that those engaged in battle must fight for their partial goals and strive in the heat of passion for victory more than harmony. Prometheus who both knows the future and yet must suffer in its unfolding, who is torn between rage and prophecy, whose opposing moods succeed each other in extreme alternations of feeling, is the archtype of man in history, committed to relentless struggle in the service of a universal ideal of peace.[56]

But *Prometheus Bound* also radiates hope, the first gift of Prometheus, without which his arts are useless. Although he defines hope as stopping mortals from foreseeing their doom (11. 248–50), as a way of giving them the courage and will to survive, such hope is paradoxically connected to foreknowledge. Prometheus's explication of the possibility of meaning in suffering or the remote promise of success arouses hope and courage in the characters struggling with their desperate situations. Despite Prometheus's warning that it will provide no cure, Io demands information about her coming journey, agreeing that "it is a relief for those in pain to know beforehand what they must suffer" (11. 698–99). Moreover, once the chorus of Oceanids understand Prometheus's purpose, they choose to suffer with him as a sign of support. Prometheus is, of course, the best example of the truth that strength comes from the hope gained from foreknowledge.

In *Prometheus Bound,* hope and foreknowledge are the symbols of man's concentration on the future to alleviate his present pain and acquire the courage to face further pain. From his sense of purpose, and his conception of new possibilities, man achieves tragic grandeur and even rivals the immortals. In himself, and in his brief lifespan, he may be helpless. But if his own sufferings can be viewed from the perspective of a better future, if his private pain can be counted as the cost of his group's survival or progress, this hope enables him to resist the debilitating knowledge of his personal doom and to find solace in the permanence of the chain of which he is a link. The suffering of Io and Prometheus gives meaning to the suffering of those in human history who struggle to preserve and advance the family and the state. The cosmogonic myth in which Prometheus's reconciliation with Zeus produces stability and justice offers the ultimate validation for all human hope that suffering has meaning because it illustrates that even gods have endured agony in order to create a better future.

Chapter Seven
Conclusion

The Other Aeschylus

The seven complete plays do not comprise all that we know of Aeschylus. The manuscripts include hypotheses (introductory summaries) to five of the seven tragedies, the *Life of Aeschylus,* and a catalogue of seventy-three titles of plays written by the poet. Other sources have revealed the names of about ten more dramas by Aeschylus. By diligent culling of citations in ancient writings, scholars over the centuries have been able to compile a collection of fragments by Aeschylus and to assign many of them to lost plays, and even group them into possible trilogies.[1]

These citations appear in many different kinds of sources. For example, the *Deipnosophists* by Atheneaus (ca. A.D. 200), a collection of literary trivia organized as a dinner conversation among savants, contains a cornucopia of verses and anecdotes about the poet. Strabo, the Greek geographer (64 B.C.–A.D. 21), sometimes quotes Aeschylean descriptions of places he is discussing, whereas Plato (*Republic,* Book 2. 380a) uses a verse from Aeschylus's *Niobe* to illustrate how poets lie about the gods. Occasionally an Aeschylean verse has been written as a note in the margin (*scholion*) to the text of another ancient author, as an ancient editor's means of identifying an allusion or explaining a word or idea. Since 1932, when a whole collection of literary papyri was discovered in a garbage dump in Oxyrhinchus, Egypt, scholars have published new fragments containing longer passages, including a piece of a hypothesis from the Danaid trilogy that indicates a later date for *Suppliants* than previously assumed.[2] Despite the uncertainty of the assignment of unidentified pieces to a particular author or play and the difficulty of interpreting fragmentary remains, our knowledge of the poet keeps increasing and our hope of finding a complete play or an indisputable new fact grows with each new discovery.

From the disjointed details, we can glean some notion of the variety of Aeschylus's work. The subject of his tragedies covered the full range of Greek myth, from plays about Dionysus (e.g., *Semele* and *Pentheus*) to the heroes of the Trojan War (*Palamedes, Philoctetes*) to women like Atalanta, Alkmene, and Penelope. The ancients commented on three of these plays in particular. Although little more than the title of *Psychostasia* [Weighing of Lives] is extant, on the basis of passages in which Plutarch (A.D. 46–120) and Pollux, a rhetorician of the second century A.D., mentioned the appearance of a god who weighed the fates of two heroes, scholars have debated whether Aeschylus actually portrayed Zeus as a character and whether his Zeus flew on to the roof of the skene̅ by crane and actually held the scales.[3] Since antiquity, both *Myrmidons* and *Niobe* have been singled out to illustrate Aeschylus's use of the silent actor. Evidently the main character was present and visible for a long time, but refused to speak until late in the play: Niobe from overwhelming grief, and Achilles because of his anger at Agamemnon and the Greeks.[4] Snell analyzes *Myrmidons* (where the Greeks beg Achilles to return to battle) as an example of a tragedy in which the hero rejects pressure from the group, recognizing his freedom of choice and willing to accept the consequences of his decision.[5] A long passage from *Niobe,* spoken perhaps by her nurse, and describing the heroine's mourning for her children (slain by the gods for her excess maternal pride), defines Aeschylean double motivation:

A god causes a fault to grow in mortals, when he is minded to utterly ruin their estate. But none the less, a mortal must abstain from rash words, carefully nurturing the happiness that the gods give him. But in great prosperity, men never think they may stumble and spill the full cup of their fortune. So it was that this woman, exultant . . . in beauty. . . .[6]

Other fragments reveal another side of Aeschylus. We know that the ancients judged him first among the writers of satyr plays. Now the Oxyrhinchus papyri have yielded enough fragments to permit tentative reconstructions of their plots.[7] In them, the exuberant and lusty satyrs meet other more serious mythic characters, who are potentially tragic or heroic. The humor may have resulted from the comic twist that the playwright gives to the tragic situation. For example, in *Dictyulkoi* or *The Drawers of Nets*, the satyrs answer the call of a fisherman of Seriphos who is trying to pull up a very heavy and strangely noisy catch. Their haul turns out to be the chest in which Danae and the baby Perseus have been exposed. After they rescue her, Danae is horrified to discover that she has attracted the love of the lecherous leader of the satyrs, Silenus. The story should end happily, however, with Danae marrying the fisherman Dictys, who is the brother of the king, instead. The parallel with the plot of *Amymone* (which followed the Danaid trilogy, and dramatized the legend where the daughter of Danaus is saved from the lust of the satyrs, only to be ravished by her savior, Poseidon) indicates that satyr plays often had fairy-tale plots where heroines in distress were rescued and then wedded (or bedded).

Although the details of plot and character are unclear, it is obvious that the thought and diction are more colloquial and the characters more realistic than in tragedy. Moreover, there is a spirit of fun in jokes such as "If I do not thank you, may——— (somebody else) drop dead!" and the playful language in which Silenus tries to soothe the whimpering Perseus.[8] These fragments suggest, in the words of Howe, that Aeschylus was "relaxing and requiring that his audience also relax from the heights and tensions of the tragic style."[9]

The papyri contain fragments of another play by Aeschylus, *Isthmiastae,* but its remains are more difficult to interpret. According to Lloyd-Jones, the satyrs have been brought to the Isthmian games by Dionysus as members of a sacred embassy. Although he expects them to dance or enter a singing contest, they sneak off to practice for the athletic games instead. If Hephestus is the unnamed character who entices them away from Dionysus, the play might be dramatizing the popular legend in which Hephestus has vanished from Olympus after imprisoning his mother, Hera, in a trick throne, and Dionysus and the satyrs, after getting him drunk, return him to the gods.[10]

Other satyr plays by Aeschylus are little more than titles to us. We know that the trilogies on the houses of Laius and Atreus were followed by satyr plays connected to their sagas: *Sphinx* and *Proteus* (about

Menelaus's return), respectively. The satyr play produced in the same tetralogy as *Persians* was called *Prometheus Pyrkaeus* [Fire-Kindler], and seems to have dramatized the god showing the fire he has just stolen to the frightened satyrs.[11] Taplin speculates that *Sisyphus Petrokylistes* [Stone-Roller] was a satyr play in which Sisyphus emerged from the underworld to the amazement of the satyrs who happen to be nearby. In their attempt to guess who or what he is, Taplin detects a stock motif of satyr plays, which is also found in *The Drawers of Nets* and Sophocles' *Trackers*: "a series of comic speculations about a person or object which cannot be identified because it is somehow unfamiliar or hard to make out."[12]

We are fortunate to have more complete satyr plays by the other tragedians. Euripides' *Cyclops* is extant in its entirety. Here the satyrs and Silenus have been enslaved on Polyphemus's island as shepherds. When Odysseus arrives, they participate in his adventure, which is more ribald than dangerous. In the end, they are freed by him when he escapes. Enough fragments exist of Sophocles' *Ichneutae* [Trackers], mentioned above, to reconstruct its plot. Having been promised a reward, the satyrs and Silenus are tracking Apollo's stolen cattle through the Arcadian weeds. Arriving at the cave of Cyllene, they try to guess what the strange sounds they hear are. Later they discover that the thief is the infant Hermes, grown to prodigious size, and that he has just invented the lyre. In the end, they foresee a happy compromise between the divine brothers, Apollo and Hermes. These few examples of the satyr play, with their rustic settings, unheroic characters, and gaiety, are tantalizing to us. We should like to know more about the genre and about Aeschylus's role in developing it.

Judgment and Rebirth

Despite Aeschylus's victory in Aristophanes' comic contest in *Frogs*, his popularity declined in the following centuries, while first Sophocles and then Euripides replaced him as the poet of Athens. His reputation suffered primarily because his language seemed archaic and monstrously difficult. According to Quintillian, the Roman grammarian of the first century A.D.,

Aeschylus invented Tragedy. He is sublime, grandiloquent to a fault, and for
the most part rugged, ill-composed. And for that reason the Athenians
allowed the later poets to produce corrected versions of his plays in
competition.[13]

Although Longinus, author of *On the Sublime* in the first century A.D.,
compliments Aeschylus for his vivid imagery in one place, in another
he uses him as an example of the tumescent or swollen style. After
quoting from *Oreithyia,* now lost, he comments:

All this has lost the tone of tragedy: it is pseudo-tragic, . . . The phrasing is
turbid, while the images make for confusion rather than intensity. Examine
each in the light of day and it gradually declines from the terrible to the
ridiculous.[14]

Despite these negative judgments, Aeschylus's dramas were transmitted from generation to generation.[15] At first, the plays were
probably passed on orally by the actors who performed them. By 330
B.C., Lycurgus, a friend of Aristotle and administrator of public
finances, established official copies of the texts of all three tragedians.
He had them deposited in the public archives and compelled actors to
keep to these authorized texts. By this time, the number of plays had
been reduced because only those which continued to be acted after the
poets' deaths could have been written down a century later. In the
second century B.C., Ptolemy the Third (247–221) borrowed the
Athenians' official copy, probably for the use of the scholars at the
Library of Alexandria, and never returned it. During the great period of
Alexandrian scholarship, critics such as Aristophanes of Byzantium
(257–180) must have contributed much to the preservation and understanding of Aeschylus's plays. Gradually, however, the number was
reduced still further, probably due as much to the increasing difficulty
of understanding the language and poetry as to accidental losses. When
the plays became only a subject for academic study, teachers produced
school editions of a selected few with explanatory notes. Through these
school texts, the Attic tragedies edited by the Alexandrians were
transmitted to the Byzantine scholars who copied, criticized, and
preserved them.

With the recovery of the Medicean Manuscript from Constantinople in 1423 and then the publication of the first printed edition of Aeschylus in Venice in 1518, the modern study and influence of Greek tragedy began. In every country in Europe, scholars, poets, and playwrights rediscovered the beauty and excitement of the dramas of Aeschylus and the others and strove to understand the form and imitate the grandeur of tragedy. From the numerous examples of Aeschylus's influence on our literary traditions, we mention only a few. John Milton modeled his *Samson Agonistes* on *Prometheus Bound,* while Shelley wrote *Prometheus Unbound,* transforming the Aeschylean rebel into a Romantic, and even Christian hero. In the twentieth century, the *Oresteia* has been more influential; Jean-Paul Sartre (*Les Mouches*), T. S. Eliot (*Family Reunion*), and Eugene O'Neill (*Mourning Becomes Electra*) have all adapted the trilogy to express their respective visions of modern life. As recently as spring 1980, John Eaton composed an opera entitled *The Cry of Clytemnestra,* inspired by the *Agamemnon* but presented as "an intense personal drama showing the agony and sufferings which lead Clytemnestra to decide to kill her husband."[16]

Interest in Aeschylean drama continues because through myth he presents universal conflicts—within ourselves, our families, and our societies—without settling for easy answers. In this, Aeschylus resembles modern man's willingness to accept uncertainty and ambiguity in his own life and to acknowledge his weakness in the face of forces beyond his control. Yet the optimism of Aeschylus, patent in the *Oresteia* and glimpsed in *Prometheus Bound,* inspires us to continue the present struggle. If Aristophanes, at the end of the fifth century, resurrected Aeschylus to recapture the past, we, at the end of the twentieth, have kept him alive to give ourselves the strength to face the future.

Notes and References

Chapter One

1. Pausanias, *Descriptions of Greece,* ed. W. H. S. Jones and H. A. Ormerod (London: G. P. Putnam, 1926), book 1, chapter 14.5. The epitaph is quoted in the ancient *Life of Aeschylus,* which was included in the Medicean manuscript and appears at the end of the Greek text edited by Denys Page, *Aeschyli septem quae supersunt tragoediae,* 2d ed. (Oxford, 1972), hereafter cited as *OCT.*

2. For the poet's biography, see the *Life* cited above. Ancient biographies generally provide little reliable information, however, because the biographers included all sorts of legendary and anecdotal material without attempting to verify or criticize the tradition. See also Albin Lesky, *A History of Greek Tragedy,* tr. James Willis and Cornelius de Heer (London: Methuen, 1966), pp. 240–41, as well as Pauly-Wissova et al., *Real Encyclopadie der classischen Altertumswissenschaft* (Stuttgart: Metzler, 1894). For further information on Aeschylus's time in Sicily, see C. J. Herington, "Aeschylus in Sicily," *Journal of Hellenic Studies* 87 (1967):74–85.

3. The problems of dating these two plays are discussed in the individual chapters. For the most complete presentations of the questions involved, see A. F. Garvie, *Aeschylus' "Supplices": Play and Trilogy* (Cambridge: Cambridge University Press, 1969), and Mark Giffith, *The Authenticity of "Prometheus Bound"* (Cambridge, 1977).

4. See N. G. L. Hammond, *A History of Greece to 322 B.C.,* 2d ed. (Oxford: Clarendon Press, 1967), for a detailed history of the period.

5. Herodotus, *The Histories,* tr. Aubrey de Selincourt (Baltimore: Penguin, 1954), book 5, chapter 78, p. 339. All following citations from Herodotus will refer to this edition..

6. Gerald Else, *The Origin and Early Form of Greek Tragedy* (Cambridge, Mass., 1965) and Gilbert Murray, *Aeschylus, The Creator of Tragedy* (Oxford, 1940).

7. For summaries of the evidence and evaluations of the various theories, see Else, *Origin,* and Albin Lesky, *Greek Tragedy,* tr. H. A. Frankfort (London, 1965), pp. 26–46; Lesky, *History,* pp. 223–40; and Sir Arthur Pickard-Cambridge, *Dithyramb, Tragedy, and Comedy,* 2d ed., rev. T. B. L. Webster (Oxford, 1962). But Oliver Taplin, in *Greek Tragedy in Action*

(London, 1978), pp. 23, 164–65, argues that the origins of tragedy, and particularly its relation to early religious rites, are irrelevant to our understanding of its essence in the fifth century.

8. E. R. Dodds, *Euripides' "Bacchae"* (Oxford: Clarendon Press, 1944), p. xviii, contains a good discussion of the character and worship of Dionysus. The works cited in notes 6 and 7 also examine the god's relation to tragedy.

9. K. G. Kachler, "Über Wesen und Wirkin der Theatermaske," *Antaios* 11 (1969):192–208.

10. For a detailed account of all aspects, with the ancient sources, see Sir Arthur Pickard-Cambridge, *Dramatic Festivals of Athens,* 2d ed., rev. John Gould and D. M. Lewis (Oxford, 1968).

11. For a concise introduction to Greek meter and further bibliography on lyric in tragedy, see James W. Halporn, Martin Ostwald, and Thomas G. Rosenmeyer, *The Meters of Greek and Latin Poetry,* 2d ed. (Indianapolis: Bobbs-Merrill, 1978). Two Greek rhythms used for dialogue, iambic trimeter and trochaic tetrameter, correspond to the English stichic verses. The lyric meters have no real English equivalent, however. They are made up of metrical phrases called *cola,* which consist of irregular alternations of long and short syllables that cannot be divided into smaller units. (In quantitative languages like Greek, long and short syllables are comparable to the stress and unstress of accentual verse.) There are many kinds of cola, with different lengths and movements, and they do not repeat themselves line after line like English stichic verse. Rather they occur in an infinite variety of combinations with other phrases to form unique lyric stanzas which are often paired and repeated exactly (strophe and antistrophe). Many of the ancient terms connected with lyric such as "strophe," which literally means "turn," indicate a close relationship between its development and that of dance. In fact, the word "chorus" itself means "a group dance performed in a set formation." For information on the origin of dance and its relation to lyric, see J. W. Fitton, "Greek Dance," *Classical Quarterly* 23 (1973):254–74.

12. Else discusses the importance of familiar lyric forms in "Ritual and Drama in Aeschylean Tragedy," *Illinois Classical Studies* 11 (1977):70–87. H. D. Broadhead, *"The Persae" of Aeschylus* (Cambridge, 1960), appendix 4, pp. 310–17, contains an analysis of these lyric forms.

13. See Else, *Origin,* and Lesky, *History,* for discussions of the theories. Else emphasizes the importance of the rhapsodes and early lyric poets to the development of the episodes.

14. Else, *Origin,* p. 76.

15. The following books discuss the various aspects of the theater and production: Peter Arnott, *Greek Scenic Conventions in the Fifth Century B.C.*

(Oxford, 1962), and *The Ancient Greek and Roman Theater* (New York: Random House, 1971); Margaret Bieber, *History of the Greek and Roman Theater* (Princeton: Princeton University Press, 1939); Taplin, *Greek Tragedy*; T. B. L. Webster, *Greek Theater Production* (London: Methuen, 1956). The article by N. G. L. Hammond, "The Conditions of Dramatic Production to the Death of Aeschylus," *Greek Roman and Byzantine Studies* 13 (1972):387–450, and Oliver Taplin, *The Stagecraft of Aeschylus: Dramatic Use of Entrances and Exits in Greek Tragedy* (Oxford, 1977), are especially valuable for study of the early theater and Aeschylus's production devices.

16. For a discussion of structural divisions, see Aristotle, *Poetics,* 1452 b, 14–27, and the comments by Taplin, *Stagecraft,* pp. 49–60, 470–76.

17. See Oliver Taplin, "Aeschylean Silences and Silences in Aeschylus," *Harvard Studies in Classical Philology* 76 (1972):89–94, as well as his *Greek Tragedy,* pp. 101–21, for an examination of Aeschylus's use of the silent actor.

18. Arnott, *Ancient Greek,* p. 44. See also Kachler, "Über Wesen," and Peter Walcot, *Greek Drama in Its Theatrical and Social Context* (Cardiff, Wales, 1976) pp. 57–58.

19. See Pickard-Cambridge, *Dramatic Festivals,* pp. 177–209, as well as Iris Brooke, *Costume in Classic Greek Drama* (New York, 1962).

20. Pickard-Cambridge, *Dramatic Festivals,* pp. 126–76, as well as Taplin, *Greek Tragedy,* pp. 58–76, and F. L. Shisler, "The Use of Stage Business to Portray Emotion in Greek Tragedy," *American Journal of Philology* 66 (1945):377–97. Walcot, *Greek Drama,* pp. 64–66, relates acting style to the mode of delivery practiced by rhapsodes and orators. Zoja Pavelonskis, "The Voice of the Actor in Greek Tragedy," *Classical Weekly* 71 (1977):113–24, considers the possible effect of the same actor playing several roles.

21. Walcot, *Greek Drama,* p. 67, and Taplin, *Greek Tragedy,* pp. 58–76.

22. See the chapter on the chorus in Pickard-Cambridge, *Dramatic Festivals,* pp. 232–62. The author argues against the theory that Aeschylus's early plays contained fifty chorus members, pp. 234–35.

23. See L. B. Lawler, *The Dance in Ancient Greece* (Middletown: Wesleyan University Press, 1965), as well as Pickard-Cambridge, *Dramatic Festivals,* pp. 246–57, and Fitton, "Greek Dance."

24. It is difficult to determine how much scenery or stage business the Greek audience expected. See Taplin's introduction to *Stagecraft* for a statement of the problems and the principles he has evolved for deciding what the production consisted of. Arnott, *Conventions,* and Walcot, *Greek Drama,* also consider this problem.

25. See Arnott, *Conventions,* Taplin, *Greek Tragedy,* and David Bain's preface to his *Actors and Audience: A Study of Asides and Related Conventions in Greek Drama* (Oxford: Oxford University Press, 1977), pp. 1–17, for an analysis of these conventions and their use in specific plays.

26. See Bain's article "Audience Address in Greek Tragedy," *Classical Quarterly* 25 (1975):13–25, as well as his *Actors,* and Taplin, *Greek Tragedy,* pp. 165–66.

27. See Pickard-Cambridge, *Dramatic Festivals,* pp. 263–78, as well as Walcot's *Greek Drama* and his article "Aristophanic and Other Audiences," *Greece and Rome* 18 (1971):35–50.

28. For information on Aristotle's opinion, see D. W. Lucas, *"Poetics" of Aristotle: Introduction, Commentary and Appendices* (Oxford, 1968). Taplin, *Greek Tragedy,* pp. 167–69; and Thomas Rosenmeyer, "Gorgias, Aeschylus, and *Apatē*," *American Journal of Philology* 76 (1955):225–60, discuss the ideas of Gorgias. For an excellent presentation of the essential elements of tragedy and the audience's response, see R. B. Heilman, *Tragedy and Melodrama, Versions of Experience* (Seattle, 1968).

29. Taplin, *Greek Tragedy,* p. 168.

30. Ibid., pp. 169–70.

Chapter Two

1. See Broadhead, *"The Persae,"* pp. 1v–1x, for a discussion of possible thematic connections between the four plays. For this chapter, I have consulted the text and commentary of Broadhead; Page's *OCT*; Herbert J. Rose, *A Commentary on the Surviving Plays of Aeschylus,* 2 vols. (Amsterdam, 1958); and Anthony J. Podlecki, *"The Persians" by Aeschylus, a Translation with Commentary,* Prentice-Hall Greek Drama Series (Englewood Cliffs, N.J., 1970).

2. See Podlecki, *Persians,* as well as his *The Political Background of Aeschylean Tragedy* (Ann Arbor, 1966), chapter 2 and appendix A, for a discussion of Aeschylus's treatment of Salamis and the Persian rulers. Harry C. Avery, "Dramatic Devices in Aeschylus' *Persians,*" *American Journal of Philology* 85 (1964):173–84, analyzes the diction by which the poet makes Salamis represent the whole war.

3. Podlecki also speculates that these lines refer to Themistocles' attempts to get the Ionians to rebel against the Persians at Salamis. See his notes on these lines and line 42 as well as *Political Background,* pp. 17–21, for a discussion of the significance of the Ionian references.

4. The translation is by Seth Benardete and appears in *Modern Library Complete Greek Tragedies: Aeschylus II* (New York, n.d.).

5. See Podlecki, *Political Background,* chapter 2, for arguments and bibliography.

6. For Themistocles' career, see Podlecki, *The Life of Themistocles* (Montreal: Queen's University Press, 1975), and Robert Lenardon, *The Saga of Themistocles* (London: Thames & Hudson, 1978). Lenardon, pp. 121–25, disagrees with Podlecki's assessment of Aeschylus as a propagandist for Themistocles.

7. Taplin, *Stagecraft,* pp. 124–27.

8. Barbara H. Fowler, "Aeschylus' Imagery," *Classica et Mediaevalia* 28 (1967): 1–3.

9. See Taplin, *Stagecraft,* pp. 39–49 and appendix F, for a discussion of the evidence for the judgment of Aeschylus's use of spectacle.

10. Ibid., p. 115.

11. Ibid., pp. 115–19, and Broadhead, *"The Persae,"* p. 309.

12. Brooke, *Costume,* p. 99; Taplin, *Stagecraft*; Podlecki, *Persians;* and Avery, "Dramatic Devices," discuss the costumes and the attention paid to Xerxes' garments.

13. Taplin, *Stagecraft,* analyzes the contrast between entrances to show that Aeschylus did not use spectacle for its own sake.

14. Ibid., p. 99.

15. Ibid., pp. 121–23. Taplin discusses the possible visual presentations.

16. The scene is loosely defined first as "this ancient abode" and later as Darius's tomb. The absence of a facade demanding definition probably accounts for the vagueness of the setting. See Taplin, *Stagecraft,* pp. 103–7, and Broadhead, *"The Persae,"* xliii–xlvi.

17. For detailed analysis, see Broadhead, appendix, on meter, pp. 283–301.

18. Both F. E. Earp, *The Style of Aeschylus* (Cambridge, 1948), and W. B. Stanford, *Aeschylus in His Style: A Study in Personality* (Dublin, 1942), present excellent discussions of features of Aeschylean style and diction, using examples from *Persians* in many sections, especially to illustrate foreign words and allusions to epic. Broadhead, *"The Persae,"* discusses the use of Persian names in his appendix, pp. 318–21.

19. Earp, *Style,* p. 55.

20. Ibid., pp. 95–113, 173–75, for a good general discussion of Aeschylus's use of metaphor and image, as well as Fowler, "Aeschylus' Imagery," pp. 1–10.

21. Fowler, "Aeschylus' Imagery," pp. 6–7, discusses the images of trampling and falling. Avery, "Dramatic Devices," analyzes the way Aeschylus uses words to stress multitude and wealth (174–77).

22. Fowler, "Aeschylus' Imagery," pp. 5–6.

23. See the commentaries of Broadhead and Podlecki for the development of imagery connected with the sea.

24. Jean Dumortier, *Les Images dans la poesie d'Eschyle* (Paris, 1933), pp. 12–26, and Fowler, "Aeschylus' Imagery," pp. 1–10, analyze this image in detail. Fowler shows how it is related to the image of balance, where weight (and mass connected to trampling) is equated with misfortune, and where Zeus weighs men's fortunes on a scale that resembles a yoke.

25. Earp, *Style,* p. 173.

26. J. A. Haldane, "Musical Themes and Imagery in Aeschylus,"*Journal of Hellenic Studies* 85 (1965):35.

27. Podlecki, *Persians,* pp. 12–13, discusses the tragedy as a "family affair."

28. Richard S. Caldwell, "The Pattern of Aeschylean Tragedy," *Transactions and Proceedings of the American Philological Association* 101 (1970):78–83.

29. See George Devereux, *Dreams in Greek Tragedy: An Ethnopsychoanalytic Study* (Berkeley, 1976), pp. 1–20, for a detailed analysis of the dream.

30. Philip Slater, *The Glory of Hera: Greek Mythology and the Greek Family* (Boston: Beacon Press, 1968), examines the frustrations of women in Greek society and their effects on Greek sons, in life and myth. Caldwell and Devereux both cite Slater in their works.

31. Aristotle, *Poetics,* 1453 a.

Chapter Three

1. Christopher M. Dawson, *"The Seven Against Thebes" by Aeschylus: A Translation with Commentary,* Prentice-Hall Greek Drama Series (Englewood Cliffs, N.J., 1970), p. 1, n. 1. Dawson suggests that this play was titled *Eteocles* after its hero, in the manner of the first two plays. In addition to Dawson, I have consulted the *OCT* edited by Page; H. J. Rose's *Commentary*; and T. G. Tucker, *"The Seven Against Thebes" of Aeschylus* (Cambridge, 1908).

2. For a convenient summary of the sources, with bibliography and interpretations, see H. D. Cameron, *Studies on the "Seven Against Thebes" of Aeschylus* (The Hague: Mouton, 1971), pp. 17–29. Antonietta Gostoli provides bibliography and a discussion of the newly discovered Stesichorus fragment P. Lille 76abc in "Some Aspects of the Theban Myth in the Lille Stesichorus," *Greek Roman and Byzantine Studies* 19 (1978):23–27.

3. For conjectures on Laius's and Oedipus's parts in the curse, see William G. Thalmann, *Dramatic Art in Aeschylus' "Seven Against Thebes"*

(New Haven: Yale University Press, 1978), pp. 8–23, and R. P. Winnington-Ingram, *"Septem Contra Thebas," Yale Classical Studies* 25 (1977):29–38.

4. Questions about the words and interpretation of the curse are discussed in A. P. Burnett, "Curse and Dream in Aeschylus' *Septem," Greece and Rome* 14 (1973):353–62.

5. See Thalmann, *Dramatic Art,* pp. 19–20, for a statement and bibliography about the problem.

6. The evidence for assuming this procedure is presented by Thalmann, *Dramatic Art,* pp. 63–69. He, Burnett, "Curse," and Cameron (*Studies,* 22–29) emphasize the importance of the imagery and action of allotment to the understanding of the play. Gostoli, "Some Aspects," analyzes the Stesichorus passage.

7. Taplin, *Stagecraft,* pp. 141–42.

8. Thomas Rosenmeyer, *"Seven Against Thebes*: The Tragedy of War," in *The Masks of Tragedy: Essays on Six Greek Dramas* (New York, 1971), pp. 9–47, discusses the dramatization of the physical and emotional aspects of war. Taplin, *Stagecraft,* pp. 152–56, stresses the military action implicit in the verbal confrontation.

9. There is a good deal of discussion about what weapons Eteocles puts on and when. Taplin, *Stagecraft,* pp. 158–61, argues against any action, but editors like Dawson and Rose assume that when he calls for his greaves (1. 676), attendants bring on his armor, and then he dresses for battle like an epic hero, as he argues with the chorus, visually exhibiting his determination. Helen Bacon, "The Shield of Eteocles," *Arion* 3 (1964):27–38, suggests an order for arming and conjectures that his shield emblem was the Curse. In any case, Eteocles' own words emphasize the spear, the weapon which the chorus later focuses on as the symbol for the fratricide and allotment (cf. 11. 730, 788, 816, 839, 885, 943–44, 962, 992).

10. For a summary of the arguments presented on both sides, see H. Lloyd-Jones, "The End of the *Seven Against Thebes," Classical Quarterly,* n.s. 9 (1959):80–115, and R. D. Dawe, "The End of the *Seven Against Thebes," Classical Quarterly,* n.s. 17 (1967):16–28. Taplin, *Stagecraft,* pp. 169–91, believes verses 861–74 and 1005 to the end are not Aeschylean, but analyzes the entire text for signs of production.

11. Podlecki, *Political Background,* pp. 29–30. Although Podlecki argues against theories which find propaganda for Cimon's campaign to build the Long Walls of Athens, Barbara Fowler, "The Imagery of *Seven Against Thebes," Symbolae Osloenses* 45 (1970):29, suggests that the ship of state imagery supports the idea.

12. See G. M. Kirkwood, "Eteocles Oiakostrophos," *Phoenix* 23 (1969):9–11, and Dawson, *Seven Against,* pp. 3–4, n. 9, for a summary of the criticism and bibliography. Major arguments inevitably concern Eteocles' freedom to act independently of the curse. Two important discussions of the problem are Friedrich Solmsen, "The Erinyes in Aischylos' *Septem,*" *Transactions and Proceedings of the American Philological Association* 68 (1937):197–211; and R. D. Dawe, "Inconsistency of Plot and Character in Aeschylus," *Proceedings of the Cambridge Philological Association* 189 (1963):31–42. Solmsen, p. 206, denies that the death of Eteocles affects the fate of Thebes. He is followed by other scholars, such as Cameron (*Studies,* 44–46), who analyzes themes and images that connect the two parts of the play, but concludes that "the split in the play is so definite and so violent that it tends to destroy its unity" (p. 96).

13. Burnett, "Curses," demonstrates the working out of both these patterns in the play. What Eteocles recognizes and how much choice he has are the subject of much debate among scholars. See Solmsen, "Erinyes"; E. Wolff, "Die Entschiedigung des Eteokles in den *Sieben gegen Theben,*" *Harvard Studies in Classical Philology* 63 (1958):89–95; and H. Patzer, "Die dramatischer Handlung der *Seben gegen Theben,*" *Harvard Studies in Classical Philogy* 63 (1958):97–119, for arguments which emphasize the power of the curse, and Thalmann, *Dramatic Art,* pp. 123–35 with notes and appendix 3, for a summary of both sides and additional bibliography. My own analysis is closer to that of Burnett, Dawson, Kirkwood, and Kurt von Fritz, "Die Gestalt des Eteokles in Aischylos' *Sieben gegen Theben,*" in his *Antike und Moderne Tragödie* (Berlin, 1962), pp. 193–226. Points of the debate will be presented where relevant throughout the chapter.

14. See Thalmann, *Dramatic Art,* pp. 26–29 and chapters 4 and 5, for an analysis of the balanced structure.

15. See Rosenmeyer, *Masks,* for a discussion of the dramatization of war as a dehumanizing activity.

16. Thalmann, *Dramatic Art,* pp. 105–35, and Seth Benardete, "Two Notes on Aeschylus' *Septem*: II. Eteocles' Interpretation of the Shields," *Wiener Studien,* n.f. 2 (1968):6–17, analyze this scene in detail. Dawson, *Seven Against,* points out the foreshadowing.

17. Benardete, "Two Notes," makes this point in his analysis.

18. The gods were probably represented visually by cult images on the edges of the orchestra. The chorus must have moved from one to the other as it prayed to each divinity, in their parodos and first stasimon. But the importance of the gods increases as the play progresses. There is some speculation that the trilogy contained a divine conflict which paralleled the

human story. Solmsen, "Erinyes," suggests, on the analogy of the *Oresteia*, that the first two plays may have included a clash between the primitive curse, represented by the Erinyes, and the newer gods of the city. Here the curse wins the death of the innocent inheritor, whereas, in the *Oresteia*, Orestes is set free. In addition, Benardete, "Two Notes," discusses the ambiguity and multiple facets of Ares on pp. 23–29.

19. In chapters 1 and 2 of *Dramatic Art*, Thalmann presents a detailed analysis of all major patterns, providing bibliography, summaries, and points of difference with his predecessors. Cameron, *Studies*, traces the ship and water imagery, and the horse to spear transformation (where he shows how the horses representing Argos are associated by nautical imagery with the enemy within and thus with the curse) as well as the imagery surrounding fertility. Dumortier, *Les Images*, pp. 27–55, analyzes the ship of state as the major image of the play. Fowler, "Imagery of Seven," studies the way the ship metaphor relates current political problems in Athens to the myth of a Thebes endangered by its cursed ruling family. Dawson's commentary in *Seven Against* explicates the metaphors implicit in the Greek he has translated. I have found it necessary to limit my discussion to the most important patterns and to refer only to passages which illustrate developments in the patterns.

20. See Burnett, "Curse," Cameron, *Studies*, and Thalmann, *Dramatic Art* for slightly different interpretations of the way the image operates.

21. Thalmann, *Dramatic Art*, pp. 131, 69–79.

22. Scholars debate the issue on linguistic, stylistic, and religious grounds. Wolff believes that Eteocles has made all his selections ahead of time, whereas Taplin and Kirkwood argue that he is making them on the spot in the shield scene. Albin Lesky, "Eteocles in den *Sieben gegen Theben*," *Wiener Studien* 74 (1961):5–17, believes he has done half before and is completing the rest, with the effect that both destiny and the hero's choice seem to bring about the catastrophe. Although Thalmann conjectures that Eteocles may himself have assigned the gates by lot while off-stage, he (as well as Burnett and Winnington-Ingram) prefers to stress his skill and recognition rather than his limited choice.

23. Several critics consider the confusion between internal and external in relation to the city and the family as a major theme of the play. See Thalmann, *Dramatic Art*, pp. 38–42, for discussion and bibliography, as well as Bacon, "Shield," pp. 27–38.

24. Some scholars do find a fault in him, however. See Leon Golden, *In Praise of Prometheus: Humanism and Rationalism in Aeschylean Thought* (Chapel Hill, 1962), pp. 42–67, for the opinion that Eteocles is an irreligious and

expedient power-seeker who uses the curse as a rationalization for doing what he wants to do. Or Cameron, *Studies,* pp. 34–35, for the judgment that, driven by Atē and concern for the city, Eteocles made a fatal error when he left his post as helmsman to become one of the warriors.

25. Some critics have suggested that the six champions are silent actors, present in the orchestra, and fully armed, to be dispatched one by one as the speeches progress. Such a spectacle would focus on the narrowing of Eteocles' options, but would weaken the illusion of the leader's singularity or ultimate isolation as the doomed son of Oedipus. See Taplin, *Stagecraft,* pp. 149–52, for discussion.

26. For a full psychoanalytic interpretation of this play and myth, see Richard Caldwell, "The Misogyny of Eteocles," *Arethusa* 6 (1973):197–231.

27. See Michael Gagarin, *Aeschylean Drama* (Berkeley, 1976), pp. 121–26, for a discussion of this point.

28. Some editors think that a Greek particle *ge,* translated as "at least," reveals Eteocles' fear that the curse might demand his own death in the battle for the city, in his prayer, "Do not blot out my city (at least) root and branch" (1. 71). See Dawson's commentary as well as Winnington-Ingram, *"Septem,"* pp. 13, 15–16, where he points out how Aeschylus calls attention to the theme of silence.

29. See H. D. Cameron, "The Power of Words in the *Seven Against Thebes," Transactions and Proceedings of the American Philological Association* 101 (1970):95–118, for a full analysis of Eteocles' manipulation of words.

30. Ibid., p. 106.

31. A full discussion of the phenomenon of double motivation appears in Albin Lesky, "Göttliche und menschliche Motivation in homerischen Epos," *Sitzungberichte der Heidelberg Akademie* 4 (1961). See also P. E. Easterling, "Presentation of Character in Aeschylus," *Greece and Rome* 20 (1973):3–19; Gagarin, *Aeschylean Drama,* pp. 17–20; N. L. G. Hammond, "Personal Freedom and Its Limitations in the *Oresteia," Journal of Hellenic Studies* 85 (1965):42–55; Albin Lesky, "Decision and Responsibility in the Tragedy of Aeschylus," *Journal of Hellenic Studies* 86 (1966):78–85; and R. P. Winnington-Ingram, "Tragedy and Greek Archaic Thought," in *Classical Drama and Its Influence: Essays Presented to H. D. F. Kitto,* ed. M. J. Anderson (London, 1965), pp. 29–50.

32. Winnington-Ingram, "Tragedy and Greek Archaic Thought," p. 50.

33. Burnett, "Curse," p. 365.

34. See Winnington-Ingram, *"Septem,"* p. 43, for this suggestion. Podlecki, *Political Background,* pp. 31–34, refutes theories that the poet was actually alluding to Pericles in his characterization of Eteocles.

35. Thalia Howe, in a paper, "Suicide and Self-slaying in the *Septem,"* summarized in the *Annual Bulletin of the Classical Association of New England* 57 (1962):11, discusses the importance of the blood connection between tribe and state, even in the fifth century, and suggests that the myth dramatizes how "civil war meant more than political discord; it was literally suicide." Gagarin, *Aeschylean Drama,* pp. 126–27, relates the conflict of the trilogy to the situation in Athens in 467, when the military domination of the civilian government by Cimon and his faction was an issue.

Chapter Four

1. In addition to Page's *OCT* text and Rose's *Commentary,* I have consulted the following editions: T. G. Tucker, *"The Supplices" of Aeschylus: A Revised Text with Introduction, Critical Notes, Commentary, and Translation* (London: Macmillan, 1889) and H. Friis Johansen, *Aeschylus "The Suppliants" I: The Text with Introduction, Critical Apparatus, and Translation* (Copenhagen, 1970). I have also referred to the translation with notes by Janet Lembke, *Aeschylus' "Suppliants"* (New York and London, 1975). In his introduction Johansen conjectures that the bold language and involved thought of *Suppliants* may account for the extraordinary number of errors and lacunae in the text; its original difficulty probably caused several errors in transcription which finally led to scribes "giving up the attempt at reproducing the worst passages" (p. 24) and simply leaving blanks.

2. For the text and discussion of the papyrus, see A. F. Garvie, *Aeschylus' "Supplices": Play and Trilogy* (Cambridge: Cambridge University Press, 1969), pp. 1–28. The fragment reports that Aeschylus defeated Sophocles with four plays, the last two of which were *Danaids* and *Amymone.* Since Sophocles did not enter the tragic contests before 468, the tetralogy of which *Suppliants* is a part must have been produced after that date and probably after 467, the year of Aeschylus's victory with the Theban trilogy. The exact date is a subject of much debate because the fragment does not give the full names of the archons by whose term of office the years are identified. Several scholars accept 463 as the most likely year, based on a restoration of the archon's name and the relationship between Athens and Argos in the early 460s.

3. Garvie examines the style, structure, and background of the *Suppliants* and summarizes the scholarship, old and new, in an attempt to reassess its place in the Aeschylean canon in the light of the new date.

4. Richmond Lattimore, *Story Patterns in Greek Tragedy* (Ann Arbor, 1965), p. 46, considers the *Suppliants* a "choice play."

5. Garvie, *Aeschylus' "Supplices,"* p. 164. See Chapter 5, "The Trilogy," pp. 163–233, for a full discussion of the evidence and the various theories.

6. Von Fritz, *Antike,* p. 166. See the entire chapter, pp. 160–91, for an analysis of the trilogy.

7. The fragment is quoted and analyzed by Garvie, *Aeschylus' "Supplices,"* pp. 204–6. The translation is by H. W. Smyth, *Aeschylus II,* Loeb Classical Library (Cambridge, Mass., 1963), pp. 395–96.

8. David Grene, tr., *The Complete Greek Tragedies: Aeschylus I* (New York, n.d.), pp. 235–36.

9. Robert P. Murray, *The Motif of Io in Aeschylus' "Suppliants"* (Princeton: Princeton University Press, 1958).

10. See Garvie's chapter in *Aeschylus' "Supplices"* on the trilogy. Von Fritz, *Antike,* also discusses the problems, pp. 169–79.

11. According to Von Fritz (*Antike,* p. 191), the satyr play *Amymone* parallels the movement of the trilogy as a whole. Like her sisters, Amymone (one of the Danaids) flees the violent advances of a suitor—this time a satyr, as required by the genre. Just as she is about to be raped, the god Poseidon rescues her. Unlike her other sisters, however, Amymone gives herself to her protector and thus imitates the positive example of Hypermestra, heroine of the third play.

12. Taplin, *Stagecraft,* pp. 193–239, analyzes the way in which the pattern affects the sequence and presentation of the entrances and exits.

13. Arnott, *Conventions,* p. 66.

14. Taplin, *Stagecraft,* calls such parallel scenes "mirror scenes."

15. Ibid., pp. 218–21.

16. Ibid., p. 239.

17. See H. Bacon, *Barbarians in Greek Tragedy* (New Haven: Yale University Press, 1961), pp. 15–63, for a discussion of Aeschylus's treatment of foreigners.

18. There is much debate about the presence of the extra choruses and the number of Danaids in the main group. For a summary of the questions and the conclusion that the Danaid chorus itself numbered only twelve, see H. Lloyd-Jones, "*The Supplices* of Aeschylus: New Date and Old Problems," *L'Antiquité Classique* 33 (1964):365–69, as well as Taplin's chapter in *Stagecraft,* especially pp. 202–3, 230–38.

19. See A. M. Dale, "The Chorus in the Action of Greek Tragedy," in *Classical Drama and its Influence: Essays Presented to H. D. F. Kitto,* ed. M. Anderson (London, 1965), pp. 17–27, for a discussion of the effects of the chorus's presence on the progress of the spoken action.

20. The passage between the herald and the Danaids (11. 825–902) is corrupt, but the rhythms appear to be lyric. Johansen prints the section as if a chorus of the herald's attendants sang them. See Taplin, *Stagecraft,* pp. 216–17, for the argument against a male chorus here.

21. Fowler, "Aeschylus' Imagery," p. 12. She analyzes the interpenetration of these themes in the imagery of the hunt and animality, as well as growth and fertility to show the legal, sociological, and religious implications in the language.

22. Dumortier, *Les Images,* traces these images as the major pattern in the play, (pp. 1–11).

23. The imagery of fertility and the Danaids' associations with water, discussed by Fowler, are particularly important in the saga. See H. P. Jacques, *Mythologie et Psychoanalyse: Le Châtiment de Danaides* (Ottowa: Lemeac, 1969), for a psychoanalytic interpretation.

24. Murray, *Motif,* studies the allusions to the legend of Io in detail and uses the ambiguities in the references to show how all but Hypermestra err in denying sexuality and marriage.

25. See Garvie, *Aeschylus' "Supplices",* p. 218, for an explanation of the problems. Interpretations depend on whether the word *autogenē* refers to the women themselves, as in "by our own act," or to the family—perhaps suggesting incest.

26. Ibid., pp. 219–20, and George Thomson, *Aeschylus and Athens* (New York, 1968), p. 291.

27. See Grace H. Macurdy, "Has the Danaid Trilogy a Social Problem?" *Classical Philology* 39 (1944):99–100, for a discussion of the relation of the play to Athenian practice.

28. Thomson, *Aeschylus,* pp. 285–95, has suggested that the play dramatizes the society's transition from exogamy to endogamy. Although the women prefer to marry according to their own choice and outside the clan (exogamy), for the good of the family and the state, they must submit to marriages within the clan to consolidate the family's property (endogamy). He conjectures that the women are compensated in the end for their lost freedom by the establishment of the Thesmophoria, their own private festival. See Macurdy, "Has the Danaid," for a refutation of this view.

29. Macurdy, "Has the Danaid," p. 99.

30. The text of the beginning of the passage (11. 291–335) is corrupt and

does not identify the speaker. Thus there is some dispute about who asks and who answers the first questions. Miss Lembke, *Aeschylus' Suppliants,* p. 86, follows Smyth's Loeb edition because she believes that his making the Danaids the interrogators reveals "their desperate cunning" and puts Pelasgus on the defensive immediately.

31. See H. P. Jacques, *Mythologie,* for a full analysis of the psychology in relation to the myth.

32. Sigmund Freud, *On Creativity and the Unconscious,* ed. Benjamin Nelson (New York: Harper and Row, 1958), pp. 198–205.

33. Ibid., pp. 202–4.

34. Devereux, *Dreams,* pp. 321–41.

35. Peter Burian, "Pelasgos and Politics in Aeschylus' Danaid Trilogy," *Wiener Studien* 87 (1974):5–14, discusses the dramatic use of Pelasgus in the episode. Bruno Snell thinks the consciousness that man is free and able to make decisions by himself was the main impetus for the development of tragedy. In *Discovery of the Mind: The Origin of European Thought* tr. T. G. Rosenmeyer (New York: Harper Brothers, 1960), pp. 99–112, Snell uses several plays by Aeschylus to make his point that the moment of choice itself is a central element of the tragic plot.

36. See Garvie's chapter on background in *Aeschylus' "Supplices,"* pp. 141–62, for an analysis of the evidence and the theories.

37. Podlecki, *Political Background,* pp. 82–83.

38. Garvie, *Aeschylus' "Supplices,"* pp. 144–56.

39. Lloyd-Jones, "Supplices," pp. 357–58, argues that Pelasgus is not so different from the kings of the *Iliad* who also consult their subjects and fear the power of their assemblies and war counsels. Although Lloyd-Jones is right, Pelasgus is much more than a conventional epic king.

40. J. T. Sheppard, "The First Scene of the *Suppliants* of Aeschylus," *Classical Quarterly* 5 (1911):228.

41. Garvie denies the connection, however (*Aeschylus' "Supplices,"* p. 156). He points out that the drama concerns the family of Egyptus, not Egypt, that Athens actually helped Egypt when it revolted against Persia in 462, and that the second play might have presented the sons of Egyptus in a favorable way.

42. For a list of terms, see H. G. Robertson, "*Dikē* and *Hubris* in Aeschylus' *Suppliants,*" *Classical Review* 50 (1936):104–9.

43. Taplin, *Stagecraft,* pp. 218–20.

44. Robertson, "*Dikē,*" p. 104. The speech imitates the actual Athenian decree which defines *metoikia,* the conditions on which foreigners became residents protected by the polis.

45. R. P. Winnington-Ingram, "The Danaid Trilogy of Aeschylus," *Journal of Hellenic Studies* 81 (1961):148–49, suggests that the sovereignty of the demos becomes a more important issue in the second play and that the people may have refused to condemn Hypermestra.

46. Robertson, "*Dikē*," p. 104. Scholars have different opinions about the sophistication of Aeschylus's religion and his conception of justice or Dikē. See H. Lloyd-Jones, *The Justice of Zeus* (Berkeley: University of California Press, 1971); E. A. Havelock, *The Greek Concept of Justice from Its Shadow in Homer to Its Substance in Plato* (Cambridge, Mass.: Harvard University Press, 1978); and Gagarin, *Aeschylean Drama,* pp. 57–86.

47. Peter M. Smith, *On the Hymn to Zeus in Aeschylus' "Agamemnon"* (Chico, Calif., 1980) pp. 36–37.

48. Sheppard, "The First Scene," pp. 223–27, analyzes this aspect of their prayer as the ritual means of persuading the gods to act in the desired way.

49. Murray, *Motif,* discusses this meaning of the analogy to Io, especially on pp. 57–77.

50. The story may provide a divine validation of the male maturation process. Their first sexual attempts are aggressive acts to satisfy their own pleasure, but in time they develop consideration for their partners and a desire for propagation. See the chapter below on *Prometheus Bound* for an analysis of the Io story from this perspective.

Chapter Five

1. The text is not free of corruption, however. For this chapter, in addition to Page's *OCT* and Rose's *Commentary,* I have used Edward Fraenkel, *"Agamemnon" wih Text, Translation and Commentary in Three Volumes* (Oxford, 1950); J. D. Denniston and Denys Page, *Aeschylus: "Agamemnon"* (Oxford, 1957); and the translations with commentary by Hugh Lloyd-Jones, *Agamemnon, Libation Bearers,* and *Eumenides,* Prentice-Hall Greek Drama Series (Englewood Cliffs, N.J., 1970).

2. Scholars make many different judgments about the sophistication of Aeschylus's religion and his comprehension of the idea of justice. For the opinion that his thought is primitive or close to Hesiod's, see Lloyd-Jones, *Agamemnon,* pp. 7–8, or Page, *Agamemnon,* pp. xv–xvi. For the contrary view see E. R. Dodds, *The Greeks and the Irrational* (Berkeley: University of California Press, 1959), p. 40, and "Morals and Politics in the *Oresteia,*" in his *The Ancient Concept of Progress and Other Essays* (Oxford, 1973), pp. 54–62. He analyzes the problems, provides bibliography, and defends his

opinion that Aeschylus is reinterpreting cruder myths for a more sophisticated age. See also H. Lloyd-Jones, *Justice*; E. A. Havelock, *The Greek
Concept*; and Gagarin, *Aeschylean Drama*, pp. 57–86.

3. For a different opinion of Apollo's place, see Thomson, *Aeschylus*, pp.
259–61, and R. P. Winnington-Ingram, "The Role of Apollo in the
Oresteia," *Classical Review* 47 (1933):97–104. On the relation of purification
to the laws on homicide, see D. M. MacDowell, *Athenian Homicide Law in the
Age of the Orators* (Manchester: University of Manchester Press, 1963), pp.
4–5, 141–50.

4. The family remained important, however, even in the legal prosecution for homicide, as MacDowell points out (*Athenian Homicide*, pp. 8–30).
For a study of this evolution, see Richard Kuhns, *The House, the City, and the
Judge: The Growth of Moral Awareness in the "Oresteia"* (Indianapolis: Bobbs-
Merrill, 1962). George Thomson also traces the development from tribe to
state and its influence on the form and ideas of drama, and on the *Oresteia* in
particular (*Aeschylus*, pp. 229–78).

5. The debate about Aeschylus's position on the reforms is summarized
by Podlecki, *Political Background*, pp. 81–92.

6. Dodds, "Morals and Politics," is a forceful spokesman for this view.

7. I have used the translation of Richmond Lattimore which appears in
The Complete Greek Tragedies: Aeschylus I (New York, n.d.).

8. See the commentaries of Fraenkel and Lloyd-Jones for analyses of the
lyrics.

9. See J. Peradotto, "The Omen of the Eagles and the Ethos of
Agamemnon," *Phoenix* 23 (1969):237–63; and Peter Smith, *On the Hymn.*

10. D. Leahy, "The Representation of the Trojan War in Aeschylus'
Agamemnon," *American Journal of Philology* 95 (1978):1–23, discusses the
allusions to contemporary warfare and their effect.

11. B. W. Knox, "The Lion in the House," *Classical Philology* 47
(1952):17–25, analyzes the parable.

12. See Taplin, *Stagecraft*, pp. 302–10, for a description of the action.

13. Ibid., pp. 310–16, discusses the manifold significance of the act. See
also R. Goheen, "Aspects of Dramatic Symbolism: Three Studies in the
Oresteia," *American Journal of Philology* 72 (1955):113–37, and Ann Lebeck,
"The Oresteia": A Study in Language and Structure (Cambridge, Mass.: Harvard
University Press, 1971), pp. 74–79.

14. See Taplin, "Silences," pp. 77–78, for a discussion of this device.

15. Although Page, *Agamemnon*, pp. xxiii–xxix, emphasizes divine compulsion, others analyze the double motivation implicit in the account of his
decision. See Albin Lesky, "Decision and Responsibility in the Tragedy of

Aeschylus," *Journal of Hellenic Studies* 86 (1966):78–85, for a definition of double motivation; and Mark Edwards, "Agamemnon's Decision: Freedom and Folly in Aeschylus," *California Studies in Classical Antiquity* 10 (1977):17–38, for a discussion of the bibliography and analysis of the passage.

16. See note 13. Fraenkel and Lloyd-Jones, however, agree that he behaves as his position and circumstances demand.

17. For a discussion of the position of women in fifth-century Greece, see Sarah B. Pomeroy, *Goddesses, Whores, Wives, and Slaves: Women in Classical Antiquity* (New York: Shocken Books, 1975), and Gagarin, *Aeschylean Drama*, pp. 89–91.

18. For the view that Menelaus in this play and Electra in the next represent the type of passive behavior necessary to cooperation rather than conflict, see Theodore Tarkow, "Electra's Role in the Opening Scene of the *Choephoroi*," *Eranos* 77 (1979):11–21.

19. For an anthropological analysis of the changing position of women reflected in the *Oresteia*, see Thomson, *Aeschylus,* especially the chapters "Exogamy" and "Property," pp. 21–51.

20. Gagarin, *Aeschylean Drama*, pp. 87–118, has an excellent discussion of sex conflict and the opposition between male and female values.

21. Ibid., pp. 91–92, analyzes the elements of the conflict.

22. The formula, "if this name is pleasing," is supposed to insure that the worshiper is using the correct address in order to attract the god's attention. But the Zeus who sits above the contention, limiting all to their proper portions and tasks, is a metaphorical complement to Plato's definition of Justice in the *Republic.*

23. For excellent discussions of this device, see Goheen, "Aspects," who concentrates on the tapestry scene, and Lebeck, *"The Oresteia,"* who traces all the major image patterns and their conversion to action in the course of the trilogy. Fowler, "Aeschylus' Imagery," pp. 23–73, shows the relation of all of the most important patterns to the central man-woman conflict. John Peradotto analyzes image in relation to action and theme in "Some Patterns of Nature Imagery in the *Oresteia*," *American Journal of Philology* 85 (1964):378–93, and "The Omen." I have discussed the four most significant images, but many other patterns (disease/cure, teaching/learning, the personification of Persuasion [*Peitho*], storm, alternating types of music, marriage, and generation) may also be traced through the trilogy.

24. See P. Vidal-Naquet, "Chasse et sacrifice dans l'*Orestie* d'Eschyle," in *Mythe et Tragédie en grèce ancienne,* ed. J. P. Vernant and P. Vidal-Naquet (Paris: Maspero, 1973). pp. 133–58, for the way the combination of hunt

and sacrifice images conveys the confusion between civilized and savage behavior in the trilogy.

25. Dumortier, *Les Images*, pp. 71–87, discusses the beast caught in the trap as the major image of *Agamemnon*, the embrace of the serpent as the major pattern of the *Libation Bearers* (pp. 88–100), and the pack losing its prey as the most important in *Eumenides* (pp. 101–11).

26. For a detailed analysis, see F. I. Zeitlen, "The Motif of the Corrupted Sacrifice in Aeschylus' *Oresteia*," *Transactions and Proceedings of the American Philological Association* 96 (1965):464–508, and "Postscript to the Sacrificial Imagery in the *Oresteia* (Ag. 1235–37)," *Transactions and Proceedings of the American Philological Association* 97 (1966):645–53, as well as Lebeck's book, *"The Oresteia,"* and Vidal-Naquet, "Chasse."

27. Goheen, "Aspects," concentrates on this spectacle and its relation to the imagery of the trilogy as a whole.

28. See Gagarin, *Aeschylean Drama*, pp. 67–86, for the pattern in all three plays as well as H. G. Robertson, "Legal Expressions and Ideas of Justice in Aeschylus," *Classical Philology* 34 (1939):209–19, for a list of technical terms and their usage in the context.

29. Peradotto, "Patterns," connects light and dark imagery to patterns of generous and hostile nature, as well as tracing the development from gloom to brilliance.

30. Lebeck, *"The Oresteia,"* has an excellent discussion of the many ways in which images, actions, and themes converge in the kommos.

31. See A. F. Garvie's discussion of the way the poet creates surprise and suspense in "Aeschylus' Simple Plots," in *Dionysiaca: Nine Studies in Greek Poetry*, ed. Dawe, Diggle, Easterling (Cambridge: Cambridge University Library, 1978), pp. 76–80.

32. G. Meautis, *Eschyle et la Trilogie* (Paris, 1936), pp. 122–28, 228, notes that the first parts of each play explicate the interior motivations of the actions that follow.

33. Ibid. Meautis emphasizes that the scene itself, the palace, attracts attention to the House as a character, and that the change from palace to tomb to palace, and then from Argos to Delphi to Athens underlines the progress from family to cult to state in the trilogy as a whole. The use of the facade of the scene building as a definite background (palace or temple), with its door used for entraces and exits and its roof as another playing area (watchman's prologue in *Agamemnon*), marks a new development in stagecraft. See Introduction above.

34. Devereux, *Dreams*, pp. 183–214.

35. See Gilbert Murray, "Hamlet and Orestes," in *The Classical Tradition in Poetry* (Cambridge, Mass.: Harvard University Press, 1927).

36. Caldwell, "Pattern," pp. 89–90.

37. See Taplin, *Stagecraft*, pp. 362–76, for a discussion of the staging and importance of the prologue. Meautis, *Eschyle*, pp. 248–63, emphasizes the move from the human to the divine plane, or from "effects to causes" (p. 263).

38. See Havelock, *Justice*, pp. 272–95, for an analysis of the development of procedures from play to play in the trilogy.

39. Taplin, *Stagecraft*, pp. 392–401, discusses the textual problems. See MacDowell, *Athenian Homicide*, pp. 90–110, for a description of the procedures for homicide trials. There is some debate about the number of jurors and whether Athena makes or breaks the tie. See Gagarin, *Aeschylean Drama*, p. 77, as well as his article "The Vote of Athena," *American Journal of Philology* 96 (1975): 121–27. See MacDowell, *Athenian Homicide*, p. 110, for the relation of the equal vote to the *Semnai* (Furies turned Eumenides), and Meautis, *Eschyle*, pp. 276–78, for mercy as a new principle.

40. For a discussion of the philosophical ideas about generation, consult A. Peretti, "La Teoria della generazione patrilinea in Eschilo," *Parola del Passato* 11 (1956): 241–262. See also Aristotle, *The Generation of Animals*, book 4, chapter 1, for a statement of the theory that male semen carries the seeds of intellect.

41. For further information, see MacDowell, *Athenian Homicide*, pp. 70–80, 110–29.

42. For the family's rights and responsibilities, see MacDowell, *Athenian Homicide*, pp. 8–32, 94–96, 107, 123–25, 133–34, 144. The family could be prosecuted for not prosecuting a murderer, and were permitted to watch the execution of a condemned killer, but not allowed to perform the execution themselves.

43. See Winnington-Ingram, "Clytemnestra and the Vote of Athena," *Journal of Hellenic Studies* 68 (1948): 130–47, for the opinion that Athena is actually the divine counterpart of Clytemnestra and that Aeschylus created sympathy for all women by exploring Clytemnestra's social problem.

44. See Lebeck, *"The Oresteia,"* for an analysis of the way in which the concept of *pathei mathos* is developed in image and action through the many episodes of question and answer and the repetition of verbs of learning and teaching. The meaning of the maxim is a subject of debate. Many critics argue that it simply implies that fools learn by painful experience what they should have already known, without the idea that suffering leads to moral improvement for sinners or others. My own view is expressed by Dodds, "Morals and Politics." See Gagarin, *Aeschylean Drama*, "Appendix A: *Pathei Mathos*," pp. 139–50, and Smith, *On the Hymn*, pp. 21–26, for a discussion and bibliography of opposing opinions.

45. For the interpretation of the cosmogony as a refinement of the cosmos, and Zeus's part in the progress, see Norman O. Brown, *Hesiod's "Theogony"* (Indianapolis: Bobbs-Merrill, 1953), pp. 7–49.

46. Dodds, "Morals and Politics," pp. 61–63.

Chapter Six

1. For general studies of the Prometheus myth, see C. Kerenyi, *Prometheus: Archetypal Image of Human Existence,* tr. R. Manheim (New York: Pantheon, 1963); Louis Séchan, *Le Mythe de Prométhée* (Paris: Presses Universitaires des France, 1951); and H. Trousson, *Le Thème de Prométhée dans la Litterature européene* (Geneva: Libraire Droz, 1964).

2. The most forceful spokesmen for this opinion are Mark Griffith, *The Authenticity of "Prometheus Bound"* (Cambridge: Cambridge University Press, 1977), and Oliver Taplin, *Stagecraft,* pp. 460–69, and "Notes on the Title of *Prometheus Desmotes,*" *Journal of Hellenic Studies* 95 (1975): 184–86.

3. The device of the silent actor has appeared before in *Agamemnon* and *Libation Bearers.* See Taplin, "Silences," pp. 78–79, for a discussion of its use in this play. When *Prometheus Bound* was dated as an early play, some scholars postulated that a large dummy represented the hero and that an actor, who had appeared in the prologue, later spoke Prometheus's lines from behind the skene entrance. Now that the play is dated later than the introduction of the third actor, most scholars have rejected the dummy theory. See Taplin, *Stagecraft,* pp. 243–45, for a discussion of the theory.

4. As George Thomson notes in his commentary to the prologue, in *Aeschylus: "The Prometheus Bound" edited with Introduction, Commentary, and Translation* (Cambridge, 1932). For this chapter, I have also consulted Page's *OCT*; Rose's *Commentary*; the translation with commentary by C. J. Herington and James Scully, *Aeschylus: "Prometheus Bound"* (New York: Oxford University Press, 1975); and E. A. Havelock, *Prometheus with a Translation of "Prometheus Bound"* (Seattle, 1968), originally published in 1951 by Beacon Press as *The Crucifixion of Intellectual Man.* I have quoted the translation of David Grene which appears in *Modern Library Complete Greek Tragedies: Aeschylus I* (New York, n.d.).

5. See H. G. Mullins, "Date and Stage Arrangments of the *Prometheia,*" *Greece and Rome* 8 (1939): 160–70; M. L. West, "The Prometheus Trilogy," *Journal of Hellenic Studies* 99 (1979): 130–48; and Taplin, *Stagecraft,* for this view.

6. M. Griffith, "Aeschylus, Sicily, and Prometheus," in *Dionysiaca: Nine Studies in Greek Poetry,* ed. Dawe, Diggle, Easterling (Cambridge: Cambridge University Press, 1978), pp. 120–21.

7. Griffith, *Authenticity,* pp. 19–102, analyzes the meters of lyric, recitative, and dialogue for such technical elements as resolution, responsion, caesura, enjambment, etc., comparing *Prometheus Bound* to the rest of Aeschylus, as well as to Sophocles and Euripides. Herington, *The Author of "Prometheus Bound"* (Austin: University of Texas Press, 1970), summarizes similar data.

8. Griffith, *Authenticity,* pp. 191–93.

9. Ibid., pp. 207–24, analyzes the evidence. Rosenmeyer, *"Apatē,"* however, suggests Aeschylus may have met Gorgias in Sicily and learned his ideas there.

10. E. A. Havelock, *The Liberal Temper in Greek Politics* (New Haven: Yale University Press, 1957), pp. 52–65, 105–7, and Dodds, "Ancient Concept of Progress," pp. 4–7, discuss Aeschylus's relation to the early scientists and anthropologists.

11. Taplin discusses all the questions and the various answers in his chapter in *Stagecraft,* pp. 240–75. See also Arnott, *Conventions,* pp. 76–78; Mullins, "Date,"; Thomson, *"The Prometheus Bound,"*; and West, "The Prometheus Trilogy." The staging of the exodus also presents a problem: the text indicates that Prometheus and the chorus disappear into Hades during a violent earthquake. But thunder and lightning machines and even a hidden exit could have been in use in 456. Therefore, this question is not so crucial to the discussion of authenticity. See the sources cited above for possible ways of representing the storm and descent.

12. West, "The Prometheus Trilogy," p. 146. See Griffith, *Authenticity,* pp. 11–12, for a discussion of possible parodies in Aristophanes' *Knights* (424) and *Birds* (414).

13. West, "The Prometheus Trilogy," pp. 135–48.

14. Griffith, "Aeschylus," pp. 117–20.

15. See theories of Griffith, *Authenticity,* pp. 224–54, and Taplin, "Notes."

16. Herington is the major spokesman for this view. In addition to his book and edition, see his articles "A Study in the *Prometheia* I & II," *Phoenix* 17 (1963):180–97, 234–43; "Aeschylus, the Last Phase," *Arion* 4 (1965):387–403; and "Aeschylus in Sicily," *Journal of Hellenic Studies* 87 (1967):74–85. See Griffith, "Aeschylus," pp. 106–17, for a refutation of his arguments, however.

17. Dodds, "The *Prometheus Vinctus* and the Progress of Scholarship," in *Ancient Concept,* pp. 35–41, discusses the various theories of incomplete composition.

18. Taplin, *Stagecraft,* p. 240.

19. The opinion that Zeus "progresses" is not universally accepted. For

surveys of the discussion, with further bibliography, see Dodds, "The *Prometheus Vinctus,* " pp. 41–43, and Alfred Burns, "The Meaning of the *Prometheus Vinctus,*" *Classica et Mediaevalia* 27 (1966):65–78.

20. For a translation and interpretation of the fragments, see the Appendix to Herington and Scully, *Aeschylus.* The Greek text can be found in Thomson's edition and the second volume of Smyth's Loeb edition.

21. Although Earth (Ge) is not a character in *Prometheus Bound,* her name appears in the hypothesis to the play. See Herington's comments for further evidence to support her intervention.

22. See West, "The Prometheus Trilogy," for arguments in favor of this view. For Chiron's part in the resolution, see D. S. Robertson, "Prometheus and Chiron," *Journal of Hellenic Studies* 71 (1951):150–55. For reconstructions of the trilogy, see Herington, "Study," and Thomson, "*Prometheia,*" in *Aeschylus,* as well as West.

23. Mullins, "Date," p. 167.

24. See S. V. Tracy, "*Prometheus Bound* 114–117," *Harvard Studies in Classical Philology* 75 (1971):59–62, as well as Rosenmeyer, *Masks ("Prometheus Bound:* Tragedy or Treatise?"), p. 56.

25. William Flint, "The Use of Myths to Create Suspense in Extant Greek Tragedy" (Ph.D. Diss. Princeton University, 1921), pp. 81–82, thinks the multiplicity of myths involved increased the suspense.

26. Dumortier, *Less Images,* pp. 56–70.

27. Rosenmeyer, *Masks,* pp. 57ff.

28. Podlecki, *Political Background,* pp. 163–67, lists the qualities and cites contemporary parallels.

29. For a comparison of Aeschylus with Hesiod, see Havelock, *Prometheus,* Appendix, pp. 185–212, and Friedrich Solmsen, *Hesiod and Aeschylus* (Ithaca, N.Y., 1949), pp. 124–66.

30. David Konstan, "The Ocean Episode in the *Prometheus Bound,*" *History of Religions* 17 (1977):65, notes the pupil-teacher imagery in the play.

31. Werner Jaeger, *Paideia: The Ideals of Greek Culture, I,* tr. Gilbert Highet (New York: Oxford University Press, 1939), p. 263 and note 14, and Herington, "Study," and appendix to his edition.

32. For the text and translation of the primary sources, see G. S. Kirk and J. E. Raven, *The Presocratic Philosophers* (Cambridge: Cambridge University Press, 1962).

33. Dodds, *Ancient Concept,* pp. 1–12.

34. Havelock, *Prometheus,* pp. 60–61.

35. Ibid., pp. 62–64.

36. See note 27.

37. Jean Dumortier, *Le Vocabulaire Medical d' Eschyle et Les Ecrits Hippocratiques* (Paris, 1975), Preface, pp. ii–iii.

38. Kirk and Raven, *Presocratic,* p. 234.
39. Dumortier, *Le Vocabulaire,* pp. 69–79.
40. B. Fowler, "The Imagery of *Prometheus Bound,*" *American Journal of Philology* 78 (1957):173–84, discusses the connection between the medical imagery and the patterns of the yoke and of musical harmony.
41. Fowler, "Imagery of *Prometheus,*" p. 173.
42. See Herington's edition, pp. 106–7, for translations and contexts of these quotations from Aeschylus by ancient writers.
43. See S. Benardete, "The Crimes and Arts of Prometheus," *Rheinisches Museum* 107 (1964):127–39, for an analysis of the signs of what Prometheus must learn; p. 134 discusses the yoke image in this context.
44. Benardete, "Crimes," pp. 134–35, and Konstan, "Ocean," pp. 68–69, develop this idea in relation to the play. Konstan also discusses Ocean's role in the cosmic development, equating his moderation with his function as earth-embracing primal water.
45. Golden, *In Praise;* Havelock, *Prometheus;* and Rosenmeyer, *Masks,* all emphasize the intensity of the conflict and consider it a reflection of the perception of dualism in the cosmos and man.
46. Rosenmeyer, *Masks,* pp. 91–98.
47. See Havelock, *Prometheus,* p. 45, and Rosenmeyer, *Masks,* p. 80, for developments of this idea.
48. Rosenmeyer, *Masks,* pp. 76–78, says that this quality turns the play from an allegory into a tragedy. Havelock also emphasizes Prometheus's vulnerability.
49. Golden, *In Praise;* Havelock, *Prometheus;* and Rosenmeyer, *Masks,* pp. 74–75, examine in detail Prometheus as an archetype for man.
50. Golden, *In Praise,* p. 108, emphasizes this point, but he, as well as most critics, points out that the cosmos contains the potential for constructive action as well.
51. Caldwell, "Pattern," pp. 92–94.
52. Devereux, *Dreams,* pp. 27–60, analyzes her dream.
53. Walcot, *Greek Drama,* p. 85.
54. Podlecki, *Political Background,* discusses specific theories about allusions, but concludes that Zeus represents all tyrants in general.
55. Konstan, "Ocean," pp. 67–71.
56. Ibid., pp. 71–72.

Chapter Seven

1. For a convenient collection of the fragments, with their sources and translations, see Smyth's *Aeschylus,* Vol. 2. See T. Gantz, "The Aeschylean Trilogy: Prolegomena," *Classical Journal* 74 (1979):289–304, for a list of the

possible trilogies. Taplin, *Stagecraft,* pp. 195–96, however, argues against the scholars' propensity to develop trilogies out of related titles.

2. The second edition of Smyth's *Aeschylus,* 2, published in 1963, contains an appendix edited by Hugh Lloyd-Jones comprising the papyri published since 1930, with bibliography, commentary, and translations.

3. Taplin, *Stagecraft,* pp. 431–33.

4. Taplin, "Silences," pp. 57–76.

5. Bruno Snell, *Scenes from Greek Drama* (Berkeley: University of California Press, 1964), pp. 1–22 and the appendix, pp. 139–44, where he prints the papyrus of *Myrmidons.*

6. Lloyd-Jones, *Appendix,* p. 562.

7. For the bibliography and literature about the satyr plays, see Thalia P. Howe, "The Style of Aeschylus as Satyr-Playwright," *Greece and Rome* 6 (1959–60):150–65. I am indebted to Ms. Howe for her ideas and information.

8. Ibid., pp. 160–62, for a discussion of these points.

9. Ibid., p. 154.

10. Lloyd-Jones, *Appendix,* pp. 442–56. See Taplin, *Stagecraft,* pp. 420–22, for further discussion.

11. Taplin, *Stagecraft,* p. 426.

12. Ibid., p. 429.

13. The quotation is taken from J. T. Sheppard, *Aeschylus and Sophocles: Their Work and Influence* (New York: Cooper Square Press, 1963), p. 62. Sheppard provides valuable information and bibliography on citations and imitations through the ages.

14. Longinus, *On the Sublime,* tr. W. Hamilton Fyfe (Cambridge, Mass.: Harvard University Press, 1953), p. 129.

15. For information on the texts and early criticism, see R. Pfeiffer, *A History of Classical Scholarship* (Oxford: Clarendon Press, 1968), p. 82; John E. Sandys, *A History of Classical Scholarship,* 3rd ed. (New York: Hafner, 1967), 1:57–58; and Rodger Dawe, *The Collation and Investigation of the Manuscripts of Aeschylus* (Cambridge: Cambridge University Press, 1964).

16. See Andrew Porter, "Musical Events," *New Yorker,* 31 March 1980, pp. 94–96, for a review of the opera. The quotation, which appears on p. 94, was taken from the preface to the libretto published by Shawnee Press.

Selected Bibliography

PRIMARY SOURCES

1. Editions of the Greek Text
Mette, H. J. *Die Fragmente der Tragödien des Aischylos.* Deutsche Akademie der Wissenschaften zu Berlin, vol. 15. Berlin: Berlin Akademie, 1959.
Page, Denys. *Aeschyli septem quae supersunt tragoediae.* 2d rev. ed. Oxford: Oxford University Press, 1972.
Smyth, Herbert Weir. *Aeschylus. Vol. 1 and 2: Plays and Fragments with an English Translation.* The Loeb Classical Library. New York: G. P. Putnam, 1922. *Appendix* to vol. 2 edited by Hugh Lloyd-Jones. Cambridge, Mass.: Harvard University Press, 1963. The latter contains fragments published since 1930, with translation and commentary.

2. English Editions of Individual Plays
with Introductions and Line-by-Line Commentaries
Broadhead, H. D. *"The Persae" of Aeschylus: Edited with Introduction, Critical Notes, and Commentary.* Cambridge: Cambridge University Press, 1960.
Denniston, John Dewar, and Page, Denys. *Aeschylus: "Agamemnon."* Oxford: Clarendon Press, 1957.
Fraenkel, Edward. *Aeschylus: "Agamemnon": Edited with a Commentary.* Vols. 1, 2, and 3. Oxford: Clarendon Press, 1950.
Johansen, H. Friis. *Aeschylus: "The Suppliants."* Vol. 1: *The Text with Introduction, Critical Apparatus and Translation: The Scholia with Introduction and Critical Apparatus by Ole Smith. Classica et Mediaevalia.* Dissertations, 7. Copenhagen: Gyldendalske, 1970.
Thomson, George. *Aeschylus: "The Prometheus Bound": Edited with Introduction, Commentary, and Translation.* Cambridge: Cambridge University Press, 1932.
Tucker, T. G. *"The Seven Against Thebes" of Aeschylus.* Cambridge: Cambridge University Press, 1908.

3. Translations into English
Benardete, Seth. *The Persians.* In *Aeschylus II: The Complete Greek Tragedies.* 1956. Reprint. New York: Modern Library, n.d.

————. *The Suppliant Maidens.* In *Aeschylus II: The Complete Greek Tragedies.* 1956. Reprint. New York: Modern Library, n.d.

Dawson, Christopher. *"The Seven Against Thebes" by Aeschylus: A Translation with Commentary.* Prentice-Hall Greek Drama Series. Englewood Cliffs, N.J.: Prentice-Hall, 1970.

Grene, David. *Prometheus Bound.* In *Aeschylus I: The Complete Greek Tragedies.* 1942. Reprint. New York: Modern Library, n.d.

————. *Seven Against Thebes.* In *Aeschylus II: The Complete Greek Tragedies.* 1956. Reprint. New York: Modern Library, n.d.

Havelock, Eric. *Prometheus.* Seattle: University of Washington Press, 1968. Published originally as *Crucifixion of Intellectual Man.* New York: Beacon, 1951.

Herington, C. J., ed., and Scully, James, trans. *Aeschylus: "Prometheus Bound."* The Oxford Greek Tragedy in New Translations. New York: Oxford University Press, 1975.

Lattimore, Richmond. *The Oresteia.* In *Aeschylus I: The Complete Greek Tragedies.* 1942. Reprint. New York: Modern Library, n.d.

Lembke, Janet. *Aeschylus' "Suppliants".* Oxford Greek Tragedy in New Translations. New York: Oxford University Press, 1975.

Lloyd-Jones, Hugh. *Aeschylus' "Oresteia": A Translation with Commentary.* Vol. 1. *Agamemnon*; vol. 2. *Libation Bearers*; vol. 3. *Eumenides.* Prentice-Hall Greek Drama Series. Englewood Cliffs, N.J.: Prentice-Hall, 1970.

Podlecki, Anthony J. *Aeschylus' "Persians": A Translation with Commentary.* Prentice-Hall Greek Drama Series. Englewood Cliffs, N.J.: Prentice-Hall, 1970.

SECONDARY SOURCES

Please refer to chapter notes for works on individual plays.

1. Books and Parts of Books

Arnott, Peter. *Greek Scenic Conventions in the Fifth Century B.C.* Oxford: Clarendon Press, 1962. A discussion of the stage, furnishings, and machinery, with specific reference to actual productions of Aeschylus's plays.

Aylen, Leo. *Greek Tragedy and the Modern World.* London: Methuen, 1964. An analysis of the relationship between tragedy and man's "need to come to terms with death and the forces with which human life is surrounded," including chapters on the background of Greek tragedy, and Aeschylus's extant plays.

Beck, Robert Holmes. *Aeschylus: Playwright, Educator.* The Hague: Nijhoff, 1965. A comprehensive study with particular attention to Aeschylus's moral philosophy.

Bremer, J. M. *Hamartia: Tragic Error in the "Poetics" of Aristotle and in Greek Tragedy.* Amsterdam: Adolf M. Hakkert, 1969. An analysis of the Greek words connected with the concept of error from Homer to Aristotle, including analyses of Aeschylus's plays from this perspective.

Brooke, Iris. *Costume in Classic Greek Drama.* New York: Theatre Arts, 1962. The development of costume, with illustrations.

Dale, A. M. *Collected Papers.* Cambridge: Cambridge University Press, 1969. Includes valuable essays on production and characterization.

Dawe, R. D. *The Collation and Investigation of the Manuscripts of Aeschylus.* Cambridge: Cambridge University Press, 1964. New collation, including papyri and rejected readings, suggests continual horizontal transmission from the editions at Alexandria to the Byzantine manuscripts rather than vertical transmission from one archetype.

Devereux, George. *Dreams in Greek Tragedy: An Ethno-Psychoanalytic Study.* Berkeley: University of California Press, 1976. Analyses of the dreams and dream metaphors which reveal the psychological depths of the tragic situation.

Dodds, E. R. *The Ancient Concept of Progress and Other Essays on Greek Literature and Belief.* Oxford: Clarendon Press, 1973. Essays which discuss Aeschylus's ideas on progress, the scholarship and interpretation of *Prometheus Bound,* and the connection among morals, politics, and the idea of progress in the *Oresteia.*

Dumortier, Jean. *Les Images dans la poésie d' Eschyle.* Paris: Société d' Édition "Les Belles Lettres," 1933. A catalogue of the principal metaphors in each play and of secondary metaphors and their use.

————. *Le vocabulaire médical d' Eschyle et les écrits Hippocratiques.* 2d. ed. Paris: Société d' Édition "Les Belles Lettres," 1975. A comparison which proves Aeschylus's awareness of the new theories and methods.

Earp, F. E. *The Style of Aeschylus.* Cambridge: Cambridge University Press, 1948. A comprehensive study of Aeschylus's diction, sentence structure, and metaphor.

Else, Gerald F. *The Origin and Early Form of Greek Tragedy.* Cambridge, Mass.: Harvard University for Oberlin College, 1965. An examination of the diverse sources of the lyric and dialogue of Greek tragedy, their combination in Athens, and Aeschylus's place in developing the genre.

Finley, John H. *Pindar and Aeschylus.* Cambridge, Mass.: Harvard University Press, 1965. A comparison of the style and world view of the two poets, with attention to Aeschylus's technique of symbolizing thought through characters and situation.

Fritz, Kurt von. *Antike und moderne Tragödie.* Berlin: Walter de Gruyter, 1962. A study of the treatment of moral problems in ancient and modern tragedy, with discussions of Aeschylus's Danaid trilogy, *Seven Against Thebes,* and the three Greek versions of the Orestes saga.

Gagarin, Michael. *Aeschylean Drama.* Berkeley: University of California Press, 1976. A study of the plays in relation to the early Greek world view, with special attention to the *Oresteia.*

Golden, Leon. *In Praise of Prometheus: Humanism and Rationalism in Aeschylean Thought.* Chapel Hill: University of North Carolina Press, 1962. An examination of context and cohesion of each play, to determine Aeschylus's religious outlook, with the conclusion that Aeschylus developed a belief that human reason is responsible for civilization.

Griffith, Mark. *The Authenticity of "Prometheus Bound."* Cambridge: Cambridge University Press, 1977. A statistical analysis of elements of diction, syntax, and meter of the Aeschylean corpus to determine whether *Prometheus Bound* is "unAeschylean."

Heilman, Robert B. *Tragedy and Melodrama: Versions of Experience.* Seattle: University of Washington Press, 1968. Analysis of the concept of tragedy and its effect, with reference to the Greek playwrights and Aristotle.

Jones, John. *On Aristotle and Greek Tragedy.* London: Chatto and Windus, 1967. A reiteration of the importance of action rather than character in Greek tragedy, with analyses of the versions of the Orestes saga.

Kitto, H. D. F. *Greek Tragedy: A Literary Study.* 2d ed. 1950. Reprint. New York: Doubleday, 1954. A useful analysis of the dramatic force of Aeschylean tragedy, although theories of Aeschylus's development are based on the early date of *Suppliants.*

Kranz, Walther. *Stasimon.* Berlin: Weidmann, 1933. On the form and function of choral song, its religious and philosophic content, evolution, and relation to action.

Lattimore, Richmond. *Story Patterns in Greek Tragedy.* Ann Arbor: University of Michigan Press, 1965. An analysis of the various patterns of tragic narrative (i.e., choice, revenge, discovery) through which personal and moral issues are dramatized.

Lesky, Albin. *Greek Tragedy.* Translated by H. A. Frankfort. London: Ernest Benn, 1965. A survey of tragedy from its beginnings through post-classical times, with substantial chapters on the concept itself and the three major poets.

———. *Die tragische Dichtung der Hellenen.* 3rd ed. Göttingen: Vandenhoeck and Ruprecht, 1972. A presentation of information and critical bibliography covering poet's biography, text and transmission, questions of dating, production, style, and ideas.

Lucas, D. W. *The Greek Tragic Poets.* 2d ed. London: Cohen and West, 1959. Introductory chapter on the social, political, and religious background of Greek tragedy, as well as comprehensive analyses of individual poets and their work.

―――. *"Poetics" of Aristotle: Introduction, Commentary, and Appendices.* Oxford: Clarendon Press, 1968. The appendices analyze the problematical terms associated with tragedy: mimesis, catharsis, hamartia.

Meautis, Georges. *Eschyle et la trilogie.* Paris: Éditions Bernard Grasset, 1936. Examination of religious ideas conveyed through the three-part form, with special attention to dramatic techniques used to underline them.

Murray, Gilbert. *Aeschylus, the Creator of Tragedy.* Oxford: Clarendon Press, 1940. An analysis of Aeschylus's use of myth, techniques, and ideas, with attention to his development of the genre and Dionysiac elements in his plays.

Owen, E. T. *The Harmony of Aeschylus.* Toronto: Clarke, Irwin, and Co., 1952. An examination of Aeschylus's plays to show how the poet dramatized the evolution of harmony out of discords.

Pickard-Cambridge, Sir Arthur. *Dramatic Festivals of Athens.* 2d ed. Revised by John Gould and D. M. Lewis. Oxford: Clarendon Press, 1968. A comprehensive sutdy of all aspects of production, with frequent citations of evidence from ancient writers.

Podlecki, Anthony J. *The Political Background of Aeschylean Tragedy.* Ann Arbor: University Michigan Press, 1966. An examination of the relation between the plays and contemporary political ideas, including presentation and criticism of the relevant bibliography.

Reinhardt, Karl. *Aischylos als Regisseur und Theologe.* Bern: A. Frankeag, 1949. An analysis of the relation between Aeschylus's dramatic technique and his religion, with special attention to *Prometheus Bound* and the *Oresteia* and the question of Zeus.

De Romilly, Jacqueline D. *La crainte et l'angoisse dans le theatre d'Eschyle.* Paris: G. Budé, 1958. On the description of fear, its religious and moral meaning, and its use as a means to wisdom.

―――. *L'évolution du pathétique d'Eschyle à Euripide.* Paris: Presses Universitaires des France, 1961. A study of scenes of suffering and violence which shows that Aeschylus concentrates on the act itself, with particular attention to the dread preceding it and the way the act is related to divine will.

Rose, Herbert Jennings. *A Commentary on the Surviving Plays of Aeschylus.* 2 vols. Hollandsche Vitgevers Maatschappij: Amsterdam, 1958. Line-by-line analysis without accompanying text.

Rosenmeyer, Thomas G. *The Masks of Tragedy: Essays on Six Greek Dramas.* New York: Gordian Press, 1971. Stimulating analyses of *Seven Against Thebes* and *Prometheus Bound.*

Smith, Peter. *On the Hymn to Zeus in Aeschylus' "Agamemnon."* Chico, Calif.: Scholars Press, 1980. An analysis of the meaning and place of the hymn in the parodos, with a comparison to the hymn in *Suppliants.*

Smyth, Herbert Weir. *Aeschylean Tragedy.* Berkeley: University of California Press, 1924. Comprehensive Study of Aeschylus's art and ideas.

Solmsen, Friedrich. *Hesiod and Aeschylus.* Ithaca, N.Y.: Cornell University Press, 1949. A comparison of the two poets' treatment of Prometheus, with consideration of other Aeschylean plays to discuss the tragedian's presentation of the gods and use of the trilogy.

Stanford, William Bedell. *Aeschylus in His Style: A Study in Language and Personality.* Dublin: University Press, 1942. An analysis of Aeschylus's use of colloquial and literary sources, choice of words, imagery, and technique of characterizing speaker through style.

Taplin, Oliver. *The Stagecraft of Aeschylus: The Dramatic Use of Exits and Entrances in Greek Tragedy.* Oxford: Clarendon Press, 1977. A comprehensive study of the staging of each play, with consideration of all questions of text and interpretation that affect analysis of the stagecraft.

————. *Greek Tragedy in Action.* London: Methuen, 1978. An introduction to the techniques of stage production, using nine plays, including the *Oresteia,* to illustrate various devices.

Thomson, George. *Aeschylus and Athens: A Study in the Social Origins of Drama.* New York: Grosset and Dunlap, 1968. An interpretation which relates the plays to the transition from tribal society to the state, with valuable discussions of the *Oresteia* and the trilogy about Prometheus.

Vickers, Brian. *Toward Greek Tragedy: Drama, Myth, Society.* London: Longman, 1973. An explication of the theory that tragedy is a representation of human suffering that results from violation of fundamental social and religious values, by examining Greek society, religion, and use of myth, with special attention to Aeschylus's *Oresteia.*

Walcot, Peter. *Greek Drama in its Theatrical and Social Context.* Cardiff: The University of Wales Press, 1976. An examination of acting, staging, and presentation of social values in the light of the expectations of a popular audience accustomed to oral performance.

2. Articles

Aylen, Leo. "The Vulgarity of Tragedy." In *Classical Drama and Its Influence: Essays Presented to H. D. F. Kitto.* Edited by Maxwell Anderson. London: Methuen, 1965, pp. 85–100. An examination of popular elements.

Bain, David. "Audience Address in Greek Tragedy." *Classical Quarterly* 25 (1975):13–25. An examination of certain passages (i.e., *Ag.* 36–39) shows that tragedy had nothing resembling the direct address typical of Greek Old Comedy.

Caldwell, Richard S. "The Misogyny of Eteocles." *Arethusa* 6 (1973):197–231. A thorough psychoanalytic examination of the entire Theban saga.

———. "The Pattern of Aeschylean Tragedy." *Transactions and Proceedings of the American Philological Association* 101 (1970):77–94. A presentation of the theory that the Oedipal pattern is the most important single element found in all the extant plays.

Dale, A. M. "The Chorus in the Action of Greek Tragedy." In *Classical Drama and Its Influence: Essays Presented to H. D. F. Kitto.* Edited by Maxwell Anderson. London: Methuen, 1965, pp. 17–27. An analysis of the effects of the presence of the chorus on spoken dialogue.

Dawe, R. D. "Inconsistency of Plot and Character in Aeschylus." *Proceedings of the Cambridge Philological Society* 189 (1963):21–62. An examination of supposed inconsistencies to show that the playwright deliberately exploits ambiguity to increase dramatic effect.

———. "Some Reflections on Atē and Hamartia." *Harvard Studies in Classical Philology* 72 (1968):89–123. The definition of *hamartia* as an error in judgment, with *Atē,* in its various meanings, representing forces that interfere with correct functioning.

Easterling, P. E. "Presentation of Character in Aeschylus." *Greece and Rome* 20 (1973):3–17. The argument that characters must and do have a continuous identity and reality to be effective agents of the tragic action.

Edwards, Mark W. "Agamemnon's Decision: Freedom and Folly in Aeschylus." *California Studies in Classical Antiquity* 10(1977):17–38. An examination of the decisions of Aeschylus's heroes to understand the extent of their responsibility.

Else, Gerald. "Ritual and Drama in Aischyleian Tragedy." *Illinois Classical Studies"* 11 (1977):70–87. Aeschylus arouses the audience to share his characters' fear and grief by assigning to the chorus the developed ritual forms for prayer and lament familiar to the audience.

Fowler, Barbara H. "Aeschylus' Imagery." *Classica et Mediaevalia* 28 (1967):1–74. A comprehensive study of the interlocking image patterns and their relation to the themes of *Persians, Suppliants,* and the *Oresteia.*

Gantz, Timothy. "The Aischylean Tetralogy: Prolegomena." *Classical Journal* 74 (1979):289–304. A presentation of the questions surrounding the development of the tetralogy, with a list of the plays that were probably connected in theme.

Garvie, A. E. "Aeschylus' Simple Plots." In *Dionysiaca: Nine Studies in Greek Poetry.* Edited by R. D. Dawe, J. Diggle, P. E. Easterling. Cambridge: Cambridge University Library, 1978, pp. 63–86. An analysis of all the plays to show how Aeschylus complicates his plots by frustrating audience expectations.

Grube, G. M. A. "Zeus in Aeschylus." *American Journal of Philology* 91 (1970):43–51. An examination of Zeus's importance to Aeschylus as a deity who developed into an omnipotent god with an inscrutable mind, but whose power does not preclude human responsibility for action.

Haldane, J. A. "Musical Themes and Imagery in Aeschylus." *Journal of Hellenic Studies* 85 (1965):33–41. A discussion of the effect of music or allusions to music in the plays.

Hammond, N. G. L. "The Conditions of Dramatic Production to the Death of Aeschylus." *Greek Roman and Byzantine Studies* 13 (1972):387–450. An analysis of the evidence about staging of drama from the earliest times.

———. "Personal Freedom and Its Limitations in the *Oresteia.*" *Journal of Hellenic Studies* 85 (1965):42–55. An examination of the choices faced by Aeschylus's characters to show interplay of freedom and limitations implicit in the apportionment of the cosmos.

Herington, C. J. "Aeschylus in Sicily." *Journal of Hellenic Studies* 87 (1967):74–85. A discussion of events and culture in Sicily with which Aeschylus had contact and which affected his plays, with a collection of the ancient witnesses to the poet's life in Sicily.

———. "Aeschylus: The Last Phase." *Arion* 4 (1965):387–403. The theory that Aeschylus's earliest plays reflect his belief in a static, undivided cosmos, whereas the last three, in which the trilogy form is fully developed, show a cosmic split where the first two plays present antitheses and third effects a synthesis.

Howe, Thalia P. "The Style of Aeschylus as Satyr-Playwright." *Greece and Rome* 6 (1959/60):150–65. An analysis of the fragments of *Dicktyoulkoi* to determine characteristics of the genre.

Kachler, K. G. "Über Wesen und Wirken der Theatermaske." *Antaios* 11 (1969):192–208. A history of the mask, with discussion of its religious, dramatic, and practical functions.

Lesky, Albin. "Decision and Responsibility in Aeschylus." *Journal of Hellenic Studies* 86 (1966):78–85. A study of crucial decisions of Aeschylus's characters to define double-determination, in which external coercion and personal readiness are fused.

Lloyd-Jones, Hugh. "Zeus in Aeschylus." *Journal of Hellenic Studies* 76 (1956):55–67. An argument against the theory that Zeus develops by proving that the religious ideas in the plays are not any more advanced than Hesiod.

Pavelonskis, Zoja. "The Voice of the Actor in Greek Tragedy." *Classical World* 71.2 (1977):113–24. The suggestion that productions made dramatic use of the same actor's portrayal of related roles in monodramas and trilogies.

Robertson, H. G. "Legal Expressions and Ideas of Justice in Aeschylus." *Classical Philology* 34 (1939):209–19. A concordance of the terms, with particular attention to their use in *Suppliants* and *The Oresteia.*

Rosenmeyer, T. G. "Gorgias, Aeschylus, and *Apatē.*" *American Journal of Philology* 76 (1955):225–60. An analysis of the way the poet exploits ambiguity and uses deceit to move or persuade.

Shisler, Famee Lorene. "The Use of Stage Business to Portray Emotion in Greek Tragedy." *American Journal of Philology* 66, sec. 4 (1945):377–97. A discussion of the action and gestures which accompany the words.

Taplin, Oliver. "Aeschylean Silences and Silences in Aeschylus." *Harvard Studies in Classical Philology* 76 (1972):57–97. A comparison of the long and meaningful silences to which the poet directs attention in *Niobe* and *Myrmidons* with the use of silent actors in other plays.

―――. "Notes on the Title of *Prometheus Desmotes.*" *Journal of Hellenic Studies* 95 (1975):184–86. An argument against the Aeschylean authorship of *Prometheus Bound* which suggests that the subtitles of plays of the same name derive from the Alexandrians and furnish no evidence for the existence of connected trilogies.

Welch, L. M. "Catharsis, Structural Purification, and Else's Aristotle." *Bucknell Review* 19, sec. 3 (1971):31–50. An examination of Else's analysis of the way in which plot effects catharsis by purifying tragic events of moral revulsion.

Winnington-Ingram, R. P. "Tragedy and Greek Archaic Thought." In *Classical Drama and Its Influence: Essays Presented to H. D. F. Kitto.*

Edited by Maxwell Anderson. London: Methuen, 1965, pp. 29–50. A
discussion of the paradox that man is both free and subject to determining powers in the tragedies of Aeschylus and Sophocles.

Index

(Theatrical and poetic terms are cited only once; reference is made only to the page where the term is defined. Greek gods, both collectively and as individuals, are cited only where there is an analysis of their role in the tragedy.)

882.01
ae253

115142